Hans Kristian Strandstuen Rustad
Situating Scandinavian Poetry in the Computational Network Environment

Poetry in the Digital Age

Edited by Claudia Benthien

Advisory Board
Frieder von Ammon · Hannes Bajohr · Jörg Döring · Julia Lajta-Novak · María Mencía · Ralph Müller · Jesper Olsson · Paweł Piszczatowski · Jessica Pressman · Antonio Rodriguez · Hans Kristian Strandstuen Rustad · Holger Schulze · Eckhard Schumacher · Henrieke Stahl · Birgitte Stougaard Pedersen

Volume 2

Hans Kristian Strandstuen Rustad

Situating Scandinavian Poetry in the Computational Network Environment

DE GRUYTER

This book series is part of the research project "Poetry in the Digital Age" that has received funding from the European Research Council (ERC) under the European Union's "Horizon 2020" research and innovation programme (grant agreement No 884177).

Views and opinions expressed in the present book are those of the author only and do not necessarily reflect those of the European Union (EU or the European Research Council (ERC). Neither the EU nor the ERC can be held responsible for them.

European Research Council
Established by the European Commission

ISBN 978-3-11-221487-9
e-ISBN (PDF) 978-3-11-100407-5
e-ISBN (EPUB) 978-3-11-100480-8
DOI https://doi.org/10.1515/9783111004075

This work is licensed under the Creative Commons Attribution-NonCommercial-NoDerivatives 4.0 International License. For details go to https://creativecommons.org/licenses/by-nc-nd/4.0/.

Creative Commons license terms for re-use do not apply to any content (such as graphs, figures, photos, excerpts, etc.) not original to the Open Access publication and further permission may be required from the rights holder. The obligation to research and clear permission lies solely with the party re-using the material.

Library of Congress Control Number: 2023934190

Bibliographic information published by the Deutsche Nationalbibliothek
The Deutsche Nationalbibliothek lists this publication in the Deutsche Nationalbibliografie; detailed bibliographic data are available on the internet at http://dnb.dnb.de.

© 2025 the author(s), published by Walter de Gruyter GmbH, Berlin/Boston
This volume is text- and page-identical with the hardback published in 2023.
This book is published open access at www.degruyter.com.

Cover image: Rebecka Dürr.
Typesetting: Integra Software Services Pvt. Ltd.
Printing and binding: CPI books GmbH, Leck

www.degruyter.com

Acknowledgements

I am grateful to my father, Arne Rustad, to the Poetry research group at the University of Oslo and to Professor Claudia Benthien and her research team at the Universität Hamburg, Rebecka Dürr, Vadim Keylin, Magdalena Korecka, Marc Matter, Wiebke Vorrath and Henrik Wehmeier, all members of the ERC project "Poetry in the Digital Age." I would also like to thank the Principal Investigator, Claudia Benthien, for awarding me a Research Fellowship in the ERC project in the fall of 2021, where I could present parts of this book and had intense and interesting discussions on poetry and media.

An early version of Chapter 5 appears in Norwegian in *Estetiske praksiser i den digitale produksjonens tidsalder* (2022). I would like to thank the editors Knut Ove Eliassen, Anne Ogundipe and Øyvind Prytz and Fagbokforlaget for giving me the permission to reuse material from the chapter and include it in the present book. Material from Chapter 7 is included in the monograph *Digtoplæsning. Former og fællesskaber* (Mønster, Rustad and Schmith 2022), though with a few significant changes.

This book is written with grants from the Department of Linguistics and Scandinavian Studies, University of Oslo, and from the Cultural Council in Norway.

Contents

Acknowledgements —— V

Chapter 1
The Digital Situation of Poetry —— 1

Chapter 2
The Computational Network Environment of Poetry —— 23

Chapter 3
Poetic Technogenesis and the Future of Poetry? Johannes Heldén and Håkan Jonson's *Evolution* (2014) —— 50

Chapter 4
Field Recordings from the Future: Astroecological Thinking in Johannes Heldén's *Astroecology* (2016) —— 73

Chapter 5
Instagram Poetry and the Logic of Media Platforms: Sabina Store-Ashkari, Alexander Fallo and Trygve Skaug —— 98

Chapter 6
Unfinished Poetry: Nils-Øivind Haagensen from Facebook to Book —— 126

Chapter 7
Digital Poetry Reading: Podpoesi.nu and @detlillarum's #digtfix —— 150

Chapter 8
Poetry Film as Political Activism: A Language for the Experience of War and Exile in Ghayath Almadhoun and Marie Silkeberg's *Your Memory Is My Freedom* (2014) —— 174

Chapter 9
Between Idea and Media: A Note on Some Preconditions for the Making of Poetry in the Computational Network Environment —— 201

Work Cited —— 211

Index of Names —— 221

Chapter 1
The Digital Situation of Poetry

Poetry in the twenty-first century finds itself in a media-technological situation that is both new and not new. On the one hand, it is not new because technology and media have always been part of poetry's environment. On the other, the situation is new because digital technology and media have configured novel frameworks and situations for the production, distribution and reading of poetry. Poetry books might contain programming languages. Using computer code, Mez Breeze, for example, has created a new language, "mezangelle." Algorithms write poetic texts, as in the case of the poet Johannes Heldén and Håkan Jonson's *Evolution* (2014) or Karen ann Donnachie and Andy Simionato's *The Library of Nonhuman Books* (2019), an autonomous art installation where artificial intelligence is programmed to create new books from old publications. Jason Edward Lewis produces visual and tactile poetry as apps to be read on a single mobile medium, preferably with a touch screen, in his series of poems called *P.o.E.M.M.*: "Speak," "Know," "Migration," "Bastard," "Choice," "White" and "Death" (2007–2013). Poetry travels between media with highly different technological and institutional affordances, i.e. between books, computers, theater scenes, performances and installation rooms.

These new technological conditions of poetry have had a direct effect on poets' and readers' everyday lives as well as on literary institutions. In Canada and the USA, the career of Rupi Kaur has been a powerful illustration of such changes. Her success demonstrates the ways in which social media intervenes with the field of poetry. The story is well known: Kaur established herself as a popular poet on Instagram, with an overwhelming number of readers. Following this online success, she made her debut with the collection of poems *Milk and Honey* (2015), topping the New York Times bestseller list. This instant success would have been unlikely without Instagram and other influential social media. Similarly, social media has played an important role for new voices such as R.M. Drake, Atticus, Nayyirah Waheed, Lang Leav, Yrsa Daley-Ward and, though on a smaller scale in terms of followers and financial success, Sabina Store-Ashkari, Alexander Fallo and Trygve Skaug in Norway.

Furthermore, in the digital era, sound poetry and poetry readings have expanded their fields of distribution and sites for performance, becoming at once more visible and audible. This phenomenon, in turn, has had an impact on poetry's appearance in physical rooms, on stages and in public and semi-public places. These shifts have not only been limited to poetry slams but have blossomed into widespread practices through which young and emerging poets have developed their own styles, as in the cases of Maren Kames, Amanda Gorman and Olivia

∂ Open Access. © 2023 the author(s), published by De Gruyter. [CC BY-NC-ND] This work is licensed under the Creative Commons Attribution-NonCommercial-NoDerivatives 4.0 International License.
https://doi.org/10.1515/9783111004075-001

Bergdahl. Recorded poetry readings may not be new, but the explosion of digital archives and distribution networks have now made it possible to reach a broad audience almost immediately, wherein algorithms as well as humans have assumed the joint role of curator (see e.g. Urrihio 2019).

Likewise, in Scandinavia, YouTube has come to serve as both an archive and a distribution platform for poetry, be it in the development of YouTube poetry, as an exhibition site for poetry films or as a place for the distribution of older and more recent poetry readings, live or recorded. In Denmark, YouTube played a central role in the reception and popularity of Yahya Hassan's debut, the collection of poems *Yahya Hassan* (2013). Videos of Hassan melodiously reading and chanting his work, in imitation of an imam's recitation of religious texts, helped to intensify certain political aspects of the poems in the book. When these videos reached social media, Hassan almost immediately became a more popular, if decidedly more controversial poet.

Johannes Heldén is one of several contemporary poets in the Scandinavian countries who creates poetic projects that travel across digital and analog platforms and that materialize as digital poems, museum installations and poems in book format, among others. Other poets such as Christian Yde Frostholm, Cia Rinne and Ottar Ormstad produce digital poetry and installations where old and new media meet, developing conceptual poetic work for presentation on computers and in books. These and other well-known "print poets" like Mette Moestrup, Marie Silkeberg and Nils-Øivind Haagensen publish and distribute their poems online and on social media. They use digital media and create a variety of poetic forms, whether they are newer forms of poetry such as algorithm-controlled poems, poems that are "born digital," including Twitter and Instagram poems or older practices that are being revitalized, such as poetry readings on digital platforms and digital poetry films. Simultaneously, the same poets continue to publish poetry in books, magazines, separate chapbooks and anthologies. The situation, as it has been described by many scholars, seems to be that literature and poetry more than ever travel between media (Kjerkegaard 2017; Müller and Stahl 2021), a description that could be applied more generally to describe a significant aspect of digital culture (Hansen 2010; Uricchio 2019). Therefore, it may well be that the printed book is still among poetry's, and the poet's, preferred medium, even if it no longer reigns hegemonic.

When the media situation, the media environment that poetry is a part of, changes, the character of poetry inevitably changes with it. This transformation becomes especially noticeable when it takes place in digital media. Poetry on web platforms, on social media platforms such as Facebook, Twitter and Instagram, as well as SMS poems and poetry in podcasts are aspects of a movement in which literature is partly released from print media and in which the non-print characteristics are a common defining feature of literary and poetic practice. Indeed, poems differ from each other, and just as much as they will vary in form, content and function on their respective platforms, they all respond to changing media conditions.

Situating Scandinavian Poetry in the Computational Network Environment investigates how contemporary heterogeneous forms of Scandinavian poetry interact with and work in a digital media environment, how digitally programmable and network media intervene with and shape new poetic forms and remediate older forms of poetry and how this poetry, through self-reflexivity, reflects on media and material frameworks of which it is a part. Thus, an examination of poetry in digital media can shed light on the media conditions of some contemporary poetry and its situation, as well as more generally on certain aspects of the digital media technology that surrounds us and is part of our everyday lives.

I am particularly concerned with how poetry interacts in and with, constitutes and is constituted by a media environment, which, I will argue, is a computational network environment.[1] This is an environment dominated by programmable and network media, a media ecology wherein poetry travels between analog and digital media, where both medialization and materializations of poems appear in an egalitarian structure, in which no media or versions are valued as more important or are given a higher aesthetic status than others. Here, poetry enters into relationships with other art forms and travels across media. It is relational, at once configured by, co-configurator of and a reflection on the interwoven machinery of digital and analog media that makes up the creative space for poetry and the arts. Therefore, a central claim of this book is that poetry not only survives in or adapts to but also actually helps to develop the digital-analog environment of which it, intentionally or not, is a part. Among others, Ralph Müller and Henrieke Stahl make a similar observation, emphasizing how contemporary poetry is in a process of metamorphosis: "More than any other literary form, contemporary poetry is in transition." (Müller and Stahl 2021, 5) These critics point to the diversity of lyrical genres that have emerged and gained new relevance in the contemporary world, where the digital media situation is part of the reason for these changes. Consequently, in order to understand contemporary poetry in the digital age, it is important to explore how poetry changes and adapts and how such changes and adaptations in poetry entail new ways of writing, reading and thinking. Digital media is part of the situation of contemporary poetry, and it is obviously part of our everyday lives, but it is also becoming a more common mode of and media for experiencing poetry. Therefore, this book poses the further question of what poetry in digital media can

---

[1] A more thoroughly elaboration of this concept is found in Chapter 2.

tell us about thinking and writing in a world that is increasingly dependent upon databases, algorithms, networks and collaborations between humans and machines. I ask what the media conditions for poetry in the digital age are, what changes have taken place in the media environment for poetry, how poetry has responded to these changing media conditions and how such changes are expressed through contemporary poetry in digital media.

It might be that some readers find the scope and intention of this book vaguely stated. This is due both to the book's explorative approach and to its material, which represents a variety of poetic genres and practices in digital media. Additionally, in order to suggest what poetry can be and to describe the media situation of poetry and the environment of which it is a part, it will be vital to apply a broad and inclusive approach. As I have already hinted at, by analyzing a small selection of contemporary Scandinavian poetry, I will examine in detail some media technological conditions for poetic genres and practices that are representative for poetry in digital media. In this respect, *Situating Scandinavian Poetry in the Computational Network Environment* is an attempt to contribute to an understanding of the situation of poetry in digital culture and to promote an awareness of the interactions between poets and digital technologies as well as poetry and programmable and network media.

I would like to elaborate on an observation made by Müller and Stahl. They claim that poetry, because of the contemporary media situation and the diversity of poetic genres, has "gained new relevance in the contemporary world." (Müller and Stahl 2021, 5) In this context, I explore how Scandinavian poetry in digital media demonstrates its relevance for and engagement with political issues. Here, relevance must be understood in relation to the new media situation of poetry. Poetry has always been pertinent to individual and/or political situations. It provides knowledge about sensations, experiences, language and literature, and it engages in societal and political issues. Poetic works and political engagements are entangled. My point is that the contemporary media situation has changed matters slightly, one consequence being that digital media have stimulated, in a positive way, the potential of poetry to have a social impact and to function as a form of political and activist literature. Therefore, the book does not exclusively explore how web technology, social media platforms, applications, computer code and algorithms are related to the understanding of what poetry in digital media can be but also what it can do and how poetry can represent new ways of engaging societal challenges. The combination of the use of media technology and reflections on commitment to societal challenges underpin the fact that media technologies give way to new methods for poets to reach readers in a socially engaged fashion.

In terms of the Scandinavia context, Stefan Kjerkegaard and Dan Ringgaard have shown how contemporary poetry, across genres and media (and modalities, including but not limited to writing) explores new ways of being political (Kjerkegaard and Ringgaard 2017). Further, Louise Mønster points out that "[in] the new millennium, poetry has to a much greater extent than in the 1980s and 1990s gone into clinch with current issues about e.g. climate, capitalism, consumerism, power relations, ethnicity and gender." (Mønster 2019, 143) Peter Stein Larsen highlights the same tendency in his study of contemporary Danish poetry (Larsen 2016). This book follows these studies and examines how a small selection of Scandinavian poetry in programmable and network media is political.

The media situation

Situating Scandinavian Poetry in the Computational Network Environment positions itself in the broader field of poetry and digital media studies. This field acknowledges that poetry cannot escape digital culture, despite how conservative or anti-technological poetry might at first appear to some readers – not to mention earlier approaches to the theory of poetry. Moreover, poetry's irrevocable situation within digital culture remains the case whether we study digital culture in terms of artistic and cultural objects, expressions and practices that are produced, distributed and read on digital media platforms or in terms of artistic and cultural objects, expressions and practices in non-digital media. Poetry is part of a media environment and, as I will argue, is always technological, whether it is a medieval troubadour reciting poetry, a situation that among others involves the body as technology or AI-generated poetry that appears on computer screens. Such an understanding reflects the fact that historical, cultural and institutional environments always shape literature. For instance, it is well documented that the hegemony of the book medium in the emergence of modern Europe, including institutions such as libraries, universities and bookstores, as well as phenomena such as nation-states, copyright and freedom of expression have been crucial to any particular view of literature (see e.g. Hillis Miller 2002; Ringgaard 2017).

To acknowledge that literature changes whenever it interacts with different media technological preconditions is an observation that can be linked to contributions by such media theorists as Marshall McLuhan, especially his emphasis on the meaning of media –"the medium is the message" (McLuhan 1964, 7–21) – and contemporary theorists such as Friedrich Kittler, W.J.T. Mitchell, Mark B. Hansen and N. Katherine Hayles. In the introduction to the book *Critical Terms for Media Studies*, Mitchell and Hansen claim that "media are our situation." (2010, xxi–xxii) The statement is a careful but significantly amended rendition of Friedrich Kittler's claim that "Medien bestimmen unsere Lage, die (trotzdem oder deshalb) eine

Beschreibung verdient." (Kittler 1986, 3)[2] The first part of the quote is well known, while the second part is included less often in quotes from Kittler's work. Kittler's claim has been mis- or over-interpreted as media-deterministic, most likely because of the verb "bestimmen," which in English is literally translated as "determine." Nevertheless, Mitchell and Hansen's observation is more open to what the media situation might be, that the situation is in flux, suggesting a variety of societal, communicative and aesthetic roles for media.

What the above-mentioned theorists – McLuhan, Kittler, Mitchell, Hansen and Hayles – have in common is that they all assume that technology and media are important for actions and events in our culture, not only for the twentieth and twenty-first century but also for a pre- and early modern cultural and social development. They all argue that media is not a neutral communicator of a content, be it a literary idea that materializes in a book or a poem that travels between books, digital platforms and a poet's body and voice at poetry readings. The lesson we have learned from McLuhan is that media has a social impact. Media structures society and is involved in creating its own content and use, as well as the meanings and experiences that unfold in the encounter with readers, viewers and users. Understood thus, this notion can be summarized in two words: media matters. It is this proposition that informs the position I take in this study on poetry in programmable and network media and its constituent medial situation.

The above-mentioned theorists apply a concept of media which is predominantly technological or denotes technical forms. In this book, I will also make use of a different concept of media, one which signals the single noun "medium" and is applicable to intermedial and multimedial poetry. Following Lars Elleström, these two concepts of medium or media represent what he names respectively technical media and basic media (Ellestrom 2010). The first involves the physical or tangible devices that are needed in order to materialize 'content' (Ellestrom 2010, 30). The second concept, basic media, which is another expansive concept, involves media in terms of social media platforms, web-pages and media as for example film, photography or computer games. This second meaning of the term is particularly engaged with such concepts as inter- or multimedia poetry, while technical media refers rather to physical objects such as printed books, human bodies, mobile phones, musical instruments and even the walls of buildings. In this regard, poetry is an art form that is materialized in several media. To be experienced, a poem in digital media needs a technical medium, like a computer; it requires a platform, like a

---

[2] In the English translation of Kittler's book, the quote says: "Media determine our position, which – in spite or because of it – deserves a description." (Kittler 1999, xxxix).

website or a social media platform; and it must engage computer codes as well as written and spoken language, often in interaction with music and images.

Poetry is another concept in which the relation to media is not easy to define. It is a verbal art form that belongs to a range of traditions in different cultures, and often definitions disclose a certain media-specific bias. For instance, when James Longenbach defines poetry as "the sound of language organized in lines" (Longenbach 2007, xi), he reveals that his main concern is the reading of printed poetry, because "organized in lines" would not apply, for instance, to sound poetry. It is important to acknowledge that Longenbach emphasizes poetry as a particular sound of language. Still, the relationship between the poem in print and the poem as a material event, between the media involved, is not made clear since one reading of the definition suggests that the poem as the sound of language is determined by the poem as organized in lines. Likewise, Terry Eagleton writes that a poem is a "statement in which it is the author, rather than the printer or word processor, who decides where the lines should end." (Eagleton 2015, 25) Eagleton's main interest is poetry as print. He is one among many who emphasize line breaks as significant for poetry. In the quote, he interestingly mentions a few technical media, which make his definition thought-provoking for at least two reasons. One is that he, like Longenbach, excludes poetry in non-print media. It seems to be, as Jason Nelson writes about digital poetry, that just as the print medium "constrain[s] the poem to line by line, pressed letter by bound page," digital technology encourages poets to search for other ways to organize their poems, such as multi-dimensional and multi-temporal organizations (Nelson 2019, 337). Secondly, and more interesting for the scope of this book, Eagleton places the human being ("the author") in opposition to technical media ("the printer or word processor"). His purpose is obvious. He wants to make a distinction between poetry and prose literature, but he ends up with (at least) two unfortunate consequences. Not only does Eagleton exclude prose poems, but he also turns media into neutral devices. In other words, Eagleton's definition does not recognize that media matters. In addition, Eagleton excludes computer-generated poetry where the computer's algorithms would at least partially decide where the line should end. These are only two recent examples of how some definitions of poetry are made print-specific, even if they are presented in terms of an ambition to define poetry prior to its medialization and materialization.

This does not mean that media are the blind spot of poetry research. Approaches to poetry the last decade address ways in which changes in the media landscape have an impact on poetic genres. Virginia Jackson (2008, 183) engages the role of media when she argues that the understandings of poetry as an expression of the poet's individuality and subjectivity has led to what she calls the "lyricization" of poetry. She claims: "an idea of the lyric as ideally unmediated by those hands or those readers began to emerge [by the early nineteenth century] and is still very much with us." (Jackson 2005, 7) With the lyricization of poetry, Jackson writes, poetic subgenres and such media as scrolls, chapbooks and recitation manuals collapsed. In other words, she points towards one moment in the history of research on poetry where media, with the exception of the poet's language as a medium, escaped the attention of researchers.

An even stronger emphasis on media is to be found in the research on the historical avant-garde and neo-avant-garde poetry and in historical research on visual poetry, sound poetry, conceptual poetry and speech performance. The research on experimental genres and movements, such as those just mentioned, has, for a long time, argued that these art works appeared among others as a reaction to the standardization of literary writing and as a consequence of the domination of the book medium. Among others, Magali Nachtergael, in her book *Poet against the Machine: Une Histoire Technopolitique de la Littérature* (2020), shows how these poetic movements attempt to rethink the social and political dimensions of poetry by searching for the materiality of language – often language close to the language of everyday life – in other media, be it on a stage or on audiotape. These attempts were carried out by media-awareness and media-sensitivity. The same goes for approaches to the neo-avantgarde. As Marc Matter shows in an essay on E.E. Vonna-Michell and Balsam Flex, media and materiality were put in the middle of the attention in experimental sound projects released by this small press publisher (Matter 2022).

Likewise, the notion of media is omnipresent in the research on poetry, such as Loss Pequeño Glaziers' *Digital Poetics: The Making of E-Poetries* (2002), a work that according to Scott Rettberg significantly expanded the field of critical inquiry towards emerging poetry (Rettberg 2019, 14), Adalaide Morris and Thomas Swiss' *New Media Poetics* (2006), Marie Engberg's *Born Digital: Writing Poetry in the Age of New Media* (2007) and Chris Funkhouser's *Prehistoric Digital Poetry* (2007). More recent studies include Hannes Bajohr's *Code und Konzept* (2015), Ralph Müller and Henrieke Stahl's *Contemporary Lyric Poetry in Transitions between Genres and Media* (2021) and Claudia Benthien and Norbert Gestring's *Public Poetry: Lyrik im urbanen Raum* (2023). These exemplary studies show that an awareness of the meaning of media has emerged in recent poetry studies.

Why *poetry*?

Situating Scandinavian Poetry in the Computational Network Environment is the first monograph to explore fully both digital and digitalized poetry in digital media and contemporary poetry as an art form that travels in the media ecology of digital and analog media.³ While the research on literature in digital media, including electronic literature, has had prose literature as their main object of inquiry, academic books on contemporary poetry in digital media are few. Scholarly studies that are engaged with the situation of digital prose include Anne Mangen's *New Narrative Pleasures? A Cognitive-Phenomenological Study of the Experience of Reading Digital Narrative Fictions* (2006), N. Katherine Hayles' *Electronic Literature: New Horizons for the Literary* (2008), Astrid Ensslin's *Literary Gaming* (2014), Jessica Pressman's *Digital Modernism* (2014) and Bronwen Thomas' *Literature and Social Media* (2020). Likewise, the field of research on poetry in digital media mostly engages with digitally produced poetry. These studies include the works referred to above by Glazier, Morris and Swiss, Engberg and Funkhouser.

The present book positions itself as a continuation of similar contemporary projects that deal with poetry and media in Scandinavia and other European countries. Peter Stein Larsen at Aalborg University and the Center for Research in Contemporary Poetry (CERCOP), led a key project on poetry and media called "Contemporary Poetry between Art Forms, Genres and Media" (2013–2016).⁴ The research group applied traditional and interdisciplinary methods and identified contemporary poetry within the framework of genre and genre-deconstruction, of interart and intermedial perspectives and media perspectives as in poetry between print and digital. Similarly, at Universität Trier Henrieke Stahl led the project on poetry in transition, "Lyrik in Transition" (2017–2021), which explored how the use of media have provided new transnational space wherein Russian poetry interacts with different languages and literary fields across geographical and national boarders.⁵ Another relevant project in this context is "Poetry off the Page" (2021–2025), with Julia Lajta-Novak at the University of Vienna as principle investigator. The goal of the project is, among other things, to write a history of British poetry performance.⁶ Here, the question of media is engaged with the focus on body and voice but also on alternative publication channels, presentational formats and institutional structures. Most

---

3 The interrogative pronoun "why" and the cluster "Why Poetry" in the section heading, should not be confused with the question "why is poetry important?" That would be misleading. As a matter of fact, the latter is a question that does not need to be posed, much less answered. By asking why poetry is important, one assumes that poetry somehow is threatened, that it needs to be defended and that its reasons need to be articulated. The fact is that the situation of poetry, as described in the beginning of this book, tells us that poetry is well, that it is visible and audible and that it demonstrates more than anything, its value, function and reason. If at all, the public and research attention given to poetry in general and, more specifically to poetry and media, shows an increasing interest in and an acknowledgment of the vast varieties of the poetic art form.
4 https://www.en.culture.aau.dk/research/academic-networks/cercop/ (5 December 2022).
5 https://lyrik-in-transition.uni-trier.de (15 December 2022).
6 https://poetryoffthepage.net/ (15 December 2022).

relevant to *Situating Scandinavian Poetry in the Computational Network Environment* is Claudia Benthien's "Poetry in the Digital Age" (2021–2025), which sets as its task not only the project of mapping the literariness and the poeticity in poems across different media but also the exploration of a range of poetic forms and formats, in order to develop analytical models and concepts for print and non- and post-print poetry and hence to grasp poetry's movement across media. Consequently, the project is concerned with the dimension of visual culture, music and performance within poetry, with the purpose of acknowledging the vast spectrum of poetic forms and practices, including artistic, cultural, social and political characteristics.[7]

These examples of recent and ongoing projects on poetry and media prove that there is an ongoing interest in poetry for understanding the media situation of the twentieth and twenty-first centuries. These projects demonstrate that poetry is a central art form to pursue if one wants to explore the digital situation of reading, writing and thinking, of new sensations and experiences and of the arts and literature more generally. By turning our attention to poetry in digital media, this book seeks to make sense of the art form's flexibility, mutability, survivability and its *raison d'être* in a rapidly changing media landscape and to study new ways in which poetry can thematize and respond to medial and societal challenges. Moreover, poetry has proven itself to be significant if one wants to study the relationship between literature and digital media. Chris Funkhouser claims in the introduction to *Prehistoric Digital Poetry* (2007) that "[d]igital poetry is the contemporary site of intense concern with poetics." (Funkhouser 2007, xvi) To this, we can add that poetry in digital media is an integral part of contemporary poetry. In other words, if one wants to explore contemporary poetry and its media-technological situation, it is crucial to include different genres and media of poetry, including the digital environments of which it is part. Additionally, poetry is a fruitful source for exploring digital culture. It commits to forms and new and unconventional materials in programmable and network media and consequently explores what poetry can be and do. As Scott Rettberg writes in defense of electronic literature: "[it] helps us understand how digital technologies and digital culture impact writing in the broader sense." (Rettberg 2019, 17) Likewise, the environment of digital media is a central, if not also imperative, place to (re)visit not only the question of what poetry is but also to find out what poetry and the poetic language can be.

Rettberg further suggests that "these [digital] works provide us with opportunities to consider what is happening to our situation within a world increasingly mediated by digital technology." (Rettberg 2019, 18) Similarly, Øyvind Prytz writes

---

7 https://www.poetry-digital-age.uni-hamburg.de/en.html (15 December 2022).

in his study of the digital environment of literature that "[a]n important aspect of electronic literature is [. . .] that it concretizes and illustrates human interaction with its digital environment."[8] (Prytz 2015, 255) Furthermore, he emphasizes "that there are certain topics that electronic literature seems particularly suitable for exploring, precisely because digital technologies are part of its tools and its design language. The media is part of the meaning."[9] (Prytz 2015, 255–256) Funkhouser, Rettberg and Prytz all argue in favor of digital literature as a resource for understanding digital culture. Their argument for its relevance can easily by transferred to poetry in a broader sense and its digital environment, both because poetic works are interacting with digital media technologies and platforms and simply because contemporary poetry is already inscribed in a contemporary media ecological situation.

Moreover, contemporary poetry is written "from within" and can thus help to make us aware of how digital technology and digital culture affect the way we read, write and think. Therefore, poetry serves as a resource for understanding language as an expression of human and non-human subjectivity,[10] and how these two subjectivities are interwoven in the digital age. Interactions between these two subjectivities, the acknowledgment that digital media matters and the recognition of digital media technologies as subjects, make the ground for exploring how media technology creates new forms of poetic expression and how poetry in analog and digital media works in a media ecology where the influence goes both ways. Digital media inspires and helps to create new forms of poetry and to re-actualize already established forms of poetry.

Why *Scandinavian* poetry?

Another question that a reader might pose is why an academic book about Scandinavian poetry would be written in English. The most obvious answer to this question is that Scandinavian poetry is poetry and that research on Scandinavian poetry is part of an international research community. The study of Scandinavian

---

[8] "[e]t viktig aspekt ved den elektroniske litteraturen er [. . .] at den konkretiserer og anskueliggjør menneskets interaksjon med sine digitale omgivelser." (My translation).
[9] "at det finnes enkelte tematikker som den elektroniske litteraturen synes særlig godt egnet til å utforske, nettopp fordi digitale teknologier er en del av dens verktøy og dens formspråk. Mediet er en del av meningen." (My translation).
[10] The idea of non-human subjectivity is elaborated in among others N. Katherine Hayles' *Unthought* (2017), in posthuman philosophy like Rosi Braidotti's *The Posthuman* (2013) and in art projects like *Nonhuman Subjectivities* at Art Laboratory in Berlin (January 2016–November 2017). See also Chapters 2, 3 and 5.

literature is international in the sense that Scandinavian literature is not solely researched in the Scandinavian countries and distributed in a Scandinavian language but is a field of study at university departments on six out of seven continents.[11] The Society for the Advancement of Scandinavian Study (SASS), located in the United States, is one of the largest academic associations to represent scholars and institutions oriented towards the study of the languages and literatures of the Nordic region.[12] One of its sister organizations in Europe is the International Association for Scandinavian Studies, established at Cambridge in 1956.[13] Needless to say, Scandinavian poetry and its research are included in the organization and work of the International Network for the Study of Lyric (INSL).[14] Scandinavian poetry research is inter-Nordic and part of a transnational and international readership. Further, a considerable amount of research on Scandinavian literature is written in English for a non-Scandinavian audience. Or, as claimed by Gunilla Hermansson and Jens Lohfert Jørgensen in *Exploring Nordic Cool in Literary History*, "an interest in Nordic literature and literary history seems increasingly to make its presence felt outside the Nordic countries." (Hermansson and Jørgensen 2020, 26)

A book in English about Scandinavian poetry communicates with the above-mentioned as well as other research communities. Moreover, it makes a contribution by reflecting on and analyzing Scandinavian poetry in a mode accessible for non-Scandinavian readers. Scandinavian poetry implies, in this context, poetry written in Norwegian, Danish and Swedish, all three North Germanic languages that are mutually intelligible for users. The book benefits from limiting the scope to poetry in a specific language region because this poetry is part of a national and inter-Nordic culture and literary history. Scandinavian poetry is, of course, also international in the sense that it is inspired by and inspires poetry in languages other than those of Scandinavia. Nevertheless, poets have the privilege to withdraw from the international scene and experience the regional community and the interchangeability between poetry across Norway, Denmark and Sweden, as well as Iceland, the Faroe Island and the Fenno-Swedish speaking part of Finland.

The material in this book opens an exploration into how Scandinavian poetry in programmable and network media is similar to but also differs from international tendencies. Further, it reveals how some Scandinavian poets are oriented towards an international readership, for instance in publishing their poetry in English in addition to one or several Scandinavian languages, as is the case for

---

11 See e.g. https://nordics.info/about-us/nordic-and-scandinavian-studies-around-the-world (15 December 2022).
12 https://scandinavianstudy.org/ (15 December 2022).
13 https://www.css.lu.se/iass/about/ (15 December 2022).
14 https://lyricology.org/ (15 December 2022).

poets like Johannes Heldén, Ottar Ormstad and Marie Silkeberg. Other Scandinavian poets write poetry in their native language or in one of the Scandinavian languages and hence signify that their primary communities are print and online readers from the national or inter-Nordic region. Other Scandinavian poets like Cia Rinne, Eiríkur Örn Norðdahl and Caroline Bergvall benefit from the language situation by applying multilingual strategies (see e.g. Schmidt 2019, Nykvist 2020).

The list of Scandinavian poets who write poetry in digital media or whose poetry travels between analogue and digital media is long and far too long for this book to treat them all with the respect and close reading that they deserve. In order to reach the above-mentioned goals of this book, I will argue for the value of closely reading poetry in programmable and network media. For this reason too, I must limit the number of poets and poems. Still, the poetry that I explore provides a variety of suggestions on the situation of contemporary Scandinavian poetry, and contemporary poetry overall, in the media environment of the twenty-first century. I write "contemporary poetry overall" to imply that even though I limit my scope to Scandinavian contemporary poetry, the situation, and the environment of which it is a part, is, despite the differences I have pointed to here, to a great extent similar to that of poetry throughout the Western world.

A critical, media-sensitive close reading of poetry

"With the increasing importance of digital media in all areas of social and cultural life, it is necessary to define a conceptual framework for understanding the social changes produced by digital media and to show students and readers how to interact with digital media and culture," Roberto Simanowski writes in his book *Digital Art and Meaning* (2011, 1). To this, we might add the need for a framework and method through which to make sense of aesthetic and poetic changes. By giving weight to the role of digital media in Western social and cultural life, an environment wherein digital art and literature are produced, distributed, transformed, read, shared, commented on and discussed, Simanowski argues for the necessity of close reading and the urgent need to develop a media-specific framework for analyzing digital works. According to Simanowski, such a framework should grasp both the surface of the texts and the media involved in aesthetic appearances (Simanowski 2011, 200–202). Both the position represented by Simanowski and the method he argues in favor of are significant for understanding poetry in digital media. This position and method demonstrate what poetry studies can add to already existing knowledge of the digital media situation. Moreover, a method for closely reading digital poetry might help us in recognizing the contribution made by poetry to the production of knowledge in the media situation of the twenty-first century.

Through analyses of contemporary poetry, I demonstrate that the situation of poetry implies that Simanowski's method could be reinvigorated in order to account for the media situation of the 2020s. Similarly, I combine methods of close reading with a media-critical and media-sensitive approach. Here, close reading implies careful attention to individual poems, while still keeping sight the poem's larger media environment. It is important to note, however, that close reading is by no means a method for "solving" a poem, in the way that one may solve a puzzle. Rather, I regard close reading as a mode of defamiliarization, one that highlights the untranslatability of a poem and demonstrates why poetry is poetry. It is, to use a popular phrase from Donna Haraway (2016), a way of making kin, of making kin with poetry, without turning it into something familiar, something other than poetry.[15] This media-critical and -sensitive approach comprises the framework for thinking about the media environment of poetry and how poetry appears different in different medializations. When combined, the two approaches make us consider poetry in digital media as both *digital(ized)* and *poetry*. A similar methodological approach, one that maintains a focus on both poetic or textual, as well as medial aspects of a literary work, is developed by Hayles and Jessica Pressman and is referred to as Comparative Textual Media (CTM). This is both a mode of thinking and a way of approaching works that draws its attention to media conditions for literary texts, including poetry. Hayles and Pressman write that CTM "pursues media as objects of study and as methods of study, focusing on the specificities of the technologies as well as the cultural ecologies they support, enable, and illumine." (Hayles and Pressman 2013, x) CTM offers a way to study systematically the significance of media technology for literature, for the development of genres and for literary history. Because of its focus on both literary texts and the media involved, it includes as part of its analytical apparatus how human and non-human agents interact in the development, appearance and experience of poetry.

One advantage of applying the method of CMT, is that it does not favor specific textual cultures, media forms or technologies over others. Rather, it establishes an egalitarian approach for discussing both print and digital media and examining how these two develop in complex relationships. In other words, this method can be used to approach code as well as print poetry. Hayles and Pressman refer, for example, to Jonathan Safran Foer's *Tree of Codes* from 2010 and argue that, since it is both a novel and an art object, it represents a new material form through its use of digital media. Further, they argue that in our time, digital and print media are so intertwined in the production and distribution of literature

---

[15] I owe a debt of gratitude to Yasmin Seals, in her presentation at the INSL's zoom seminar on translation on 9 June 2022, for the idea of close reading as a way of making things stranger.

that in order to understand the processes in which literature is involved, we must look at them comparatively (Hayles and Pressman 2013, xiv). In other words, Hayles and Pressman's description of contemporary literature is close to the situation of contemporary poetry that I referred to in the beginning of this chapter.

In the study of poetry in the age of programmable and network media, CMT offers a preferable and adequate approach because of its egalitarian view of literature in different media. As I will show throughout this book, the media environment that contemporary poetry works in, foregrounds intermedial kinships where no one text and no one medium is valued more than any other. Simultaneously, because of the focus on texts and media, this method provides the opportunity to disclose how central terms in poetry studies are, as described above, media-specific, even though they might be concepts developed from, adapted to and entrenched in a print culture in which the book or other media have been the preferred medium.

CMT is, according to Hayles and Pressman, developed out of a range of genres, art forms and media, such as "film, installation art, electronic literature, digital art, emergent narratives, and a host of other computational and analog media forms." (Hayles and Pressman 2013, xiii) One can, of course, discuss to what extent a general text and media analytical method that is developed to fit a wide range of art forms, genres and media, is suited for conducting media-specific and media-sensitive analysis. Such a sweeping ambition always risks the attempt to become universal. Still, in the approach to poetry in programmable and network media, where the poems include and combine a great variety of genres and art forms, I claim that one is in need of an approach that is both sufficiently broad and fine-tuned.

In addition to being a method that is suitable for capturing poetic features and medial affordances, the comparative text and media perspective can disclose how poetry in digital media might reflect on itself as poetry and as materialized and medialized works and events situated in a computational and network environment. Hayles has suggested elsewhere that these metareflective aspects of a text turn it into "technotext". The term refers to the ways in which a text emphasizes and reflects on "the physical form of the literary artifact [that] always affects what the words and other semiotic components mean." (Hayles 2002, 25) In the CMT model, these metareflective dimensions, contained in the concept of technotext, serve, according to Hayles and Pressman, as the starting point for the analysis. They write that "it would recognize that recursive feedback loops between form and content are not only characteristic of special cases [. . .] but are necessary ground from which inquiry proceed." (Hayles and Pressman 2013, x) In this way, studies of poetry in digital media can, as previously argued, make important contributions to the understanding of the ongoing changes in the field of poetry. By shedding light on its own situation, poetry reflects how the new sensible worlds of digital media contain and develop in collaboration with new literary forms and genres of poetry.

Finally, I will argue that a critical media-sensitive approach to poetry in digital media is much needed. The poems are part of a revolution where the scope and commercialization of programmable media and its networks have established, and continue to establish, new technologies and platforms for writing, reading and thinking. If it is true that we are not even close to grasping the larger consequences of digital media, then the need for a critical text- and media-sensitive method is imperative. For instance, a media-sensitive approach to poetry in digital media serves as an alternative to a post-critical position, one of the most discussed methods in literary studies of the last decade. Post-critique has evolved during the past decade as an attempt to find alternative approaches to literature other than those offered by post-structuralism and post-colonial theory and which includes critical, ideological and allegorical interpretations. This position uses among others digital culture to fuel its argument that critical theory and suspicious, close readings are out of date and need to be replaced. In the introduction to a special issue on post-criticism in *New Literary History* in 2014, Rita Felski argues that a digital culture requires a post-critical position. She legitimizes such a claim by placing traditional concepts of reading, often associated with critical theory, in opposition to alternative and, according to Felski, more attractive concepts of reading: "close reading versus distant reading, surface reading versus deep reading, and reading suspiciously versus reading from a more receptive, generous, or post-critical standpoint." (Felski 2014, v) Based on her construction of these binary reading positions, Felski argues that digital culture calls for generous approaches, and she claims that established interpretative and reading practices in literary studies, and critical reading based on a hermeneutics of suspicion in particular, have outlived their usefulness.

Furthermore, Felski and Elisabeth Anker call for a study of literature and the humanities that facilitate more attractive approaches: "At a time when higher education is under siege, it seems urgent to articulate more compelling accounts of why the humanities matter and to clarify to larger audiences why anyone should care about literature, art, or philosophy." (Anker and Felski 2017, 19) It is hard to disagree with the idea that humanities need to demonstrate their relevance to society, though I will refrain from entering into a more comprehensive discussion of Felski's post-critical reading and literary studies. Rather, I will confine myself to clarifying Felski's notion of digital culture. Even though I broadly follow her main argument that we need reinvigorate methods for reading literature, I regard several of her reflections as examples of post-critical shortcomings in the approach to literature in programmable and network media. I argue that while the post-critical method might be of relevance for analyzing some aspects of digital culture, it lacks a necessary notion of the role of media and medialization. To illustrate this, I will consider an example taken from the work I have already cited by Simanowski. In the poetic installation *Text Rain* from 1999 by Camille Utterback and Romy Achituv, letters fall down on a screen as if they were raindrops. The installation is interactive in the sense that when the letters hit the silhouette of the viewers that is also projected on the screen, they change course, and with it, the poem changes too. It is fair to say that one approach to the digital installation is to take part in it and enjoy the visual event, embrace the affective dimension of the work and read receptive and generously, as would be the case with a post-critical approach. Still, it would also be necessary to read critically, to explore the role media technology plays in the work and to what extent *Text Rain* is also a comment on our contemporary digital situation. The poem ends with the line "turn to nothing. *It's just talk.*" Perhaps a receptive reading could be one that recognizes this as a comment on the poem itself, that the poem has turned into nothing, that it was just talk. Simanowski gives a satisfying interpretation of this line when he writes that it "is understood as a celebration of the aimless conversation, which does not turn into a linguistic message as a practical result. Such aimless talk is exactly what users do in their interaction with the letters in the installation." (Simanowski 2010) Still, could it not also be that it is a non-celebration, a somewhat dystopian comment on how conversations in our contemporary time, whether or not they take place on a digital platform, might have been transformed into mere talk, that is, as if letters and words, though shared by humans, never really reach us – that they inspire, in other words, neither feeling (the readers, cannot of course, feel the letters as they hit the silhouettes of their bodies projected on the screen) nor thought (the letters just bounce off the silhouette)? If so, the installation and the poem make a critical comment on society and call for a critical approach that is appropriate for what the installation (also) does. Furthermore, this example demonstrates the need for an approach that also pays attention to how the installation creates an environment of poetry and new technology. In *The Literariness of Media Art*, Claudia Benthien, Jordis Lau and Maraike M. Marxsen describe this environment in more general terms as "complex, interwoven connections among media technologies, culture, and script." (Benthien, Lau and Marxen 2018, 81) The collaboration between poetry and digital technology is one that is both egalitarian and reciprocal, that is, one wherein the poetic event makes us aware of the presence of technology and the technology makes us aware of the text and the way it moves.

Felski legitimizes a post-critical approach to digital culture by claiming that new media technology has made practices of critical interpretation less relevant, writing that the media technological situation requires what she calls generous, receptive and post-critical ways of reading. Among others, she refers to Hayles' research, which has shown how reading, writing, drawing and thinking evolve in accordance with digital technology (see e.g. Hayles 2012, 55). It is, for instance, in such a framework that Hayles develops three modes of reading: deep reading, hyper reading and machine reading (Hayles 2012, 55). These three modes signify that reading is an activity that involves both human and non-human agents and actions. Further, Hayles also underlines how deep and hyper reading are human activities developed in and adapted to different media cultures, e.g. print culture and digital culture, respectively. Lastly, Hayles describes the reading of digital texts as "reader directed, screen based, computer assisted reading" (Hayles 2010, 66) and stresses once again that reading in digital culture is a human action that is partly assisted by a computer. Similar to the case of *Text Rain*, this tells us that we are in need of theories, methods and analyses that enable us to critically grasp the notion and role of media technology. Such approaches would make us able to reflect deeper on the appearance of texts, the development of genres, medializations and digitalizations in the digital age. In so doing, we are better positioned to understand some of the impacts of non-neutral programmable and network media on poetry.

In Hayles' model, deep and hyper reading are not conflicting activities, as Felski claims. Rather, the digital media situation contributes to the development of both modes of reading. According to Scott Rettberg, digital texts require both modes: "The process of reading any configurative or 'ergodic' form of literature invites the reader to first explore the ludic challenges and pleasures of operating and traversing the text in a hyperattentive and experimental fashion before reading more deeply." (Rettberg 2009) Rettberg argues, in line with Hayles, that without this combination of deep and hyper reading, the reader is at risk of losing vital information. To this, I can only add that the combination of these two, which includes a critical media-sensitive approach, like the one provided by CMT, is crucial because in interacting with digital technology, neither we nor poetry can escape machine reading, the algorithms and network. These are among the fundamental features of digital media and therefore highly important for understanding digital culture, how media technology works and the impact that digital media have on our everyday life. Consequently, reading digital poetry from a "more receptive, generous, or post-critical standpoint" would imply that we would lose sight of how media technology works and how programmable and network media involve processes and information, "shadow texts", as Shoshana Zuboff calls them (Zuboff 2019), that affect the production, distribution and reception of poetry. Poetry is an important source for revealing mechanisms and ideologies that might control the contemporary media situation, including technologies that connect machines with machines, people with machines and people with people in a network that affects our sensory life in decisive ways.

In order to uncover and reflect on the complexity that follows digital medializations of poetry, a media-critical and media-sensitive approach is required. It may well be that poems on social media ask for compliant readings and ordinary readers, a concept developed by Torill Moi (2017) that reflects some of the same critique of critical theory as the one Felski employs. Further, it might also be that some of the responses by readers of social media poetry, whether in the form of "likes" or comments, are receptive and generous and have a phatic function. Nevertheless, in the digital age both poets and ordinary writers and readers engage with extraordinary or non-human writers and readers. A computer with its algorithms would be an extraordinary agent, one who conducts machine reading by collecting and categorizing huge amounts of data over a large timescale, by identifying patterns and by generating outputs such as recommendations on digital platforms. Therefore, it is evident that digital culture strengthens rather than weakens the need for critical, media-sensitive analysis.

The material and organization of the book

The selection of works to be analyzed in this book is motivated by how each text creates a simultaneously surprising and apparent connection between the poem and its contexts, including the programmable and network media environment of which they are a part. Some of the chapters focus on single works, while others examine a small cluster of poems. The material includes both digital and digitalized poetry, i.e. poetry that is "born digital" and poetry that has been transferred from an analog medium to a digital medium. Examples given in the beginning of this chapter demonstrate the media ecology of poetry in practice, that is, how poetry travels between digital and analog media, a journey that, as I will argue in Chapter 2, challenges the relevance of distinguishing between digital and digitalized poetry. The term "digital poetry" denotes poetry that is produced to be distributed and read in a digital medium. Technically, "digitalized poetry" refers to poetry that was "originally" published in an analog medium and has later been reproduced as digital data, as combinations of the digits zero and one (see e.g. Prytz 2015, 15). This means that even if a digitalized poem was not written to be published, distributed and read in a digital format or exclusively for a digital medium, the poem has through the process of digitization materially changed, and medial properties have been added as a consequence of the medium in which the poem is presented. Furthermore, as I will argue in this book, contemporary poetry is part of a computational network environment in which the poems float between analogue and digital media, in a media ecology that exceeds the digital network and in an environment that is more-than-human.

Some of the chapters in this book address technology in an explicit way. This is for instance the case with poetry that partly or wholly is written by self-learning algorithms, where genetic codes challenge our conception of the poet's autonomy, subjectivity and creativity. Other chapters explore a small selection of poems by contemporary poets with the purpose of investigating how they use social media and what role social media can play in the creation, distribution and presentation of poetry. Here, the selection criteria include popularity, for instance, the most popular Instagram poets in Norway, and noteworthiness, meaning that the poems in question have received significant attention, are widely distributed and have qualities that make them interesting in a book about poetry in programmable and network media. Again, other parts of the material draw attention to how digital media has led to a remediation of poetic genres and practices, such as poetry film and poetry reading. In addition to the focus on the encounter between poetry and digital media technology, all chapters show how digital genres and practices engage in the question of poetry and its role in society and how the genres and practices are constituted by and constitute the computational network environment.

Chapter 2 deals with the historical and theoretical situation of poetry in digital media. It presents a history of poetry in digital media, a historical review that includes both digital and digitalized poetry and argues for a rationale for a computational network environment for contemporary poetry. The term "computational network environment" serves as an alternative to what Hayles calls "the regime of computation" and what Alan Kirby calls "digimodernism." Additionally, it comprises a discussion of how to understand the relationship between poetry and digital media, how to overcome the question of media as neutral and the concept of media determination. As an alternative, I suggest how to grasp media as an environment, especially as one that includes both human and non-human subjectivity. Consequently, the chapter ends with a clarification of poetry in relation to concepts like programmability, network, events and intermediality.

While Chapter 2 concerns historical and theoretical frameworks for the study of poetry in digital media in general, Chapters 3 to 8 are comprised of analyses of Scandinavian poetry in digital media. **Chapter 3** discusses the role of the poet in the computational network environment, in particular the relationship between the poet and the computer in terms of poetry and genetic algorithms. This is done partly through the framework of what Hayles calls "technogenesis" and partly by reading the algorithm-based and media-ecological work *Evolution* (2014) by the Swedish poets Johannes Heldén and Håkan Jonson. The purpose is to show how *Evolution* creates new understandings of what poetry and poetic language can be. I argue that with *Evolution*, Heldén and Jonson perform a poetic thinking about and an exploration of a possible future relationship between poetry and artificial intelligence. Therefore, *Evolution* can be regarded as a collaboration between Heldén, Jonson and the computer's algorithms where they, as creative and cognitive subjects, as assemblages, create the poem that is constantly evolving on the screen.

Further on, **Chapter 4** pays attention to another poetic and media-ecological work by Johannes Heldén, namely *Astroecology* (2016). The chapter looks into what *Astroecology* can tell us about the situation of poetry in the twenty-first century, how poetry in the computational network environment can contribute to knowledge of the Anthropocene and engage in questions regarding imagined futures. I argue that Heldén's work is an attempt to develop poetry in the computational network environment, as both a response to the Anthropocene and a poetic and astroecological thinking about a future horizon that is disconnected from human consciousness. Heldén makes visible the coexistence of nature as an ever-ongoing evolutionary process alongside technological medializations, demonstrating how media prefigure archives and memories of the past (and the future).

In **Chapter 5,** I focus on Instagram poetry, particularly in terms of how the logic of Instagram prefigures the what, how and when of this poetry. Through the concept of media logic, developed by José van Dijck and Thomas Poell (2013), and by integrating the existing research on Instagram poetry, I argue that Instagram is not a neutral platform, not even for poetry, and that it largely determines the genre of Instagram poetry, including how the poets write, what they write and when they publish. The chapter explores texts that can be analyzed as platform-specific poetry. In particular, it focuses on Instagram poetry in Norway. Because the poems are written in a language understood only by a fairly small community of Norwegian and other Scandinavian-language readers, this material offers poems that in some respect differ from the poetry that seems to dominate the international field on Instagram.

Chapter 6 continues with a focus on poetry in the context of social media and is concerned with poetry that moves between Facebook and the medium of the book. Here I read a few poems by the Norwegian poet Nils-Øivind Haagensen. These poems were first published on Facebook before later being republished in one of Haagensen's book collections. Haagensen is a well-established Norwegian poet who, since his debut in 1995, has written print poetry and prose. In recent years, he has included Facebook as a platform for exploring how many of his poems work, i.e. as occational or political poems. First, I conduct a media-comparative analysis that emphasizes changes that appear in the poems as they travel from Facebook to print and ask how the function of the poems differs in the two media. Then I discuss the value of intermedial analysis and concepts such as "intermedial poetry" and "unfinished business."

For the past three decades, we have witnessed a significant increase in poetry readings in public and semi-public spaces (Middleton 2005). According to recent studies in poetry and sociology (cf. Benthien and Gestring 2023), public spaces do not include event sites such as bars, theaters etc., since you need to pay to enter these places. Public spaces allow entrance without restrictions. With the digital revolution, the number of public event sites for poetry readings have risen even further. That is why **Chapter 7** explores two digital platforms in Scandinavia that offer poetry readings, either as live performances or as recorded poetry readings that are archived. The chapter includes a discussion of what a poetry reading is, what a poetry reading online is, the function of poetry readings in digital media and how to analyze poetry readings in digital media. The chapter includes poetry readings in Swedish and Danish on social media platforms, as podcasts and on "regular" websites.

As with poetry reading, poetry film has become a more visible, usable and accessible form of poetry in the digital age (Orphal 2014; Benthien, Lau and Marxsen 2019). Therefore, **Chapter 8** discusses what a digital poetry film might be and consists of an analysis of a multilingual poetry film in Swedish, Arabic and English by Marie Silkeberg and Ghayath Almadhoun. The poetry film titled *Your Memory is My Freedom* (2012) deals with the war in Syria, the persecution of minorities and the question of how to find a language to describe or deal with the situation of being in exile. Therefore, in addition, the chapter discusses the contribution of digital poetry film as a form of politically-engaged literature and activist poetry.

Chapter 9 concludes the book by revisiting the concepts and arguments that have been developed across the analytical chapters with the purpose of situating these in the framework of specific media, platforms, genres and practices explored in the respective chapters. Since one of the main arguments throughout the book has been that computational network environment includes human and non-human subjectivity, forming a constitutive and creative environment for the making of poetry, the concluding chapter focus on the preconditions for the understanding of the making of poetry in the digital age and how to account for media in poets' "freedom to make."

Chapter 2
The Computational Network Environment of Poetry

One consequence of the media situation for poetry in the twenty-first century, as I alluded to in the introduction to Chapter 1, is that poetry travels between media. This movement takes place in an egalitarian media structure. In this way, questions about the value of a particular medium, as well as the various art forms that poetry interacts with, appear to be inadequate. Such questions of comparing art forms and media have long been posed and will be familiar for instance from Gotthold Ephraim Lessing's discussion in *Laokoon oder Über die Grenzen der Malerei und Poesie* (1766) or more recent debates e.g. the "pictoral turn," as suggested by W.J.T. Mitchell (1992). Rather, poetry can take the form of a written text and/or oral text, combined with images, still and/or moving, and music; it can appear on commercial social media platforms, independent platforms and on a screen in a movie theater or museum, and, indeed, it can be printed in a book. This is a media-ecological practice in which the question is not about which of these materializations, in terms of form and media, has the most value, is the most poetic or is the most appropriate and significant. Nor is the question about which of these materializations is the most "original."

Still, there is something else, or rather more, going on here. What I am proposing is not a mere version of the ancient approach that looked for analogies between art forms, as in Horace's *ut pictura poesis* (c. 18 BC). Nor am I describing the tradition of the sister arts, in which art and literature inspire new art works and literature, nor, indeed, the idea of a *Gesamtkunstwerk*, first coined in 1827 by Carl Friedrich Eusebius Trahndorff in his *Ästhetik oder Lehre von der Weltanschauung und Kunst* and later made famous by Richard Wagner. Finally, I am also attempting to get at something beyond newer ideas about the ekphrastic relationship between art forms as encounters (Kennedy 2012). Rather than reflecting a "total work of art," as was the original idea of a *Gesamtkunstwerk*, the different medializations of a poem complement each other and reflect a potentially never-ending process.[1] We might call this potentiality an unfinished poetics, which I see as related to Peter Lunenfeld's "unfinished business" (Lunenfeld 1999; see also Chapter 6), a concept that seeks to account

---

[1] The idea of art works complementing each other is a pre-Raphaelite approach, described by Aaron Kashtan as "resulting in a double art work whose poetic and pictorial components produced a combined aesthetic effect." (see http://victorianweb.org/painting/prb/kashtan12.html) This is a potential connection to art and literature in digital media that could be explored further.

for the mutability, variability and instability of texts in digital culture. Like myself, N. Katherine Hayles also grapples with the problem of incompleteness in programmable and network media. She asks for

> a theoretical framework in which objects are seen not as static entities that, once created, remain the same throughout time but rather are understood as constantly changing assemblages in which inequalities and inefficiencies in their operations drive them towards breakdown, disruptions, innovation, and change. (Hayles 2012, 13)

This claim has a number of implications for the context of this book. First, there is a question about the relationship between poetry and media; next, there is a question about the interplay between human cognition and artificial intelligence, which Hayles calls unconscious cognitions (Hayles 2017); and, finally, there is a question about understanding poetry as event, performed by programmable and network media. Moreover, as poetry travels between media platforms, digital and analog, both the poems and their surroundings change: every new materialization adds something to the media-ecological history of the particular poem. Therefore, the poems do not "remain the same" but are constantly in transition.

The aim of this chapter is to suggest a framework for the study of poetry in programmable and network media that recognizes poetry's "constantly changing assemblages," as Hayles calls them, which are, I argue, a result both of computational and network dimensions of digital media. I call this framework the "computational network environment." The chapter discusses some of the media conditions for poetry in the digital age and poetry as intermedial event, including how to understand the relationship between media and poetry, applying a perspective in which poetry and media cannot be totally separated. Rather, the two need to be acknowledged as being in a reciprocal interaction with one other. This is especially true when poems are made exclusively by or in collaboration with advanced computers. The latter case, in particular, engages a posthuman perspective and recognizes non-human subjectivity. In the following, I will first briefly describe the development of poetry in digital media. This development convincingly demonstrates the impact of programmable and network media on poetry and makes evident how poetry today is in a media ecological situation and is part of a computational network environment.

A short history of poetry in digital media

The history of poetry in digital media can be traced back to the 1950s. Chris Funkhouser offers a chronological overview of digital-poetic works and refers to Theo Lutz's text-generating computer poem "Stochastische Texte" from 1959 and Ian Somerville's "I am that I am" from 1960 as early examples (Funkhouser 2007, xviii).

Despite the fact that these early literary experimentations with digital technology were in poetry, and due to projects that aimed to develop more "useful" or convenient hypertext writing programs, hypertext fiction and narrative digital texts like *afternoon, a story*, by Michael Joyce, originally written for Storyspace in 1987, and Stuart Moulthrop's *Victory Garden*, another Storyspace classic, from 1992, for a while, dominated the broader field of digital literature. Likewise, in Scandinavia, Karl-Erik Tallmo's *Iakttagarens förmåga att ingripa* (*The Watcher's Ability to Interfere*) from 1992, written on HyperCard and published on disc, is an early example of digital fiction.

The intimate interweaving of literature and digital media technology has so far manifested itself in four generations of digital literature. The two first are often referred to as hypertext literature and multimedia literature. In addition, the development includes cybertext literature as the third generation and social media literature as the fourth generation (Rustad 2012; Bell, Ensslin and Rustad 2014). These four generations highlight different aesthetic and medial strategies, strategies that are related to specific developments in media technology and digital culture.

In the first generation of digital literature, we find texts that particularly emphasize the use of hypertext technology. Narrative hypertext works received much attention from the research community in the late 1980s and 1990s. They represented, so to speak, the status quo of digital literature at that time. Prominent examples include the works mentioned above by Joyce, Moulthrop and Tallmo, and in the field of poetry, Deena Larsen's *Marble Springs* (1993) and Stephanie Strickland's *To Be Here as Stone is* (1999). In these works, the potential of hypertext technology to create texts with numerous possible parallel courses of action and event with different endings (that is, if they had one) is prominent. With the turn from a hypertext-oriented digital literature towards multimedia digital texts (see Ensslin 2006; Hayles 2007; Rustad 2012; Bell, Ensslin and Rustad 2014), one can once again recognize an expansion of digital poetry and other poetic experimentations outside the narrative field. By the turn of the millennium, digital poetry had developed into what Adalaide Morris and Thomas Swiss describe as largely made in "DHTML, JavaScript, Java, QuickTime, Macromedia Flash, Shockwave, and other programs that combine verbal elements with graphics, images, animation, sound, and other multimedia effects." (Morris and Swiss 2006, 14) This second generation, which Hayles refers to as "postmodern electronic literature" (Hayles 2007, 7), comprises multimedia narratives and poetry and, as Morris and Swiss propose, makes use of forms of expression and media such as writing, photography, graphics, film, animations, speech and sound.

Works in both of these first two generations are mainly structured according to hypertext technology, where readers make choices and partly control how the text develops and which events that will take place on the screen. In contrast, the creation and development of literature in the third generation is more or less algorithmically driven. In her book *Literary Gaming* (2014), Astrid Ensslin writes that the term cybertext is applied to digital literature to emphasize how literature plays with the role of the reader (Ensslin 2014, 47). The term "cybertext poetry" denotes the ways in which software codes are given a more prominent role as an agent, partly in control of the reception of the work, though without suspending readers' possibilities of interaction. To call these works representative for the third generation does not mean that "cybertext poetry" first appeared after the millennium. Lutz's "Stochastische Texte" is only one example of early poems in which the computer is partly in control of the evolution of the text.

Given the flexibility of poetry and the intimacy between poetry and digital technology, it should come as no surprise that the fourth generation of digital poetry has found its way to social media. In blogs and on Twitter, Instagram, Facebook and TikTok, texts in different literary genres are flourishing. As a result, poems on these platforms might correspond with terms like blog poetry, Twitter poetry, Instagram poetry, Facebook poetry and TikTok poetry. This is poetry that has been introduced, tried out or exclusively published on a social media platform and that utilizes social media's affordances towards literary and artistic ends. They turn social media into literary media and make them literary and artistic sites where readers and viewers can experience poetry alongside other communicative activities on the platforms. Social media offers literature an opportunity to be in direct and continuous contact with its readers, mediating the possibility of a social reading in which readers qua "followers" experience a sense of belonging to a community of followers and readers with a preference for similar kinds of poems.[2]

The development of digital poetry, conceptualized in terms of generations, suggests both a chronology and causal relation between poetry in digital media and innovative developments in digital technology. The four generations discussed above demonstrate how in just a few decades poetry in digital media has responded swiftly and in a diversity of ways to changing media conditions. This evolution shows how poetry is media sensitive: rapid changes in media technologies lead to equally rapid changes in poems, making way, in turn, for new poetic genres. Additionally, this development reveals a continuity. Some of the poetry works that I have mentioned, like Larsen's *Marble Spring*, are written on predefined writing programs, such as Storyspace and Hypercard. They are thus early examples of platform literature. Today, platform literature is more or less synonymous with literature on social media platforms such as Youtube, Facebook, Twitter, Instagram and TikTok.

---

2 For a further discussion of this "generation", see Chapter 5.

Concerning the relevance of platforms, there is a significant difference between works on Storyspace or Hypercard and poetry on social media. One difference involves the affordances of the platforms that to some extent will differ from platform to platform, which makes the poetry in question platform-specific. Another important difference between platform literature in the late 1980s and today concerns the processes of distribution. First-generation works were mainly distributed through floppy disks, with a distribution model similar to that of print literature. For instance, the Eastgate systems is one well-known online publisher and bookstore for digital literature.[3] Today, however, poetry on social media is made available through network connectivity and various algorithm-driven feeds, giving way to different literary systems that also alter the long and stable "Gutenberg galaxy". Furthermore, other forms of poetry in digital media are accessible via archiving projects and websites with collections of links. Besides, the first three generations contain poetry where the digital media technology is more directly intervening in the poetic expression. In contrast, social media platforms mainly serve communicative and distributive possibilities for poetry in digital media, in addition to providing and supplying poems with paratexts and visual frameworks.[4]

Digital and digitalized poetry

The development of poetry in digital media demonstrates an evolution towards a contemporary situation in which digital, digitalized and analogue poetry are all entwined. Still, in much of the research on poetry in digital media, there has been a strong tendency to distinguish between digital and digitalized poetry, despite the fact that both categories of poetry appear in a digital medium and operate in an environment of programmable and network media. "Digitalized poetry" is poetry that has traversed media borders, from a non-digital medium to a digital medium. The process is a technical transfer of analog information to digital data. In most intermedial events, this transfer across media ontologies and borders would have an effect on the poems and on how they appear on a screen. Furthermore, it has an impact on the internal structures and functionalities of the poems in question and, consequently, on how they are distributed, archived and read. In contrast, the term "digital poetry" is frequently used synonymously with poetry that is born digital. It refers to poetry written in order to be published, distributed and read on programmable and network media (see e.g. Hayles 2006; Engberg 2007; Strickland 2009).

---

3 http://www.eastgate.com/ (15 December 2022).
4 The affordances of social media will be thoroughly discussed in Chapter 5.

Strickland is one of many who emphasizes that digital poetry interacts with and depends on digital media affordances. She writes that digital poetry "relies on code for its creation, preservation, and display." (Strickland 2009, n.p.) So far, this definition would hold true for both digital and digitalized poetry. Strickland then continues by insisting that "there is no way to experience a work of e-literature unless a computer is running it – reading it and perhaps also generating it." (Strickland 2009, n.p.) Strickland's definition serves to distinguish between poetry that is born digitally and poetry that is non-digital. Her definition is a strong appeal to later research: digitally born poetry should be researched and treated differently from non-digitally born poetry. This is because its ontological status is fundamentally different from that of poetry in other media; it is "code born" and is typically composed and produced in order to be read in a different medium than print poetry. For this reason, one might regard this poetry as a media-specific form that offers other poetic and aesthetic experiences than poetry in other media.

To distinguish between digital and digitalized poetry thus appears to be a reasonable approach to an early phase of digitally born poetry and, with regard to some poetic genres, it still makes sense to maintain this distinction. For a genre like code poetry, for example, which is digitally born, it makes sense to differentiate between digital and digitalized poetry because the former is dependent upon computer codes that are part of the poems.[5] Still, in respect to the media-ecological situation that I described in the introduction to this book, this distinction does not always hold. Actually, one could argue that to separate digitally born poetry from the ecology of media and poetry in which it is entwined, would be to isolate it from its network situation. Moreover, Strickland's strict and rather exclusive definition ignores much digitally born poetry.

When Strickland claims that "there is no way to experience a work of e-literature unless a computer is running it," she does not take into account digitally born poetry that can be experienced without a computer running it. Digital poetry that is not interactive and does not include sound and moving images and letters can, usually, be transformed from screen to paper without this transformation involving significant changes to the aesthetic and semiotic expression of the poem. Even further, with regard to an increasingly popular genre such as Instagram poetry, there is good reason to acknowledge it as digitally born poetry. One could, of course, argue that Instagram poetry, in its poetic and aesthetic expressions, does not exploit in any significant way the potentiality of computer codes and other media affordances. It might be written on a computer program, but

---

5 See e.g. Wiebke Vorrath's article "Unter der Oberfläche? Programmierte Schriftlichkeit in digitaler Lyrik" (2022).

often it is published on Instagram as a photographed page from a book. Moreover, as described earlier, the most popular Instagram poets publish their poems both on Instagram and in books. Although it is possible to experience these poems without a computer running them, they are born out of and constitute a digital culture. In fact, Instagram poetry has become a powerful genre because of the way digital culture, of which it is a part, works (see e.g. Korecka 2021; also see Chapter 5).

Given the dominance of digital media technology in all areas of society, which has led poetry (and literature and art) into a computational network environment, there are good reasons for including digitalized poetry in the concept "poetry in digital media." Both digital and digitalized poetry rely on computer codes to run in order for the poems to appear on the screen and through speakers. In respect to understanding the impact of the digital media situation on poetry, and in order to locate similarities and differences between forms of poetry, it is necessary to look at both digital and digitalized poetry. In the framework of this book, the question of origin is of less significance. It would be like asking for the beginning and the end of a network ecology. In fact, to ask about a poem's original medium, is, I claim, to ask the wrong question. It is as I will explain and argue in the following, not a question fit for the logic of the computational network environment. The evolution of poetry in programmable and network media has come to a point where the distinction between digital and digitalized appears less relevant, or not relevant at all, for the understanding of the digital situation of poetry. Therefore, in this book, both digital and digitalized poetry are included, and they will henceforth be regarded as poetry in the computational network environment. This consolidation is not only for practical reasons. It is based on the argument made above and the scholarly position of this study. Poetry always already conveys the traces of the media environment in which it participates, a media environment where multiple media and several materializations of poetry exist in an ecology and continuously influence each other.

Computational network environment

Contemporary poetry in digital media constitutes and is constituted by what I call a computational network environment. "Computational" implies that the environment in question involves, among other things, communicative and aesthetic practices that are conducted exclusively by or in collaboration with advanced computers. Following the argument made by Hayles in *My Mother Was a Computer*, computation is a concept that originally denoted humans who would conduct the intellectual work of calculation. It then came to refer to computational machines that conducted similar labor, including complex calculations that processed massive amounts of information in a split-second. In this way, we witness a transition from "Homo sapiens to Robo sapiens, humans to intelligent machines" (Hayles 2005, 1), an evolution that entails new and advanced collaborations between humans and computers, in short, a new form of kinship.[6] This is not to say that all contemporary poetry in and outside of Scandinavia is produced by artificial intelligence, but that twenty-first-century media, programmable and networked media, have become so dominant in our society that it affects how we read, write and think. This implies, simply and inevitably, that digital media matters and, more than that, that the environment for contemporary poetry involves both human and non-human subjectivity.

Today, the significance of exploring the relationship between poetry and digital media and to question the roles or functions of digital technology for the creative process that leads to the materialization and medialization of poetry, are strengthened by the fact that we are witnessing, as Luciana Parisi writes in the article "Critical Computation: Digital Automata and General Artificial Thinking" (2019), a new form of algorithmic processing that learns from collected data without following explicit programming and a formal mathematical language. Therefore, we have to ask not whether but how the computer should be thought of as intertwined in the poet's thinking, writing and creative practice. The theoretical framework that I suggest, is one that enables us to grasp how digital media facilitate poetry and how we can account for algorithms, whose ability to select, combine and make decisions turn them into non-human agents or what Hayles calls "non-conscious cognizers." (Hayles 2017, e.g. p. 30)

Furthermore, the notion of the computational network environment emphasizes digital media's power of connectivity. This includes networks that connect the many to the many, humans to other humans, computers to other computers and humans to computers on a large scale. Such networks are partly or wholly supported, that is, established and maintained, by the capacity of computers. It is an environment wherein poetry is floating and is centered on both human and non-human agents. In this environment, there is a continuous cooperation between coexisting entities, where none, neither media nor artistic or poetic ideas, can be completely defined in advance. It is a network, in which no medium, no genre and no text is considered more valuable or more important than any other configuration. Of course, "network" has for some time been a buzzword in our electrified society. Marshall McLuhan described the electronic age as "a global network" and metaphorically compared it to the human body's central nervous system (McLuhan 1964, 4). The idea of a network is embedded in Vannevar Bush's

---

[6] Hayles borrows the term "Robo sapiens" from Peter Menzel and Faith D'Aluisio's book *Robo Sapiens: Evolution of a New Species* (2000).

idea of a memory extender, the Memex (Bush 1945), and it has been a central term in hypertext theory since Ted Nelson's "Complex Information Processing: A File Structure for the Complex, the Changing, and the Indeterminate" (1965). In contemporary theory, Bruno Latour, with his actor-network theory, is one of the main contributors to the "network turn" (see e.g. Latour 2007). Mark B. Hansen also underlines digital media's power of connectivity and argues that the meaning of digital media – in other words, that which is mediated in what he calls the regime of networked computation – "is the technical capacity to connect on a massive, many-to-many scale." (Hansen 2010, 180) Furthermore, William Uricchio names the networked era as one of the changes "in cultural production that suggest[s] a powerful change in the situation" of texts in the age of algorithms (Uricchio 2019, 24; 28–29).

Still, network is not an exclusively technical phenomenon but is, in a broader sense, a cultural and aesthetic concept. In this respect, the network also refers to media ecology. Media ecology highlights relational dimensions in which events are given their function, as well as their meaning, in a system and in their relations to other events. Media ecology can thus broadly be described as a system in which media are thought of as connected to each other and their surroundings, both in a technical sense, like in a digital network, and in a non-technical sense, as in poetry that travels across borders of analog and digital media.

In media ecology, objects, which are considered as events, are regarded as parts of a media system – a network of media. These objects, or events, are distinct but relational. In media ecology, according to Matthew Fuller, events refer to "processes embodied as objects, as elements in a composition." (Fuller 2005, 1)[7] This implies that one will not regard an object, a text or an event as isolated or as the exclusive center of attention and experience. This is a form of knowledge embedded in the notion that (print) literature alone is not at the center of literary experiences.

For example, Instagram poetry appears not only on Instagram but also in books. Similarly, poems printed in books can appear on Instagram. However, this description not only holds true for poetry in social media. Indeed, it is also applicable to poets such as Johannes Heldén, Caroline Bergvall, Cia Rinne, Marie Silkeberg, Ghayath Almadhoun, Scott Rettberg and a number of other contemporary artists and performers, whether they are primarily linked to digital culture or to

---

[7] In this book, media ecology is not used as a method for approaching poetry in digital media, even though this would be an understandable approach to the field. It is rather used as a descriptive term for the situation of contemporary poetry. I will constrain myself from taking part in a wide-ranging discussion of the history and the many meanings of the concept, the method and the ontological and epistemological status of media ecology.

print poetry. In this context, we might also think of an artist like Björk, who, on her 2011 album *Biophilia*, not only combines music, song lyrics, music videos and live performances but also a mobile phone application, which, in addition to the ten songs from the album, also includes supplementary texts, as well as sound and graphic art. Moreover, materials from the album were included in a MoMa exhibition and art catalog. Likewise, Johannes Heldén's *Astroecology* from 2016 is an evolving work that so far has materialized as print poetry, digital poetry, art installations, a music album and theater (see Chapter 4). These materializations and medializations are not mere adaptations but intermedial collaborations. They complement each other in their meaning-making processes. Therefore, one could even argue that we have reached the end of generations of poetry existing solely in digital media because contemporary poetry exploits, in a variety of ways, the power of computer programmability, the network organization of digital media and/or the media ecology of literary culture. Hence, the computational network environment includes digital, digitalized and analog poetry and is simultaneously a technological and cultural concept.

Media as environment

As I suggest with the term "computational network environment," media are conceived as an environment, as a milieu.[8] This implies that media constitute the environment in which we think, write and read. We cannot step out of this environment because media are always already our situation. As much as media surround us, they are part of what define us. Likewise, they contribute in forming out conception of poetry. As Jacques Rancière writes in his discussion of art and media: "the milieu in which the performances of a particular artistic arrangement come to be inscribed but also the milieu that these performances themselves contribute to configuring." (Rancière 2011, 2) Consequently, just as media are part of the definition of poetry in digital media, poetry is part of the structuring and development of a media environment.

The concept of environment is distinctive to Rancère's notion of "the aesthetic regime"; he argues that media offer "a new environment of experience, a new technical world that is simultaneously a new sensory world and a new social world." (Rancière 2011, 36) Rather than conceiving of media as suppressing the

---

8 The conception of media as an environment is also put forward by others, such as Thomas Weber in "Der dokumentarische Film und seine mediale Milieus" (2016), Erich Hörl's "Introduction to General Ecology: The Ecologization of Thinking" (2017) and Jesper Olsson's "Shifting Scales, Inventive Intermediations: Posthuman Ecologies in Contemporary Poetry" (2021).

ways poetry appears, media as environment reflects the ways in which poetry and media are involved in each other. In a reciprocal interaction, they constitute a specific environment for experiences and perceptions, whose goal, if there is such a thing, is not defined exclusively by either poetry or media technology. Therefore, the result cannot be traced back to the one or the other.

The conception of media as an environment is crucial because the notion of a computational network environment suggests that poetry is freed from the notion of media as neutral or determining actors. To regard media as neutral implies that media are perceived as neutral platforms for materializing and distributing poems and that they in no way significantly influence the poet's idea or the conception of a work as poetry. Rancière claims that this notion of the role of the medium has been dominant in much art theory until recent times (Rancière 2011). Likewise, Hayles writes that the dominant thinking of literature since the eighteenth century has been one where the literary text is an expression of an immaterial essence "the idea of the work as an immaterial verbal construction." (Hayles 2005, 107) Hayles' argument is that in the contemporary situation of programmable and network media, one can no longer ignore the role media play in our understanding of what literature might be.

Similarly, in much theory of poetry, the relevance of other media than language and the materiality of the poet's voice and breath has been neglected. From the Romantic period onwards, poetry has frequently been seen as the most intimate, subjective and non-material type of literature. It has been regarded as an alternative and often even in opposition to the mechanical and technological world. Hegel, for instance, claims that what is significant for (romantic) poetry is the self-conscious subject that is expressed in poetry through experiences and utterances (Hegel 1975, 1113). According to Dieter Burdorf, Goethe, Hegel and the Romantic period still have a strong impact on interpretations of poetry, at least in German Studies, even if this conception is "not necessarily adequate for earlier or more recent texts." (Burdorf 2017, 23)[9] Still, the Hegelian comprehension of poetry has less resonance in recent theory. Jonathan Culler departs from Hegel's idea in *Theory of the Lyric* (2015), introducing an elaborate and up-to-date conception of the lyrical poem. Nonetheless, Culler fails to address the function of media. In a Scandinavian context, Atle Kittang and Asbjørn Aarseth in their book, *Lyriske strukturer* (*Structures of the Lyric*), which continues to be one of the main reference works on poetry studies in Scandinavia since it was first published in 1968, too suggest an understanding of poetry that deviates from the Hegelian conception of

---

[9] In regards to English Studies, Virginia Jackson in "Who Reads Poetry?" (2008) makes a similar argument.

poetry. However, Kittang and Aarseth also define the structure of poetry, treating respective media, whether it is the book medium or the poet's body, as neutral.

In contradistinction to the idea of media as neutral, media could be regarded as that which sets the premises for poetry. In his conceptualization of art and media, Rancière claims that "[t]he medium, then, is no longer the means to an end. It is properly speaking that which prescribes this end." (Rancière 2011, 35) This point indicates that the medium has some predefined properties that limit the artist's freedom and that he or she is forced to follow in order for the art to be true to itself and its medium. Rancière argues that in this conception, the medium takes on a specific materiality that defines the essence of art. This implies that a medium becomes the framework that sets the terms for aesthetic practices. Not surprisingly, Rancière refers to Clement Greenberg's conception of modernism. The use of a canvas means that, in order to realize the medium's properties, one paints "flat" abstract art, rather than figurative images that imitate a three-dimensional medium, thus breaking with the properties of the canvas as a representational medium. Paradoxically, in modernist, non-figurative art, art becomes an art that reflects both limitations and freedom or emancipation. Again, according to Rancière, art has made itself free from the idea of art as imitation, but, at the same time (and in some cases subconsciously), it also began to obey material and media affordances.

A consequence of a poetry determined by media is that media become what poetry realizes. As follows, media and media's affordances are, to phrase it in the extreme, the goal of poetry. In this sense, the medium is not a neutral instrument for realizing a poem but an agent that opposes the idea of the poet's creative freedom. By emphasizing restrictions made by media or creating new literary methods, for instance based on mathematical models like Oulipoian exercises, one might argue that one constitutes new conditions for creativity and poetry, simultaneously as one realizes literary potentials for a medium or for a mathematical model. Twitter fiction, a genre whose goal among others is to create a story or an episode in as close to 280 characters as possible (see e.g. Thomas 2014), constitutes at once a story or an episode and makes Twitter a literary medium. Likewise, as I will argue later in the book, Instagram poetry is a form of poetry that not only exhibits but also realizes Instagram. It is developed in accordance with the conditions or the logic of Instagram as a platform. In this respect, we might argue that Instagram, to a large extent, determines Instagram poetry and that this form of poetry realizes and mediates the meaning of the respective social media platform (see Chapter 5).

Neither of the two latter conceptions of poetry and media that I have discussed – media as neutral to and media as agents which determines poetry – is, as I see it, adequate for the media situation of most contemporary poetry. The first of the two involves considerations of medium as neutral, as something that is not of concern for the poet and is based on a concept of poetry being more or less as materially solipsistic. That is, one does not recognize the fact that the poet's immaterial idea must be "tested" against something, that it needs resistance. The second conception indicates that poetry is unfree, that it is dictated by the media in which it is involved and, as a consequence, that poetry rather than realizing itself, realizes the potential of one or more media. The two conceptions give the upper hand to either poetry or media and hence maintain a structure where one of the two is neutral to or rendered passive to the other. Consequently, both views lack the ability to regard the two as mutually dependent. In contrast, the computational network environment implies reciprocal relations in order to dissolve binary thinking like subject-object, human-computer. Therefore, in the following I will argue that the contemporary media situation of poetry, what I am calling the computational network environment, is a posthuman environment wherein poetry and media, the poet and technology, are internalized. In this environment, media technology can be regarded as a creative agent.

Posthuman environment

With the dominance of programmable and network media and the introduction of contemporary posthuman thinking in our contemporary culture, the question of the role of media for poetry and the notion of media as an environment have been further intensified. Due to programmable and network media, the ecological situation of contemporary poetry differs from previous historical periods. By defining media ecology as "thinking about media not in terms of thought referred to as technical artifacts, but in terms of their connectedness to their surroundings, and centered upon the human agents in these surroundings," Solveig Daugaard makes a significant contribution to research on literature and media (Daugaard 2018, 74). Still, one should notice that while she emphasizes human agents as being at the center of the network, the computational network environment is an ecological posthuman environment in which no one center can be recognized, and even if such a center should be constructed, it would be an assemblage of human as well as non-human agents.

At the end of her book *How We Became Posthuman* (1999), Hayles proposes a version of posthumanism that recognizes contemporary culture as an interplay between the human and non-human. She rightly argues for the importance of recognizing bodily and material aspects as part of aesthetic and meaningful actions and interactions in digital media. In her later work, in *My Mother Was a Computer* (2005), Hayles states that discussions about human beings and machines, aesthetics and technologies in the future will be to a lesser extent about tensions between traditional conceptions of the humanities and posthumanism and more about different versions of posthuman approaches to the world (Hayles 2005, 2). She justifies such a claim by pointing to the fact that digital technology "has penetrated even further into the infrastructure of developed countries." (Hayles 2005, 2) Digital technology has become "naturalized," so to speak. It has restructured Western societies, and it has become an invaluable part of our everyday world. This means that in many, if not all, of the fields of interest in historical-philosophical topics, including poetry, it is necessary to consider digital technology, computers, artificial intelligence and social media as providers of the contexts and conditions for culture and aesthetics, as well as as independent agents that interact with human activity. This also applies to literary studies and to the study of poetry in the computational network environment.

Posthumanism's insight that humankind does not alone act upon the world, but that change in the world is brought about by human and non-human agents, is relevant for the evolution of genres and literary texts. For this reason, Hayles points out that print literature today appears to be far less privileged and can no longer be regarded as having a natural or exclusive place at the center of literary experiences (Hayles 1999; 2005). Her claim can be positioned in the above-mentioned rationale for posthuman thought, but it is also based on an empirical observation of the media ecological situation of literature as I have described it. As claimed in Chapter 1, today, literary texts are distributed through and experienced via various platforms such as print, audiobooks, e-books, social media and podcasts, and they interact with other art forms and non-literary genres. Although the media ecological perspective is included in Hayles' exploration of the media situation of contemporary literature, the statement above also includes literary works and their individual media. Therefore, poetry must be considered as a product of the interaction between human and non-human agents. Non-human agents include media technologies that, in various ways, are involved in the production and dissemination of poetry and which influence assumptions about, prerequisites for and practices related to poems, whether they are printed in a book, read aloud on a stage or available on a digital medium.

Poetry and media constitute a posthuman environment in which binary relations like subject-object are dissolved and wherein creativity is embedded in the reciprocal interaction of human and non-human subjects, poetry and media. The environment is reciprocal, one in which poetry acts upon a medium and a medium acts upon poetry. The media in question are agents in the creative process of making poetry. In this environment, everything, including poetry and media, are subjects and objects for each other. Because a work of poetry relates to a media environment to which it already belongs and poetry itself performs in and is a co-creator of this media environment, we might understand this relationship as a media-ecological relationship and as comprising "constantly changing assemblages." (Hayles 2012, 13)

The posthuman subject can be perceived as "a collection of heterogeneous components, a material-information entity whose boundaries undergo continuous construction and reconstruction." (Hayles 1999, 3) Tamar Sharon argues that it is "a heterogeneous subject whose self-definition is continuously shifting, and that exists in a complex network of human and non-human agents and the technologies that mediate between them." (Sharon 2013) An alternative way, I would suggest, is one that is in accordance with the notion of media as environment, one that include media technologies as non-human agents rather than, as Sharon suggests, to regard them as mediators between agents. In such a view, media technologies can be regarded as internalized in the creative process because humans and technology have a shared history and are part of the same evolution. In his historical study of humans and memories in *Technics and Time* (1998 and 2008), Bernard Stiegler offers a ground for understanding human and technological beings as internalized. He refers to paleontological studies of prehistoric tools and weapons and points to the causal correlation between their use and changes in the human cerebral cortex. Further on, he connects this correlation to McLuhan's idea of media as prosthesis and writes that "the evolution of the 'prosthesis', not itself living, by which the human is nonetheless defined as a living being, constitutes the reality of the human's evolution as if, with it, the history of life were to continue by means other than life." (Stiegler 1998, 50) In *Philosophising by Accident* (2017), Stiegler summarizes his position as "technics is the condition of culture" (Stiegler 2017, 59) and repeatedly claims that technology and culture are not separate entities but have, from their origin, a necessary coexistence. Hansen, in his comment on Stiegler, puts forward that

> the evolution of the human can be characterized in terms of a long series of 'new media' revolutions: what our material history teaches us is that human beings evolve in correlation with the evolution of technics; the long line of once-new new media would simply be the index of this coevolution. (Hansen 2010, 177)

Similar to Stiegler and Hansen, Hayles too claims a co-evolution between human beings and technology and humans as technical beings. She also argues that the human way of writing, reading and thinking are intimately connected with the history of technology since these activities always have developed in accordance with media-technological evolution. Hayles names this co-evolutionary process "contemporary technogenesis" (Hayles 2012, 1–18) and explains that technogenesis involves a continuous reciprocal-causal evolution of the human and technology. As such, this evolution is important for understanding the development of art and literature in the digital area. The adjective "contemporary" emphasizes the role of computers in meaning-making processes, including the production, distribution and reading of literature, which makes technogenesis different from earlier phases in the history of humans and technology. It is only when the computer takes on such a significant role as it does with programmable and network media, that we really see the significance of contemporary as well as previous media's role in our culture. This posthuman environment where human and computer interact in the making includes not only digital poetry but has, as I will demonstrate later in this chapter, its effect on digital, digitalized and analog poetry because of networked media and the ecology of poetry described above.

Environment as an alternative

Computational network environment is an attempt to grasp in a single concept a major shift in the situation of contemporary poetry (as well as in literature and the arts more generally). Still, the notion of contemporary network environment might suggest both a continuation and a change in paradigm. The term does not propose another Kuhnian paradigm shift. It is not an attempt to suggest a revolutionary alteration of how we think about poetry. Rather, it is fair to claim that the concept "contemporary network environment" contributes to an understanding of the contemporary epistemic situation of poetry. Michel Foucault defines *épistémè* as "the conditions of possibility of all knowledge, whether expressed in a theory or silently invested in a practice." (Foucault 1970, 183) While Foucault uses the concept of episteme to describe how knowledge is conditioned, the computational network environment here concerns the digital media conditions of poetry. Even though one could argue that the computational network environment points toward a situation that is applicable to cultural artifacts and communication in general, I will limit my argument to poetry.[10]

Close to the computational network environment is what Hayles calls the "regime of computation." The regime of computation also denotes that we have entered an environment in which programmable and network media penetrate and affect all areas of communication and aesthetics. Hayles writes that to consider such a regime can "serve to deepen our understanding of what it means to be in the world rather than apart from it, co-maker rather than dominator, participants in

---

[10] For those who are interested in the situation of cultural artifacts in the digital age, William Uricchio provides an intriguing account of the shift of conditions for texts in "Reassessing the Situation of the Text in the Algorithmic Age" (2019).

the complex dynamics that connect 'what we make' and 'what (we think) we are.'" (Hayles 2006, 242) As in the computational network environment, Hayles' regime of computation is fundamentally characterized by a relationship between human and machine that transcends the understanding of these as opponents or in binary structures like dominant-dominated. In fact, Hayles is among those who argue that the evolution of humankind and technology have never been separate. Therefore, she argues in favor of "technogenesis," as a "reciprocal causality between human bodies and technics." (Hayles 2012, 123)[11] In the computational network environment, the "natural" and interdependent relationship between human and technology, technogenesis, has developed into, among other things, an interaction between human language and computer code, human reading and machine reading, where computer code, according to Hayles, has brought about cognitive and neural changes for humankind (see also Hayles 2005, 2; 2012, 10).

Hayles' version of posthumanism, expressed through the regime of computation, emphasizes that "humans are distinct from intelligent machines even while the two are becoming increasingly entwined." (Hayles 2005, 242) What makes the interaction between humans and technology different in the computational network environment is that computer codes are linked to an advanced media technology that not only perform actions but also develops by learning from the outcome of its own actions. In other words, in order to consider the act of writing poetry in the digital age, we need to take the environment in which poetry is inscribed into account, where both humans and machines make choices and combinations and are subject to choices and combinations.

One could argue that there is substantial overlap between the computational network environment and Hayles' regime of computation. Beyond the fact that "regime" might not imply the most positive political connotations, it can also be misinterpreted and read as if computational media are in control and determine the situation of poetry. In his well-known introduction regime as a theoretical concept, Foucault uses it in the formula "regimes of truths" to point to discourses that control truth, and to how societal power structures produce knowledge (Foucault 2010). Programmable and network media are actors that contribute to knowledge production (see Ingvarsson 2021) and the creative process of making poetry. Hence, they are not in themselves a power structure but rather part of such structures – or, as I suggest in this book, an environment. Obviously, Hayles is not a media determinist. Rather, she develops a theory for collaboration and reciprocal interactions between literature and media, between authors and digital technology. Therefore, I will continue to employ Hayles' reflections on the computational regime and notion

---

[11] The idea of technogenesis is elaborated further in Chapter 3 of this book.

of the posthuman but will situate poetry in a more specifically computational network environment, rather than within the broader scope of posthumanism. When I refrain from calling the computational network environment a paradigm or a regime, or to claim that it represents a paradigm shift in the research on contemporary poetry, it is because it does not present a new scientific tradition and is neither determining nor representing a model for how to approach the situation of contemporary poetry. Rather, it suggests a theoretical framework for understanding poetry in digital media, and it offers one of many ways of approaching poetry. Indeed, to claim that this theoretical framework and approach should serve as a model, as if it should provide a new standard for solving challenges in poetry research, would be to create a hierarchy and a new origin. This is a way of thinking that is counter-productive to egalitarian and ecological structures in the computational network environment.

Further, the conception of the computational network environment corresponds with Hansen's argument that the media situation in the new millennium consists of "multi-scalar computational networks and [. . .] intelligent sensing technologies ranging from environmental sensors to the smart phones and other portable devices we now carry with us as a matter of course." (Hansen 2015, 23) Hansen describes a media-technological situation that connects humans and non-humans, events, expressions, experiences and sensations. This situation has an impact on how we experience and perceive the world. Perhaps the situation for poetry too has come this far, that media not only archive and serve as platforms for poetry, but that the future of poetry is inherent in new media systems that anticipate how poets write and readers read.[12]

One could also argue that contemporary poetry has entered "the age of digimodernism." With "digimodernism," Alan Kirby suggests another alternative cultural and aesthetic concept for our contemporary age and emphasizes the role of the digital:

> '[D]igimodernism', properly understood as a contraction of 'digital modernism', is a pun: it's where digital technology meets textuality and text is (re) formulated by the fingers and thumbs (the digits) clicking and keying and pressing in the positive act of partial or obscurely collective textual elaboration. (Kirby 2009, 1)

According to Kirby, digimodernism is characterized by new opportunities for communication and production of texts on social media platforms. He includes new popular cultural phenomena and what he calls endless narratives as one of many "new" features of texts and cultural expressions. Furthermore, digimodernism can be described through texts that are "characterized by onwardness, haphazardness,

---

[12] I discuss this question more in detail in several of the analytical chapters of this book.

evanescence, redefined textual roles, evolving authorship, fluid textual boundaries, electronic digitality and evincing aesthetics of earnestness, apparent realness and infantilism." (Kirby 2009, 155) In this enumeration, Kirby blends content-determined terms with form-oriented ones. It is fair to say that many of these terms sound familiar from poststructuralist hypertext theory such as Jay Bolter's *Writing Space* (1991), George Landow's *Hypertext: The Convergence of Contemporary Literary Theory and Technology* (1992) and Jane Yellowlee Douglas' *The End of Books – or Books Without End?* (2001). More generally, they reflect poststructural thinking and postmodern aesthetics more than they provide an alternative to postmodernism.[13] Many of the concepts of aesthetics pesented by Kirby, are representative for postmodernism while others, e.g. infantilism, suggest an alternative aesthetics, though not necessarily because of digital media technology.

Furthermore, it is striking that Kirby does not include digital genres and text practices in his reflections on digimodernism. In fact, he claims that these genres and practices are missing so far. Kirby asks rhetorically: "Where are the digimodernist novels, poems, and plays? Who are the digimodernist writers?" (Kirby 2009, 218) Moreover, he answers: "it would be truer to argue that digital modernist literature is yet to come." (Kirby 2009, 218) These questions and conclusions make it difficult to follow the argumentation in favor of digimodernism. The digital genres that Kirby calls for have made their entrance in the literary field long ago and represent those literary and aesthetic practices that best and most concretely testify to how literature has changed in the digital age. Digital narratives, poems and plays have been around for some decades, and the list of authors of digital literature is long, indeed too long to be rehearsed here.[14] All together, these genres, practices and authors offer knowledge about the impact that digital media technology has on the way we communicate, as well as on how we write, distribute and read texts.

Most crucially, Kirby's digimodernism does not take into account how deep digital media technology, not least algorithms and network organization, are involved in our culture and how they alter conceptions of human-machine relationships. When Kirby writes at the end of his book that "[i]t is almost possible to argue that digimodernist literature does not exist" (Kirby 2009, 218), he does not

---

[13] Timotheus Vermeulen and Robin van den Akker make a similar argument (Vermenulen and van den Akker 2010, 3).

[14] It should be enough to point in the direction of ELO's collection, https://directory.eliterature.org/, ELMCIP's international knowledge base, https://elmcip.net/, the archive of afsnitp, http://afsnitp.dk/plogultra/ or larger digital collections like Deutsche Nationalbibliothek's Digital collection, https://www.dnb.de/EN/Sammlungen/DigitaleSammlungen/dgitaleSammlungen_node.html (5 December 2022).

grasp that contemporary literature in and across different media has long since become part of a digital culture, where computers at the most obvious level are involved in the production of literary texts.

I have claimed that poetry in programmable and network media is an event. To further qualify such a claim, I will in the following develop this idea and argue that in the computational network environment, poetry is an intermedial event on at least four levels: as poems, as code-based poems, as (most commonly) multimedia poems and as media-ecological poems. Therefore, to argue that poetry in the computational network environment is an event does not only concern the nature of ecology, where objects as events (according to Fullers notion quoted earlier in this chapter) are processes in a composition. More to the point, this claim engages both specific aspects of poetry as an art form and certain media-specific elements.

Computational events and flickering poems

It comes as no surprise that poetry has a temporal dimension and is an event. Poetry appears as sung poetry or as poetry film, is performed as poetry reading or poetry slam and includes performative media in its appearance on the page, specific site or screen. Moreover, Culler holds that a performative dimension is fundamental to and is embedded in all lyric poems. He argues that the lyric is a performative type of poem, contending that a poem is an "iterative and iterable performance of an event in the lyric present, in the special 'now', of lyric articulation." (Culler 2015, 226) These notions of performativity and event are not exclusive to lyric poetry but are appropriate for other genres of poetry as well, especially due to the significance of the poetic utterance and the poem's "nowness" in its articulation. Likewise, Derek Attridge argues that poetry is an event that occurs when it is read in a certain manner. "The poem is a human event," Attridge writes (Attridge 2019, 1). He emphasizes "human" because the poem depends on a human reader to experience it as a poem. Even poetry in digital media requires a human reader to recognize it as a poem. In this respect, the poem becomes an event when a human reader reads it. Due to language's semantic resources and physical properties, "its sounds, its silences, its rhythms, its syntactic sequencing, its movement through time", it is, according to Attridge, recognized as a poem since its meaning "is something that happens." (Attridge 2019, 2) Culler too is attentive to the articulation of the poem, whether this articulation is audible or represented by the imagination of a voice. He writes that the nowness of a poem is "a moment of time that is repeated every time the poem is read." (Culler 2015, 295) The word "read" denotes, as it does in Attridge's notion, a human activity.

In addition to recognizing the art form of "poetry-as-an-event," regardless of the medium in which a poem is performed, poetry in digital media is also an event on a different level. In order to appear and perform on the screen and through speakers, this poetry is dependent upon computers that read codes. In programmable media, poems have a surface and a depth. They are, as Hayles puts it (not with regard to poetry, though), both "flat and deep." (Hayles 2004) Poems in digital media are "deep" in a technical sense because they are processes run by computer codes.[15] These processes are time-based events that take place below, or, taking account of cloud technology, above the surface. The poems are "numerical representations" (Manovich 2001), presented with the help of programming languages and binary codes, symbolized by 0s and 1s for electronic voltage curves. Poetry becomes, according to Hayles, "an event brought into existence when the program runs." (Hayles 2006, 181) The phrase "brought into existence" implies that poetry in digital media has a non-fixed materiality, which means that the poems appear on the screen as "flickering signifiers," (Hayles 1999, 25–28) a term that suggests poems to be brought to the screen in a continuous process, that is, as events. Therefore, Hayles writes that "it would be more accurate to call a digital text a process rather than an object." (Hayles 2006, 184–185) Poems always presuppose a continuous distribution of data files between the underlying codes and the deep surface of the screen. Consequently, the two dimensions, the flat surface and the codes, are not separated. They are connected, held together by the machine that reads and writes (Hayles 2006, 182), since what appears on the surface is the result of algorithms that execute commands and machine-read information stored in computer cells and databases.

Hayles is concerned with how computer codes evoke poems on the surface and transforms them into events. For most poetry in digital media, the distinction between the two layers, the flat surface on the screen and the deep layer of codes, is clear. Again, code poetry, poetry in which the computer's codes appear in whole or in part as print poems (see e.g. Funkhouser 2012, 255, Vorrath 2022), is an exception because the computer codes become part of the poem on the surface, that is, computer codes exist on the surface and below the surface. In this respect, code poetry transgresses media borders and reveals itself to be an intermedial genre. It contains and is based on what Irina Rajewsky in her theory of intermediality would call "intermedial references" (Rajewsky 2005, 50–52). The term is suggestive of how one medium refers to another medium, "as the structural adaption of media-specific aesthethic techniques." (Rajewsky 2005, 52; see

---

15 This is a central argument in Rita Raley's article "Code.surface || Code.depth" (2006) and a perspective that is critically discussed in Wiebke Vorrath's sub-project "Beneath the Surface. Coded Writing and Writing as Code in Digital Poetry," as part of the research project Poetry in the Digital Age, at Universität Hamburg.

also Benthien et al. 2019, 40) Intermedial references in poetry are e.g. ekphrasis or language used in a way that mimics another media. For instance, to write "photographically" is an intermedial reference (Rustad 2020). Now, most code poetry is digital but some also appears in books, where the codes are meant to be enjoyed and interpreted by a human reader. When codes appear in print, they cannot function as computer codes. Instead, they become intermedial references to computer codes in digital media and their numerical representations. Still, regardless of whether the poem appears on the screen in a human language or a computer language, it is run by the computer and is, for that reason, also an event.

Even though it is fair to claim, as Attridge does, that computers are not able, at least thus far in the history of artificial intelligence, to experience a poem as a poem (Attridge 2019, 2), computer codes conduct a form of reiteration in making the poem appear, and re-appear, on the screen. The process of "flickering signifiers," or, if you like, "flickering poems", is necessary for a poem to appear on a screen and is a performance that reiterates the poem. The computer makes the poem appear in the world again and again, and thus, it manifests the poetic and lyric present in moments of time.

However, the nowness of poetry in digital media is also a moment in time that is repeated every time the machine reads the code of the poem. On the one hand, this repetition can be a repetition that repeats a repetition. A quote is a decontextualized repetition in Culler's theory, while recitation is a doubling of the quote's "first" decontextualization. On the other, the repetition can be a repetition that drives the poem "towards breakdown, disruptions, innovation, and change." (Hayles 2012, 13) In both cases, the nowness of the poem is repeated, but in the latter case, the machine does not perform the poem in a circle but in a spiral, in feedback and feedforward loops. Therefore, poems become events that change because they adapt to their medial environment, the computational network environment, upon which they feed.

Medial combinations

Whether as a second or later generation of poetry, poetry in digital media is most often multimedial, combining words, images, videos, music, etc. They are media combinations that more generally is "determined by the medial constellation constituting a given media product, which is to say the result or the very process of combining at least two conventionally distinct media or medial forms of articulation."

(Rajewsky 2005, 45)[16] Combinations of media move digital poetry closer towards other digital art forms. In this regard, it becomes a challenge to poetry research because it offers difficulties associated with categorizing these kinds of works in terms of genre. For this same reason, Hayles calls digital works in general "hopeful monsters" (Hayles 2008, 4). There is not enough space here to discuss all possible art forms and media to which poetry might refer, in print or on the screen. Therefore, I will only briefly discuss the relationship between poetry in digital media and media art here, two aesthetic media practices that in some cases have certain similarities. Even though I agree with those who claim that the field of media art might be a fruitful companion for understanding poetry in digital media, I also argue that it is helpful to uphold the attention on poetry through which to view the digital art form in question.

Media art is a term applied to art works that combine different art forms and art systems. From a literary point of view, the meaning in media art is, according to Claudia Benthien, Jordis Lau and Maraike M. Marxsen, "established through language [when it] inevitably enters into a relationship with other elements." (Benthien, Lau and Marxsen 2018, 2) These scholars argue that media art can stage experimental encounters between visual, acoustic and textual dimensions; that it reconstructs, deconstructs or dissolves literary and textual practices; and that it brings forward frictional processes that lead both to the semantization and desemantization of sign systems (Benthien, Lau and Marxsen 2018, 2). This description of media art could be applied to works of poetry in digital media as well. The experimental strategies and destabilization processes in poetry (and literature) are among the most explored features in the early research in the field of digital literature, as mentioned earlier, particularly as they are related to narrative structures in digital literature. Likewise, poetry in digital media has contributed to these experimental practices.

Because of the many semiotic and aesthetic possibilities that come with network computers, Jason Nelson calls his digital poetry "a poetic playland." (Nelson 2021, 337) Nelson uses hand-written language, graphics and interactivity in a combination of poetry and computer games. His digital poem "game, game, game and again game" (2007) expands our notion of what poetry can be and how it can work and be experienced. Nelson names this poem a retro-game, as it represents an alternative to the dominant clear-lined design in digital culture by re-entering "the hand-drawn, the messy and illogical into the digital, via a retro-game."[17]

---

16 Rajewsky refers to the combination of basic media such as text, photography, graphics, video, speech and music. For a clarification of "basic media," see Elleström (2010) or Chapter 1.
17 See http://www.secrettechnology.com/ (15 December 2022).

Poetry game, or game poetry, as media art and digital poetry, contributes to new art forms, to a continual destabilization of ways to categorize art and to a negotiation of established boundaries between genres and art forms.

Interestingly, Nelson himself terms his poetic computer games both digital art and digital poetry. In so doing, he suggests that there are no clear boundaries between the two and that a good alternative to discussions of genre is, rather than making a distinction, to approach a digital work as both. This notion goes well with Hayles' description of digital work as "hopeful monsters" and the recognition made by Roberto Simanowski in *Digital Art and Meaning* (2011) regarding challenges in categorizing digital works of art. Simanowski closely reads visual and concrete poetry, computer-generated poetry and interactive poetry and names these and other art forms that he engages with "digital art." In contradistinction to this view, Scott Rettberg, who in *Electronic Literature* (2019) includes many of the same genres as Simanowski does, regards these works as literature. These examples confirm that works in digital media struggle against fixed and final categorizations. In other words, they fulfill what Benthien, Lau and Marxsen describe as one of the functions of media art, namely to reconstruct, deconstruct and dissolve established boundaries.

Following Benthien, Lau and Marxsen's approach to media art through the lens of literariness, I argue that even though poetry in digital media often combines media and art forms and therefore could be regarded as media art, the poetic language and the combination of text, images and sound are significant for the works and how they appear. Letters and words – spoken or written – and poetic structures like rhythmic and metric forms, repetitions, syntactic sequences and eventualizations of poems as they move, for instance on a computer screen, are physical properties that make us experience and read the works as poetry. This is also a central approach in Benthien, Lau and Marxsen's exploration of poetic structures in media art (see Benthien, Lau and Marxen 2019, 113–122). The above-mentioned features are significant to the understanding of poetry in digital media as poetry. They relate to Attridge's claim about what it takes to experience a poem as a poem (Attridge 2019) and are parallel to what Culler calls "effects of voicing, of aurality" (Culler 2015, 37); effects that not only appear in lyric poems but also in other genres of poetry. I contend that this effect is important in reading the respective texts in this book as poems, because many of the poems have a structure that creates the experience of "voicing." To quote Culler on this point, "to read something as lyric is allegedly to lend phenomenal form to something like a voice, to convince ourselves that we are hearing a voice." (Culler 2015, 35) These features are central to poetry on a printed page and to poetry on the screen and make a good argument for maintaining the focus on these works, or events, as poetry.

Ecological intermediations in the computational network environment

The fact that many poems wander between digital and analog media turns them into media ecological events, where the relevance of the distinction between digital and digitized poetry is, as I claimed earlier, lessened and replaced by an emphasis on reciprocal intermedial interactions. Indeed, one can argue that this intermedial travelling challenges the before-mentioned generations of poetry in digital media. The situation is one in which various generations are often placed in synchronic dialogue with one another. Indeed, a single poem might contain aspects from more than one generation. The change from first and second generations of poetry in digital media to the third and fourth does not suggest that poetry based on hypertext technology has reached the end of its history. Hypertext technology may still be engaged but is less prominent than it once was. Even though hypertext literature reached its climax in the late 1980s and early 1990s, contemporary poetry still involves hypertext poems. Nelson's digital poems are hypertextual and poetic games. In Scandinavia, the hiphop band Karpe published one of their lyrics, "Sasplussaspussy," as a hypertext poem (2019).[18] Cautiously, one can contend that this synchronic dialogue between generations and the entwining of digital, digitalized and analog poetry are what define a fifth generation, a contemporary media ecological generation of poetry. Less cautiously, I argue that this entwining describes the situation of poetry in the computational network environment.

Poetry's wandering across media platforms too engages an intermedial approach, one that is similar to what Rajewsky terms "medial transposition" (Rajewsky 2005, 51) and which concerns the migration of texts between media, such as the adaptation of a novel into a film or the migration of a poem between a book and Instagram. It is a form of intermediality that engages media as technical media and emphasizes the intermedial travelling of poems. Still, in the case of poetry in the computational network environment, the migration is not linear but networked, that is, poems move between analog and digital media platforms in a network structure. This media ecology of poetry substantiates the obvious fact that print poetry no longer exists in isolation from other media, as if it ever did. Therefore, in order to grasp such a movement in which media do not exist in isolation from each other and in which no particular medialization is to be regarded as more important than any other one, I suggest to apply the term "intermediation." The term, which is theorized by Hayles among others, denotes "the spirit of multiple causality in

---

[18] https://sasplussaspussy.no/tekst.

emphasizing interactions among media." (Hayles 2005, 33) Intermediation refers to non-linear relations of media and of literary works that do not proceed from one medium to another in a single direction. Rather, the interaction is a result of intertwined causal relationships and multiple co-existing feedback loops. In this way, as Hayles notes, texts can "converge into digitality and simultaneously diverge into a robust media ecology in which new media represent and are represented in old media." (Hayles 2005, 32) In other words, intermediation draws attention towards the complexity in poetry's migration between media. It represents an alternative to concepts that present intermedial migrations as linear movements from one original medium to another. In this respect, one may pay too much attention on whether a poem is originally born in an analog or digital medium. Therefore, intermediation supports the blurring of the distinction between digitally born and digitalized poetry since both concepts draw attention to an origin/original.

With the purpose of addressing the situation of poetry in the framework of the computational network environment, I have described some of the recent changes in structures and processes concerning the production, distribution and reception of poetry. Therefore, I have outlined the computational and media ecological environment of contemporary poetry. I have included in the discussion three theoretical positions for approaching the relationship of poetry and media (media as neutral, media determinism and media as environment) with the purpose of arguing in favor of viewing media as an environment. Although media as a posthuman environment is the one that is the most adequate for the situation of contemporary poetry in the computational network environment, all three are to be regarded as theoretical or ideal models. In practice, the relation of poetry to media will vary and the outcome of the interaction between the two will differ from poem to poem. The point is that much contemporary poetry is inscribed and functions in a media environment that to varying degrees has an impact on the poems, simultaneously as the poems influence the media environment.

I have suggested that the relationship between poetry and media has historically been recognized either as non-existent or as media deterministic. The former position is dominant in much work in the theory of poetry, while the latter is apparent in poetic experimentations with media technologies. Both of these positions, media as neutral and media viewed as determining the making of poetry, maintain the subject-object relationship. Entering the realm of the posthuman, media as environment obviates binary thinking. Poetry and digital media can be thought of as being the subject and object for each other. So, rather than regarding media as neutral or as part of the goal of poetry, a new sensible and social environment of poetry and media should be postulated. Further, by combining Hayles' posthumanism with the idea of media as environment, media become not only a source of inspiration but an agent that resists the poet's creative process.

Programmable and network media are regarded as creative subjects in a posthuman media environment wherein poetry can be seamlessly articulated with machine reading. Concurrently, poetry might be an art form that makes machine reading and artificial intelligence visible and thus reflects on the computational network environment of which it is a part.

Chapter 3
Poetic Technogenesis and the Future of Poetry? Johannes Heldén and Håkan Jonson's *Evolution* (2014)

"Welcome to evolution. Start by selecting language" reads the opening of the digital-poetic work *Evolution* (2014; see Fig. 1).[1] The opening page shows a photograph of a wooden desktop with an open book on it. The desktop is shabby and seems old and well used. It is full of scratches, stains and dry marks; there is even, perhaps, a mark where water had been spilled. The book appears to have a stiff cover; the pages of the book are creased and have slight folds. The book is opened to the colophon page, which lists information about the release, including an ISBN number, information that is historically and legally specific for the institutionalization of the book. So far,

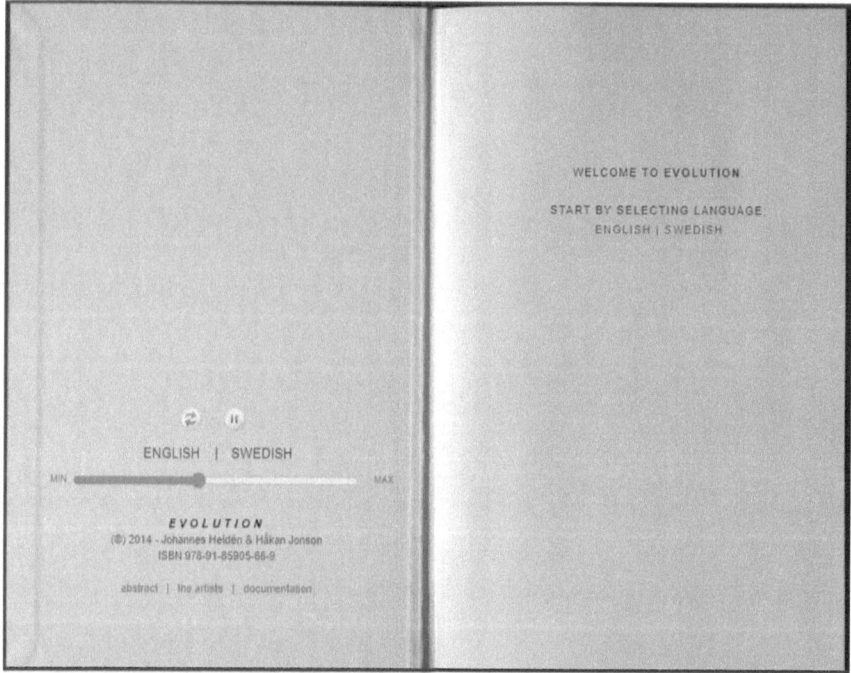

Fig. 1: The opening screen of the digital work *Evolution* (2014) by Johannes Heldén and Håkan Jonson.

---

1 http://www.textevolution.net/ (15 December 2022).

this could simply be a page with a photograph of a desk and a book. But the page also contains interactive links with functions such as "restart" and "pause" and a device that allows one to control the pace of the process. Moreover, there are three links that lead to information about the present poetic project and its authors, marked respectively as "abstract", "the artists" and "documentation." On the opposite page is a link to the English and Swedish versions of the project. All of these functions emphasize that the book is not a book but an image of a book, a remediation that makes the digital work something different from what it would be in print.

Evolution is a collaborative work by the Swedish artist and poet Johannes Heldén and the Swedish poet and programmer Håkan Jonson. The image I briefly described above is from the digital part of this intermedial project that consists of a physical book and a digital work and involves several multimedia presentations and poetry readings. As a whole, it includes a potentially endless ecology of medializations and materializations. Parts of the project are presented at different physical and digital occasions and locations.[2] It is a multimedia work combining not only technical media but also graphics, photographs, words and computer codes, and it transgresses genre conventions.

The book *Evolution* includes code poetry, scientific tables and reports and scholarly essays. In 2014, it was awarded the N. Katherine Hayles' prize for Criticism of Electronic Literature, by the Electronic Literature Organization.[3] In their announcement, one of the jury members writes:

> Perhaps the book was written, compiled, designed by *Evolution* itself. Even the table of contents looks like computer code, laid out the way that a piece of software might prefer. I'm ranking this book first on my list because of its challenges to the form of criticism – there is a creativity and unexpectedness in the way that these responses to the text are presented that is very engaging and that contributes to the work and to the field in general.

While the book is both performative and fixed, the digital part is, in principle, a never-ending and ever-changing poetic event. This chapter concentrates on the digital part of *Evolution*, in order to grasp how certain aspects of the work are connected. Moreover, I explore how the work engages in its situation and media environment. It will therefore also be necessary to look at the print book *Evolution*. The purpose is to show how *Evolution* creates new understandings of what poetry and poetic language can be. I argue that with *Evolution* Heldén and Jonson practice and explore poetic thinking about a possible future relationship between

---

[2] An overview of this activity and the many events are to be found on Heldén's artistic website: https://www.johanneshelden.com/news (5 December 2022).
[3] See http://eliterature.org/2014/06/announcing-winners-of-1st-coover-hayles-awards/ (5 December 2022).

poetry and artificial intelligence. Therefore, *Evolution* is a collaboration between Heldén, Jonson and the computer's algorithms. This collaboration forms a creative and cognitive assemblage and creates the poem that is constantly evolving on the screen. In this respect, I will also argue that the work draws the attention to technology as a creative agent and thus to the idea of technogenesis. For poetry in the computational network environment, this is perhaps the singular point, namely that point at which digital technology and artificial intelligence intervene in poetry in a way that dramatically changes both what poetry can be and how it works.

One of the most intriguing and pressing questions for poetry in the computational network environment concerns the role of media and how to understand the encounter between the poet, the poetic idea and so-called self-learning algorithms. The solipsistic idea of the poet, isolated from the world and everyday life, who receives inspiration through tranquility or in deep connection with God or an untouched nature is long gone. In our digital age, this idea is, as I discussed in Chapter 2, challenged by an understanding of the reciprocal interconnectedness of human and technology, put forward by philosophers like Bernard Stiegler or in theories of the posthuman such as N. Katherine Hayles' "technogenesis" (Hayles 2012). As mentioned, Hayles develops the idea of technogenesis in order to understand how aesthetic and social processes in the digital age work in networks of conscious and unconscious cognitions (Hayles 2017). Likewise, Heldén and Jonson explore a similar idea in their poetry.

The poetic event of *Evolution*

Evolution is an algorithm-based poem and event, a poem in which the computer's algorithms continuously create and change the poem on the screen and make it into an event. Words, word clusters and blank spaces appear, disappear and change on the screen, brought forward by the computer's algorithms. The poem performs itself on the right-hand side of the screen, while information about the ongoing process is given at the bottom of the page, below the poem. Here, the number of transactions that have been conducted by the machine is shown. Further, information about designations of atmosphere ("ambience") is displayed together with the title of the sequence that the computer is working on (e.g. see Fig. 2).

By clicking on the button marked with a play-sign on the left-hand page, the work is activated. On the right-hand page, a poem with a postmodern typography appears with single words and word clusters with blank spaces between them. The left-hand margin is straight, while the one on the right has a ragged edge. The poem follows just a few, if any, grammatical rules. None of the words are

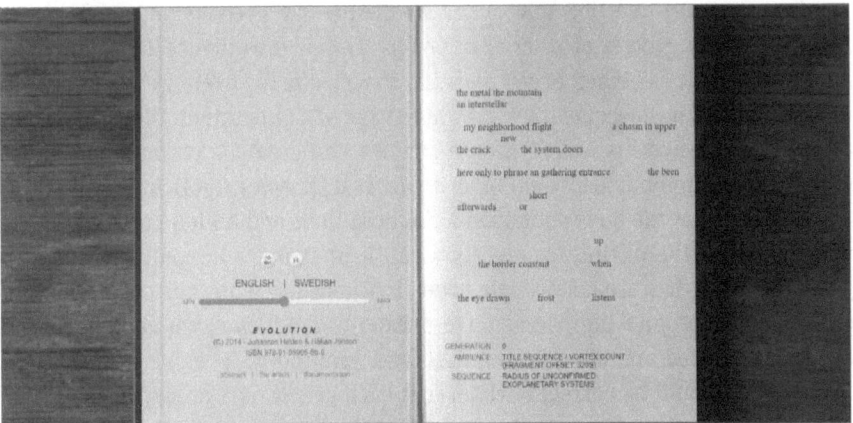

Fig. 2: A screenshot from a random place/page in the evolutionary process of the poem in *Evolution*.

written with capital letters or begin with a capital letter, and it lacks grammatical symbols and punctuation marks.

The poem gradually changes. New words appear, some fade from the screen immediately, others again stay on the screen for a long time and become part of different contexts. At an early stage in one of my readings, the first two lines read: "a metal door // an interstellar." Later in the same reading, "a metal door" has been replaced by "a comic door" and the word "interstellar" has been moved to the first line: "a comic door open my interstellar travel gargoyles". There seems to be no poetic or logical explanation for the changes, except that the changes and the event are the meaning of the work. The work is an event both because of its underlying code, its flickering signifiers, and because it is a continually changing assemblage. As I described in Chapter 2, poetry should be regarded as an event, including in those cases when poems change, vary or are disorganized to the extent that they end in breakdown or continue to change (see e.g. Hayles 2012, 13). Here, the lack of punctuation and other grammatical symbols strengthens the ongoing evolutionary process, since a full stop would mark, for example, the end of a sentence, a larger sequence or the poem as a whole. Likewise, a comma would signify a grammatical break. But, rather than including such breaks, computer-generated algorithms cause pauses to appear in the poem. Blank spaces and single words are kept on the screen during several sequences, perhaps for the sake of continuity or perhaps to make the poem readable for a human being. Evolution never stops, never pauses, but moves forward through both continuity and change. So does *Evolution*. As long as the computer is kept running and there is no technical breakdown, as long as the computer program continues to read code and is able to complete the predefined instructions, the poetic event will continue.

An important question that arises is whether the event is one single poem that continually evolves or a series of poems – a poetic sequence. More provocatively, one might ask whether the question concerning the event as a single poem or many poems has become irrelevant in the age of computation. When Raymond Queneau published his book with ten sonnets and created, as combinatory poetry, "poésie combinatoire," *Cent mille milliards de poèmes* (1961), he suggested in the very title that the book contained a hundred thousand billion poems. In other words, even if the poems are merely a result of changes in combinations of a given material, they are not a single poem. In Queneau's work, the pages separate each print poem and the poems have a fixed organization. On each page, the event has stopped and materialized itself as a print poem. This is not the case in *Evolution*. It would be correct to claim that each generation, or sequence, is only one materialization. However, such a claim would also imply that the reader must pause the process and interfere with the poem that continues to flow like a river. Still, the event is marked, quantified with the number of generations in the specific reading and qualified with a title on each sequence. In one reading, twenty generations yield the following poem:

> of the new　　　　　　　　　　　　　in
> high dragonflies came around me
> not leaves　　　　　　　　　　　　take another one
> 　　　　　　　　messages sent

In addition to information about the number of generations, the work tells us that the ambience is "Title sequence / corporations (fragment offset 140S)" and that the poem belongs to the sequence called "Radius of confirmed exoplanetary systems." The title of the sequences changes every eight to ten generations, while the information concerning the ambience changes less often or each time the reader pauses the performance, consequently interrupting the event. On the one hand, one could argue that because of the sequences, each containing eight to ten generations, the work could be treated as a sequence of poems. Sequence here is not to be understood as the genre elaborated by Sally M. Gall and Macha Rosenthal's classic study of the poetic sequence. Gall and Rosenthal claim that the poetic sequence is a long poem structured through association, juxtaposition and connection (Gall and Rosenthal 1983). These qualities in the process of selection and combination would assume a human being to associate, juxtapose and connect. Rather, in *Evolution* it is the computer that selects and combines, without any consciousness about why the words are selected and combined. Further, in *Evolution*, sequence is a technical term that denotes the number and logical steps that the algorithms perform and complete in performing one specific task. This implies that the name of one sequence does not necessarily have anything to do with the poem or the words that appear on the screen in a specific sequence.

The first sequence in one reading is called "Cups of coffee per episode of Twin Peaks," while one of the generated poems in this sequence says: "so // phanerogams known / would probably be change / shining // out / something // is." Except for the fact that the poem appears to be as illogical as the fictive universe of David Lynch and Mark Frost, it would take some interpretative work to connect the information that is given in the title of the poem to its content. Therefore, the connection between changes in the knowledge of plants that carry seeds (phanerogams) and the number of cups of coffee that special agent Dale Cooper and the other characters drink during one episode of *Twin Peaks* is most likely random. Furthermore, from the tenth to the eleventh generation, the sequence shifts from "Cups of coffee per episode of Twin Peaks" to "Radius of unconfirmed exoplanetary systems," but the poem does not change with the change of title. In this specific reading, the first visual change in the poem takes place at the fourteenth generation. Taking into consideration the fact that the poem does not change much during one sequence or in the transition from one sequence to another, it seems reasonable to regard the sequence as a technical concept and to treat the title of each sequence as separate from the form and content of the poem that evolves. Additionally, the titles and ambiences of sequences represent the organization of a process that is continually taking place, not on the surface but below the surface, in the world of computer code.

In generation 3197 of one particular reading, the sequence is called "Mass of exoplanets detected by timing." The title denotes discoveries of planets outside of our solar system and signifies the fact that the poem is either referring to scientific facts – planets that have been detected – or that it is revealing itself to be a science fiction poem. Therefore, the generations and sequences are of importance for understanding the poem as an event, just as they emphasize both the performance and role of the computer in the performance. One could even ask whether the titles of the sequences constitute a poem or narrative in their own right and to what extent they provide information useful for the interpretation and experience of the poem.

To read an intermedial event

Another intriguing question is how to read *Evolution*. We might even go so far as to ask whether a concept like "reading" is applicable at all, since the poem continually evolves. What would it mean to "read" a media-ecological work presented as, among other things, digital and print poetry? Further: who, or what, is reading and when? What takes place under the surface is a computer performance, what Hayles calls "machine reading" (Hayles 2012, 75–79). The computer selects and combines words, organizing them into a poem that appears on the screen for a human being to read.

To read *Evolution* does not require much interactive work. The poem evolves on the screen through repeated computer generations. The readers first need to choose a language, and then they can control the pace of the event and the changes that take place. They can also choose to read the above-mentioned information about the work in order to contextualize the poem. While the latter information functions as a fixed contextual framework for the poem that evolves, the poem is always in flux. The notion of the poem as an evolving event means that the poem is always different and that one (at least in theory) never reads the same poem twice. Every poem, the result of every generation, is unique.

Erika Fischer-Lichte (2004) reminds us that an event on a theater's stage is unique and cannot be repeated. With theater performances as her main material, Fischer-Lichte emphasizes how performances take shape through an interaction between the audience and what happens on stage. According to Fischer-Lichte, a feedback loop arises in which the interaction is unpredictable and the event unique (Fischer-Lichte 2004, 59ff; 116). Therefore, she also emphasizes that a performance should not necessarily be understood but rather experienced as an action (Fischer-Lichte 2004, 17). To this, it is crucial to add that Fischer-Lichte strongly insists upon a physical co-presence of actors and audience. Therefore, her concept of event is not easily transferrable to the digital situation of *Evolution*, even though one might argue that in the events on the screen there is a strong physical presence of the computer as a co-creator of the generated words and phrases.

Evolution is a poetic event to be experienced, in which the computer functions as a platform and a stage where the poem unfolds and acts as a co-creator of the poem. One can press start, sit back and observe the poem that appears and changes on the screen. However, at the same time, *Evolution* invites the reader or viewer to reflect upon what is taking place on the screen and below the surface. It implicitly asks the reader to pay attention to the premises put forward by the media technology, to what is happening and to how the relationship between poetry and digital media, humans and algorithms and an alphabetical-conventional language and computer code can be understood.

To conduct a hermeneutic close reading of the digital poem is made almost impossible because the event that takes place on the screen is unpredictable, unique and never-ending. Consequently, there is no obvious or fixed correlation between individual parts and the whole. Rather than a hermeneutic circle, readers are left with a line, a stream of words that constantly feeds the changing poetic event. In this sense, we might say that readers are put in a situation where they can experience the poem. This is what Fischer-Lichte would claim, in a more general way, about the proper way to approach performance. Nevertheless, in *Evolution*, two aspects are noteworthy. First, the poem develops in a pattern of repetition and change, which, as I will explain later in this chapter, is related to the technogenetic environment of the poem and its reflexivity. The other relevant aspect for a reading of *Evolution* is that readers are given the opportunity to interfere in the process. Either they can choose to watch the changes and experience the event, or they can pause at each generation, at each new sequence, to closely studying the words and combinations and thereby viewing each generation as a "whole." The flipside of such an approach is that the reader disrupts the event and turns the poem into something other than what it is, namely an evolution. It is possible to do both, to approach the poem as an event and, at the same time, to pause the poem in order to closely read specific moments of the event. A combination of these two approaches implies that one regards *Evolution* as a poem and as an event and that one concurrently keeps in mind that both the generations and the event are framed in a human-computer collaboration.

The print book *Evolution* contains the computer codes that run the digital poem. As mentioned, the book received the N. Katherine Hayles Award for Criticism of Electronic Literature in 2014. In their statement, the jury writes that the book is both "a work of literature and multi-voiced, multi-modal criticism". Further, they claim that it provides "responses to the generative [digital] poem *Evolution* by Johannes Heldén and Håkan Jonson and plays with the genre of criticism by enclosing the essays within over 200 pages of code."[4] The book is not pure but includes a mix of genres. Most striking is the many pages of code that in the book are combined with Heldén's poems, photographs and essays written by researchers in the field of digital literature: John Cayley, Marie Engberg, Jesper Olsson, Jonas Ingvarsson, Jakob Lien and Cecilia Lindhé.

The book is in itself a product of aesthetic and epistemological considerations in the computational network environment. With the computer codes, the human responses to the work and results of technological measures that are presented in graphs and lists, the print book too is a human and non-human work. It is a network, and it is part of a network of texts, media, codes and events. In the opening of the book, it says:

---

4 See https://eliterature.org/2014/06/announcing-winners-of-1st-coover-hayles-awards/ (5 December 2022).

```
Package net.evolution.text.domain:

import net.evolution.text.domain.generation.Generation:
import net.evolution.text.domain.rule.ConsecutiveWordsRule:
import net.evolution.text.domain.rule.IllegalEndingFragmentRule:
(. . .)
Private static final Rule RULES []= {
        new LineBreakCommaRule(),
        new WhiteSpaceCommaRule(),
(Heldén 2014b, n.p.)
```

A human reader will most likely feel addressed in the encounter with the six essays and Heldén's print poems. In contrast, the computer code that fills most pages defamiliarize the work, as if the code is out of place in such a context. This response may occur because few readers can read computer code and because the pages of code appear in print, that is, in an analog rather than a digital medium. Additionally, one could argue that the code has an ambivalent, or double, addressee. Code is the language of and for computers, and is, in most cases, addressed to computers. Computer codes are commands, most often input by humans, which are meant for computers to execute. A human programmer speaks to the computer in a language it understands. This is also how the appearance of print code in the book can be read. It represents the codes and instructions that Heldén and Jonson have used in order for the digital part of *Evolution* to work. Anyone who wants to can enter all the print codes from the book into a computer and thus copy or change the digital poem.[5] The book is, in other words, a recipe book for the digital work *Evolution*, and, therefore, even though it has a double addressee, it turns its attention from what is present, the book, towards what is absent but present through codes, the digital work.

Furthermore, due to the medium, the print codes are also addressed to a human reader. A strong argument presented in the field of critical code studies is that codes used in code poetry could be made an object for human interpretation (Marino 2020, Vorrath 2022). Still, it is fair to ask how to read the book or whether we should read the 200 pages of code at all. Is it perhaps the case that a human reader should preferably read the code aloud, as in a poetry reading, so that the sound of the poems when uttered covers for the lack of linguistic semantics. In this respect, the poems may sound like Dadaist sound poetry. Or perhaps the effect of the sound of the repetitive commands can be recognized as a pattern, as anaphoric repetitions in an analog medium that has nevertheless become digital.

---

[5] See "documentation" here: http://www.textevolution.net/ (5 December 2022).

In this way, the reading will reveal the poems as code poetry, a poetic work that mixes poetry with computer codes.

In the book, the codes cannot run, the commands cannot be executed by computer algorithms, but they can be executed, read, by a human reader. Still, I find it fair to claim that, as a response to the digital part of *Evolution*, the book needs to be regarded as a post-digital phenomenon because it occupies a space between analog and digital and because the term post-digital suggests how analog and digital cultures have merged. Florian Cramer defines the post-digital pragmatically as a description of "either a contemporary disenchantment with digital information systems and media gadgets, or a period in which our fascination with these systems and gadgets has become historical." (Cramer 2015, 13) Codes have become mainstream, also in poetry, whether we are conscious of them or not. When code appears in print, it denotes binary language at the same time as it differentiates itself from it, because in print it is analog, undivided and continuous.

The concept of the "post-digital" obviously does not mean that the digital era has ended, but it implies that, in the digital era, programmable and network media are "everywhere". Moreover, the term underpins the fact that in the computational network environment, analog and digital media, print and digital poetry, are entwined. Digital code has even invaded the print book, not only by amending the visual and material aspects of the book or by changing how we write and read but simply by being included on the surface of a poetry book as code poetry and combined with texts written in conventional English in humanistic genres like essays and scholarly reports. Therefore, the print book *Evolution* strengthens the hypothesis in this chapter: *Evolution* explores the relationship between humans and computers, and, more specifically, it explores poetry in the encounter with computer's genetic algorithms. Indeed, the book is precisely a materialized result of poetic technogenesis, that is, of the human-technological evolution of poetry.

Generative poetry and a poetic technogenetic feedback loop

Algorithm-based poetry belongs to the genre of generative poetry, what is also termed "combinatory poetics," and it is an early genre in the history of poetry in digital media, as the short presentation in the beginning of Chapter 2 tells. Indeed, according to Scott Rettberg, it is "the oldest genre of electronic literature." (Rettberg 219, 20) Produced by a computer, generative poetry implies a practice in which the selection and combination of words and other semiotic resources are based on predefined formal rules, commands for the computer to perform and a collection of characters, words and phrases in a database. Jean-Pierre Balpe points out that generative literature is literature "of which the author does not write the final texts but which only works at the level of the high rank components such as: conceptual models, knowledge rules, dictionary entries and rhetoric definitions." (Balpe 2005, n.p.) Balpe's definition of generative literature is media-specific and assumes that the genre always involves processes with algorithms powered by a computer. However, generative poetry can also be performed in other media. The defining feature of generative poetry, however, does not have to do with the question of media but to what extent a generative poem is performed in accordance with predefined rules. Rather than computer algorithms, a human being could perform and execute the rules and instructions that she herself or others have made, as in the case with mathematical poetry where the poet follows predetermined mathematical rules for how to choose and combine words. As I pointed out earlier, this would be a creative process in which the purpose might be to diminish the role of the poet for the benefit of the rules and restrictions.

Still, concerning computer-generated poetry, two aspects are, in this respect, of particular interest. One is that the selection and combination of words and phrases are performed partly by a human being who sets the premises for the action that takes place and partly by a computer that performs the actions. Selection and combination are two processes, each belonging to its own axis. Roman Jakobson regards the two processes as significant for the poetic function. In his elaboration on the poetic function, the poetic quality is linked to the axis of selection and combination and, more specifically, to a transfer of the principle of equality from the axis of selection to the axis of combination:

> The election is produced on the base of equivalence, similarity and dissimilarity, synonymity and antonymity, while the combination, the build up of the sequence, is based on contiguity. *The poetic function projects the principle of equivalence from the axis of selection into the axis of combination.* (Jakobson 2014, 240)

For computer-generated poetry, these two processes are redefined from being human-centered processes to being rule-based and (partly) computer-centered. This means that when the computer takes over selection and combination processes, it takes over part of the poet's role, performing tasks that are regarded as significant for the poetic function and the quality of both poem and poet.

Even though the role of the poet in the process of making poetry, her freedom to create, has been changed, she is by no means rendered completely peripheral. Computer-generated poetry is based on computer code or "numeric representations." Therefore, the code, and with it the poem, can easily be changed or adopted. As Lev Manovich points out in *The Language of New Media* (2001, 36), one of five principles of digital media is "variability," a principle referring to how digital texts are not fixed but can easily be amended. As a result, the digital text can potentially exist in infinite versions, either because of genetic or self-learning algorithms or because the poet is in a position to interfere in the process. In a mathematical print poem, the poet can choose to break the chain of rules and, in so doing, transform the poem into something other than a formal-based, mathematical poem. In a generative poem run by a computer, the poet, or programmer, can interfere in the process by applying new rules or changing existing rules during the potentially endless event.

Actually, during several presentations of *Evolution*, Heldén has explained that after they launched *Evolution*, he and Jonson discovered that the word "Toyota Land Cruiser" appeared much more frequently in the poem than other words. They could not identify any reason why the computer seemed to have a preference for the name of a car over other nouns and decided to change the rules by instructing the algorithms not to choose "Toyota Land Cruiser." This short anecdote shows not only that rules in computer-generative poetry can be altered, but it also serves as an example of how the poem is a collaborative event by poets and computers, human and non-human agents.

According to Hayles when people, technology and cultural representations migrate across networks, changing configurations, interpretations and opinions also emerge, circulate, interact and are disseminated through networks. In her book *Unthinkable*, Hayles therefore develops the term "cognitive assemblage" as a specification of the term "assemblage" from the network theories of Deleuze and Guattari (1987) and Bruno Latour (2007). In this respect, Hayles' term "cognitive interconnections" refers to networks that are characterized by the circulation of information and interpretations produced by both humans and artificially intelligent machines. The latter is what Hayles describes as "cognizers," i.e. actors who have cognition. She defines cognition as the ability to perform interpretations of information (Hayles 2017, 22) and suggests that not only humans but also computers can interpret information in contexts and create meaning. Here, artificial intelligence is an obvious example to use because it can process and even interpret information. Furthermore, Hayles notes that "cognizers direct, use, and interpret the material forces on which the assembly ultimately depends." (Hayles 2017, 22) In this sense, the actors in a network who act as cognizers have an important role because they can make decisions and perform tasks of selections, combinations and interpretations that make them appear flexible and adaptable. There are features that provide them with the opportunity to develop based on feedback information from their environments.

Cognizers have degrees of cognition or degrees of ability to interpret and create meaning. On a continuum, humans will be considered sophisticated, while plants will be deemed primitive or simpler forms of cognizers. Similarly, we can imagine that computers can be positioned at different stages on this continuum, depending on the technological standard and on what kinds of tasks they are designed to perform. This is likewise the case with poetry. Furthermore, the question is not so much whether cognizers, such as genetic algorithms, can create poetry by themselves. After all, genetic algorithms are not autonomous geniuses. The question is rather how we consider the collaboration between humans and non-humans, poets and genetic algorithms, in computer-generated poems like *Evolution*.

In her article "Literary Texts as Cognitive Assemblages: The Case of Electronic Literature" (2018), Hayles comments directly on Heldén and Jonson's *Evolution*: "[It] reveals the power of literature conceived as a cognitive assemblage, in which cognitions are distributed between human and technical actors, with information, interpretations and meanings circulating throughout the assemblage in all directions, outward from humans into machines, then outward from machines back to humans (Hayles 2018, n.p.). According to Hayles, *Evolution* demonstrates a collection of cognitions at work. Three of these are Heldén, Jonson and the computer that works in collaboration. The first two act as conscious cognitive participants, while the computer is what Hayles calls an unconscious cognition. Pertaining to poetry, an interesting question arises regarding the idea of a cognitive accumulation of connections between human and non-human actors: what happens to our understanding of the quality of poetry and poetry as poetry? Keeping the anecdote above in mind, it is evident that poets are still partly in control of the poetic event and apply certain preferences and poetic judgments to the sequences that appear on the screen in order to improve them. This is a poetic technogenetic feedback loop. There is a movement from the computer to Heldén and Jonson (and other readers) in the form of a poem that contains, for instance the frequent use of the word "Toyota Land Cruiser." Then, there is a movement from Heldén and Jonson back to the computer in the form of a new instruction that again changes the poem. Then again, the changed poem moves from the computer back to Heldén, Jonson and other readers. It is in a loop that potentially never ends.

The evolution of poetry

The title of the work, *Evolution*, can be applied on three levels. First, it reflects the evolution that takes place on the screen because the poem is an event. As a digital poem, it is based on computer codes running under the surface. Second, it highlights what happens in the poem. Not only is the poem an event, but the poem also evolves continuously. Third, the title signifies that poetry as an art form is evolving and is in constant flux. Finally, this evolution implies that the relationship between humans and computer technology, in the arts in general, is also in the process of development. In this respect, it is relevant to ask how the relationship between

Heldén, Jonson and the algorithms, human and non-human cognizers are explored in the work.

The work presents itself as an exploration of a rivalry between computer technology and poetry, AI and the poet Johannes Heldén but ends up showing the fruitful reciprocal relations of the assumed "opponents." In their presentation of the work, Heldén and Jonson write: "Evolution is an online art work-in-progress designed to emulate the texts and music of poet and artist Johannes Heldén with the ultimate goal of passing 'The Imitation Game' as proposed by Alan Turing in 1951." (Heldén and Jonson 2014a) They explain that they want to explore the role of the author and challenge established conceptions that distinguish the role of the author from the role of the programmer. "Is it [the distinction] even relevant?" they ask, a question that is highly appropriate to the computational network environment. In *Evolution* and in computational network environments, the question does not only actualize the distinction between author and programmer. Just as significant is the question of the relationship between author and algorithms, as well as human and non-human actors.

The above-mentioned reference to Turing evidently concerns his idea and ambition to develop a machine that could perform intelligent behaviors equivalent to human behaviors, with the aim of being able to pass a test. Basically, the Turing test involves the idea that a human receiver of a machine's response would not be able to distinguish a machine's response from the response of a human being. The Turing test as a framework for understanding *Evolution* is fascinating. Nevertheless, it is reductive because it is based on a situation and a scenario in which a human being sets the premises for the evaluation of the capacity of the computer. The computer is measured against human capacity, while a human being evaluates the output. Therefore, in the Turing test, the human is still the center of attention. Consequently, the development is human-driven and the computer perceived is as a tool, the value of which is measured by its capacity to imitate human behavior.

It should not come as a surprise that I will suggest as an alternative that *Evolution* demonstrates an evolution that puts the development of the poem and poetry in the hands of both the poets and the computer. In this respect, it demonstrates a contemporary poetic technogenesis. The collaboration between the computer and Heldén and Jonson is of a posthuman "nature". Except for those cases in which Heldén and Jonson intervene in the algorithm-driven event by changing the rules, for example with the anecdote about the name "Toyota Land Cruiser," one can ask whether it makes sense to distinguish between human beings and computer algorithms, to treat these two in a subject-object relationship and to think of them in a user-tool dichotomy. In the framework of posthumanism, Hayles emphasizes the human-computer relation: "the posthuman implies not only a coupling with intelligent machines but a coupling so intense and multifaceted that it is no longer possible to distinguish meaningfully between the biological organism and the informational circuits in which the organism is enmeshed." (Hayles 1999a, 35) Consequently, we might say that *Evolution* demonstrates the posthuman ideal. Here, digital poetry becomes a collaborative environment for humans and computers. This notion stands as an alternative to the conception of a post-biological future developed by Hans Moravic (1990), connoting a future (for poetry and the arts) dominated by intelligent and self-learning machines. Still, it is relevant to ask to what extent the posthuman ideal is fully realized in *Evolution*. We might ask, in other words, how far the technogenetic evolution of poetry has come in this work.

Evolution is the result of an encounter and collaboration between Heldén's previous publications of poetry and Heldén and Jonson's genetic algorithms. Heldén's publications are collected in a database. Genetic algorithms work within an evolutionary model and perform the selection and combination of words and phrases. The algorithms have evolutionary properties, which means that they develop from selections, recombinations and mutations. At each generation, a group of algorithms is developed on the basis of previous algorithms. Further, this process means that new algorithms are constantly being developed, and these again produce new combinations of Heldén's words.

On the one hand, one could argue that there are some similarities between how the computer works in *Evolution* and Tristan Tzara's idea of Dadaist poems. When asked to clarify what Dadaist poems could be, Tzara once explained that one should cut out words from a newspaper. Then pick one word at a time from a hat and put them together into a text.[6] Nevertheless, this comparison is a simplification because Heldén and Jonson's work is a poetic thinking with and through a programmable medium; they think with, through and together with the algorithms. In Tzara's example, it will be a human being who chooses, while in Heldén and Jonson's work, it is a computer that, through a process of cognition, is responsible for the selection and shaping of the poem. Furthermore, the creative process in *Evolution* is not a game of chance, as it will be in Tzara's version of Dadaism but rather an interplay between repetitive patterns and small changes. One consequence of the fact that the evolutionary process is run by genetic algorithms is that the poem continually changes and that an identical poetic expression – unless the algorithms are told differently – will never be generated twice.

Thus, a poetic practice is established, further developing Heldén's original style. In this respect, it is fruitful to recall Hayles who claims that it "is precisely

---

[6] See Tristan Tzara's "Pour faire une poème dadaïste" here: https://www.gommeetgribouillages.fr/Presse/poemedadaiste.pdf (5 December 2022).

when these multilayered, multiply sited processes within humans and machines interact through intermediating dynamics that the rich effects of electronic literature are created, performed, and experimented." (Hayles 2008, 119) Beyond the fact that the computer provides performative dimensions to the work on the three levels mentioned above, it is fair to question whether it also makes a contribution on a syntactic level of the poem, which would indeed imply an even deeper poetic technogenetic evolution.

Poetic technogenesis

Evolution demonstrates a media environment in which poetry can perform. It is a reciprocal environment: the environment constitutes the work as the work simultaneously constitutes the (local) environment. Hayles describes this environment as programmable and reflexive. Thus, such reflexivity can be understood through the model of a pendulum, a feedback-loop of what I described earlier as a pattern of repetition and change rather than as a circle or spiral. In other words, when a computer creates texts, it is not a process of reproduction but a reproduction with a difference since the algorithms create small variations with each new generation. To look further into these possible small variations, let us consider two examples. In respect to the work as written in a Scandinavian language, the two examples will be given in Swedish.

The two screenshots above are selected at random from the same reading, at generation 44414 and 72833, respectively. It is, of course, impossible to determine whether Heldén could have written the two generations, but they are both so far out in the performance that we must assume that the algorithms have left some marks on the poem. The first of the two generations (Fig. 3) shows a poem that consists of 12 words. It includes several voids and caesuras, and it appears fragmented with several blank spaces. The disruptions of syntax are of semantic significance and give space to and highlight each word or cluster of words. These disruptions indicate that, if read aloud, the poem should be read slowly, since the silence between words and clusters reflects the empty spaces that are visualized on the screen. In the continuous development, the algorithms have led the poem into a phase where it has been given many pauses, which together with the relatively few words provides the poem with a sense of silence and emptiness. It is worth noticing that the reader, by controlling the speed of the generations, can slow down the process and thus establish a correlation between the slowness and silence in the poem and its visual appearances on the screen. Otherwise, the reader can speed up the process, speed up the evolution and by that conceal or compensate for the impression of silence and stagnation in the poem. Also, the poem appears without verbs, which strengthens the indication of an atmosphere of stagnation established by the words and the visual form. There are no pronouns in the poem at this generation either, which underlines the lack of action and an acting subject.

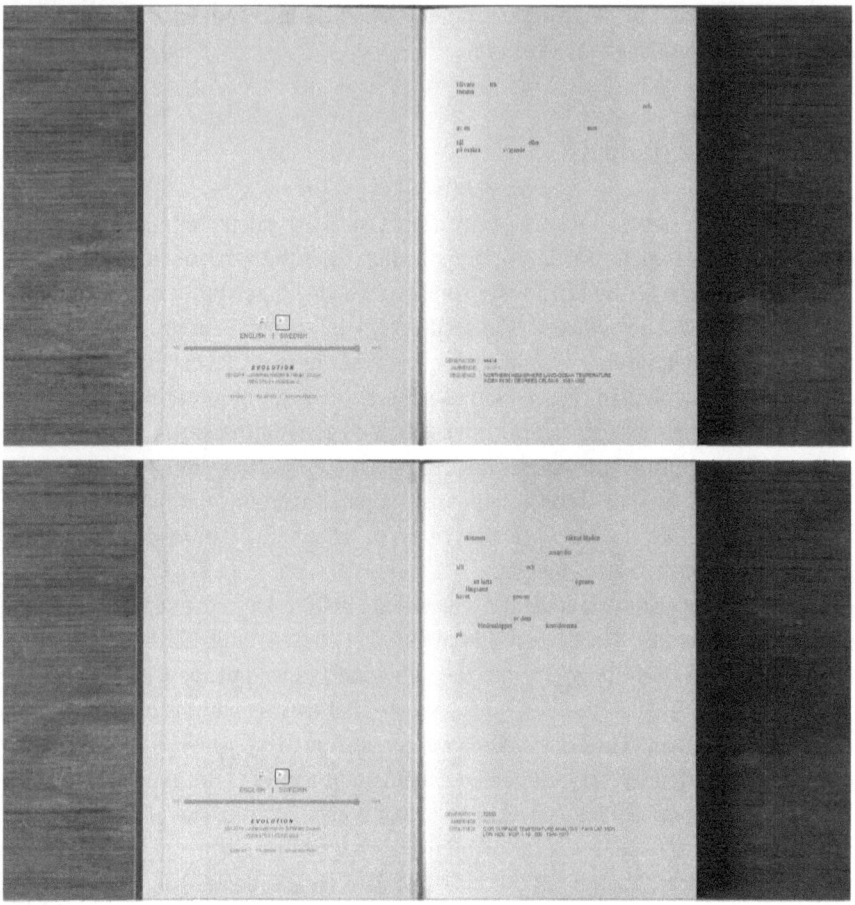

Figs. 3 and 4: Two screenshots, both randomly chosen, from Heldén and Jonson's *Evolution*.

The second example (Fig. 4), taken almost 30000 generations later into the process, contains only five words more than the first. Still, it has a different character due to the composition of word classes. Besides the fact that it includes several nouns, seven against two in the first example, one of which is the name of a flower ("amaryllis"), we find two verbs in contrast to none in the first example. One of the verbs is in the present tense, "räknar" ("counts"), while the other is in the infinitive "att hitta" ("to find"). The two verbs provide the poem with action, making it more dynamic than the previous one, indicating an acting subject as if someone or something counts, observes and searches. Actually, here we might recognize a connection between this sense of something counting or making observations and the graphs and lists that are presented in the book, *Evolution*, based on the results of technological measurements of the atmosphere. It might be a coincidence, but it is nonetheless a coincidence that occurs and offers to the reader the possibility of reading and experiencing a relationship between the digital work and the book.

Caesuras appear frequently in both examples, and there is no punctuation in the two generations. Lack of punctuation supports the poem as an event and as a continuous generative process with no ending. The blank spaces and caesuras have similar functions. Both the blank spaces and the caesuras serve as representations of rhythmical pauses and as syntactical amputations and are visual traces of conscious or unconscious omissions, as if a line's syntax and meaning had been cut off and single words and phrases have been taken out of their original context. Interestingly enough, in *Evolution* words and phrases have been severed from their original contexts, rearranged and replaced by the algorithms. At the same time, the occurrence of caesuras along with the blank spaces indicates that the text on the screen might be erased poetry, i.e. poetry that has "been added through erasures [or] exclusions," as Lisa Schmidt defines the genre (Schmidt 2018, 253). In erasure poetry, according to Schmidt, it is assumed that the text as a palimpsest is literally written over another previously materialized text. Applied to *Evolution*, we might say that the algorithms write texts not over but based on, beside and as an extension of Heldén's previously published poetry. Furthermore, while erasure poetry is an act of consciousness, in *Evolution* the selection of words and phrases involves both a conscious and unconscious act. Still, with a few exceptions, it is not an act of intentional omission. The blank spaces do not mark the absence of anything that has been, because the poem is an event that occurs here and now.

The caesuras are of semantic significance because they remind us that the texts could have been different. The absence of words could have been, and in the evolutional process will be, replaced by the presence of other words. In the process, this is what happens as some words and phrases remain on the screen through several computational generations while others disappear. Likewise, the blank spaces carry with them multiple representations. They signify both the presence of what has been, that something has been erased by hand, nature or technology, and a promise of something that is yet to come, that the process of repetition and change at some point will replace a blank space with words. In addition to these two, the blank spaces are digital spaces. Actually, the blank spaces are not empty but filled with codes that are constantly running underneath. They remind us that both the words and the blank spaces are computer-generated, and, for this reason, the meaning of the blank spaces is not only conditioned by the absence of words but also by the presence of the meaning of the codes. Again, the digital work points towards its non-digital sister, or companion, the book *Evolution*, which contains the algorithms that the digital work conceals underneath words and blank spaces.

In addition to the poem being an event, a process in which the poem gradually becomes less Heldén's than the computer's, the work and the poem establish an atmosphere and an affective environment. In one of the poems I presented earlier (Fig. 4), in generation 44414, the nouns "tilvaro" ("existence") and "tomma" ("empty") and the adjectives "osäkra" ("uncertain") and "svajande" ("swaying") appear grammatically decontextualized, only surrounded by a few prepositions, conjunctions and subjunctives. It expresses, with both words and blank spaces, an existence that is unfilled, as if it is referring to itself as an empty poem that needs to be filled with running codes. Each of these words may not give much, but read together they create an uncanny feeling and signify a situation and a development that is uncertain, out of balance, just like the poem that never rests and therefore in the next second will be different.

Evolution as imitation and mutation

In the framework of technogenesis, blank spaces and broken syntax – produced in a collaboration between humans and computers – indicates, perhaps, that the computer is running the poem towards the death of language, grammar and poetry reading as we know it. In poetry, we are familiar with blank spaces and broken syntax, but in *Evolution*, these elements are largely unintentional. Further, the poem does not follow any syntactic rules; therefore, it makes less sense to look for branches with linguistically and logically concerned semantics. Likewise, because of the collaboration between humans and algorithms, conscious and unconscious cognizers, it might not make sense to stress potential correlations between form and content. This also holds true for the algorithms' interpretations, since they are linked to word classes and not to single-word semantics. Furthermore, because the algorithms are to be regarded as unconscious cognitions, it is fair to say that the poem does not exhibit metapoetic consciousness. The algorithms do not know that they are performing a poem or a poetic event. Algorithms do not know poetry and poetic traditions.

Evolution is a work that, according to Heldén and Jonson, is designed to pass "The Imitation Game," meaning that it produces poetry that could have been written by Heldén. Therefore, the pattern of repetitions and changes is also an evolutionary process of imitations and modifications. As long as the computer only imitates a predefined poetic form and tradition, evolution will not take place. When it makes small changes during its imitation game, evolution will occur. The genetic algorithms work by executing the instructions given by Heldén and Jonson, but, as they learn, they slowly amend these instructions and create differences. In other words, *Evolution* points towards an evolution of poetry that is structured around imitations and differences and that follows the allegory of evolution, patterns and mutations. The point is that evolution cannot take place unless there are sequences that disrupt or change existing patterns. "Mutation", a concept that Hayles develops in accordance with her technogenetic model, "is crucial because it names the bifurcation point at which the interplay between pattern and randomness causes the system to evolve in a new direction." (Hayles 2012, 33) Hayles describes the interplay between pattern and chance as mutations. Mutations are then the productive outcome of the encounter between pattern and coincidence, where fractures occur and create a new and hitherto unforeseen development. With *Evolution* and its poetic tradition in mind, we might ask how far the mutations have come or to what extent *Evolution* is an imitation or mutation game.

The form of the poem, with the blank spaces, is similar to many of Heldén's poetry as it brings with it a poetic shape and includes words of a certain kind that have become a watermark of his art and poetry. Further, the poem can be linked to poetry in Scandinavia in the 1980s and 1990s, including by such poets as Agneta Enckell and the late Eva-Stina Byggmästar. It also shares much in common with the poetic style and environment around OEI in Sweden, often referred to as *språkmaterialism*, which renewed the idea of language as concrete materiality. This poetic style, inspired by Language poetry in the US, includes poets such as Anna Hallberg, Malte Persson, Lars Mikael Raattamaa, Johan Jönsson and Johannes Heldén. Therefore, one may argue that *Evolution* as a poetry machine imitates the poetry of Heldén and the poetic tradition out of which his poetry is born. This is why Marie Engberg points out that Johannes Heldén as a poet is ubiquitous in the poetic event, even though, as she claims, it is generated by algorithms (Engberg 2014b, n.p.).

The algorithms imitate Heldén's poetry and evoke moods and emotions similar to those Heldén creates in his poems. The algorithms then develop these elements until they can no longer be regarded as Heldén's but as the algorithm's and the computer's. On the one hand, such a project is in danger of becoming overly limiting or of being read ironically, as was the case for early literary experimentations with artificial intelligence. One example of this is Christopher Strachey's *Love Letter Generator* from 1952, which was programmed to automatically generate love letters. As Roberto Simanowski points out, this program can be understood as an ironic commentary on the genre of love letters (Simanowski 2011, 94). Rather than replacing Strachey, it imitates the feelings and intentions of Strachey and of any sender of love letters. On the other hand, poetry events like *Evolution* invite us to reflect on and look for the technological point of singularity, i.e. the point where what we think of as human-made cultural and aesthetic expressions is taken over by artificial intelligence (see e.g. Shanahan 2015).

Just as Heldén is omnipresent in the work, so too are the algorithms and the computer ubiquitous. They are ubiquitous to such an extent that Heldén and the computer's algorithms have become inseparable. Poetic technogenesis and the idea of imitation and evolution are based on an organic model. The poem is continuously developing and is, therefore, similar to how nature evolves organically. It is, of course, obvious to think of an ecological evolution where nature is programmed to repeat actions but where mutations and other changes also break with such patterns. Existing patterns can for instance be written algorithms, while changes, or mutations, occur when the predictable patterns are broken, which leads to a difference. The latter may occur, for example, because of genetic codes. The algorithms work in a pattern, but because they can contain generations that break with a pattern, coincidences will also occur. The title *Evolution* must be considered in a similar dialectic because mutations create an unpredictable development. This unpredictability can be described as the poetic strategy of the digital poem. It is also this that allows Heldén to distinguish between what he considers to be his poetry and the generations in the poem's development that differentiate it from his poetry. As he once stated in a presentation of *Evolution*, the poems were considerably better after about 30,000 generations. At this stage, which takes some time to reach, the algorithms have created connections that are new and different, and the digital poem appears to be more detached from Heldén's poetry.

Posthuman poetics

A note from the "about" section of *Evolution* reads that "The release of *Evolution* will mark the end of Johannes Heldén writing books of poetry. He has, in a sense, been replaced." (Heldén and Jonson 2014) The reference to the work's intention, which is not only to imitate Heldén's poetry but also to replace him, hence making him superfluous as a poet, is striking at a time when literature has become dominated by autofiction and self-presentation. However, it is worth noting that on the opening page of the digital part and on the front of the print book, Johannes Heldén and Håkan Jonson are listed as authors with legal rights over the work. They also represent and present the work in poetry readings and conversations about their works. In other words, the exploration of the computer that replaces the poet goes far, but it does not exceed paratexts, literary conventions or the legal and institutionalized dimensions of literature and poetry. Perhaps it is fair to say that just as much as *Evolution* challenges understandings of what poetry can be in the computational network environment, the work is also an attempt to incorporate the computer and its poetry into the print publishing institutions, a system that is to a high degree humanistic. In this sense, the work does not represent a movement from human to machine, from poet to genetic algorithm, a movement that would emphasize the play of presence and absence but an interconnection of conscious and unconscious cognitions, poet and algorithms, analog and digital materialities, a reciprocal interaction of repetitions and changes.

It would be difficult to determine whether or not we would be able to distinguish the computer's poem from Heldén's in a blind test. This task is interesting precisely because technogenesis is not about the separation of humans and technology but of their co-existence. In *How We Became Posthuman*, Hayles writes: "the posthuman appears when computation rather than possessive individualism is taken as the ground of being, a move that allows the posthuman to be seamlessly articulated with intelligent machines." (1999, 34) In such a perspective, Heldén and Jonson become posthuman subjects, and *Evolution* becomes a poetic event and posthuman poetry, or at least *Evolution* explores the possibility of such a development for poetry, where there is a seamless connection between poets and computer.

The goal to emulate Heldén as a poet immediately reflects the co-existence of humans and computers: media are neither neutral, nor do they entirely determine the process. Rather, *Evolution* depicts new sensibilities in the computational network environment wherein Heldén and Jonson choose to (try to) outdo the poet and his poetry. Heldén and Jonson embrace the media technological situation with which they are entwined and regard genetic algorithms as their possibility. They recognize both the poet and poetry as always already being technological. Both are, in the contemporary media situation, intertwined with environments of programmable and network media. They demonstrate what poetry can do and be and what computers can do and be. Here, in the posthuman environment of *Evolution*, media obviously matter and both the poets and the algorithms determine the process and the result. Therefore, *Evolution* and the technogenetic perspective demonstrate that in this media environment, in which the poet and poetry are already entangled, it is not a question of either poet or media, human or non-human. The poem is made up of conscious and unconscious decisions, selections, combinations and interpretations that make the environment, and therefore the work *Evolution*, flexible, changeable and evolutionary.

With respect to the technogenetic feedback loop of repetitions and changes, *Evolution* demonstrates that an outcome, a poem, could be different and that the outcome is unpredictable and promised. Evolution always promises change and so does the work *Evolution*. This is a freedom to create, that is, to try to let go of one's responsibility as a poet and leave the poetic event partly to the computer. Still, the omnipresence of Heldén, in addition to the presence of Heldén and Jonson in the work's paratexts and the poetic tradition that the poem reflects, are a reminder that poets still can make a difference. The poem as an event is always different, and even this is something that could be different.

It is fair to claim that *Evolution* invites readers to press play, lean back and enjoy, or be confused, amazed or provoked by the event on the screen. If so, it gives space to a less critical and more compliant reading, as Felski contends. But again, rather than making this the only mode of reading, I would argue for a combination of modes of reading and that a media-specific close reading is crucial if one is not to miss what it implies when genetic algorithms or AI takes over ancient human activities like writing and performing poetry. The close reading that I have conducted in this chapter demonstrates that even though *Evolution* is a performance, a close reading can make the experience richer, more thoughtful and stranger. *Evolution* opens up a reflection on the future of language and technology and, it turns out, as it often does in the course of the history of literature, that the work does something other and more than what its authors say it does or that they claim they want to achieve.

Chapter 4
Field Recordings from the Future: Astroecological Thinking in Johannes Heldén's *Astroecology* (2016)

A desk with two screens, one is large, the other small. The large one shows an image of a forest landscape with a lonely house and garden. A fence encloses the garden from the forest that surrounds it. A small road passes through the woods. The year is 2016. The image alternates between day and night. A black bird flies over the landscape in a repetitive pattern. Random clicks with the mouse create small changes. Words and text fragments perform on the screen and become poems. Glimpses of nature photography appear while encyclopedic texts about extinct plants and animals open upon command. The world is slowly advancing at ten-year intervals towards a future, a predictable and final end at which time the world as we know it, or knew it, will have become non-retrievable. This world appears lifeless in a static image of planetary nebula, cold, full of waste and unfriendly. Here, we encounter an imagined end of history, civilization and nature. The impact from humans and evolution has transformed the landscape into a post-anthropocentric world. The sound of wind and gloomy music with dark, long tones and a slow rhythm run continuously in the background. It is as if these are the sounds of evolution; as if we are being spoken to from a remote and imagined future; as if what we witness on the screen are "field recordings from the future."[1]

Technogenesis and the idea that artificial intelligence has replaced human subjects, which I discussed in the previous chapter, are further explored in Johannes Heldén's *Astroecology* (2016a). *Astroecology* is a work of science fiction in which a specific landscape is lifted into a spaceship. Here, one or several subjects observe how the landscape evolves from 2016 till its final collapse in 2156. The work reflects poetically on nature, technology and human cognition in the Anthropocene; it serves as a real and fictitious archive of the past and of a future in which artificial intelligence has replaced human beings as observers, archivists, storytellers and poets.

Like *Evolution*, *Astroecology* is a media-ecological work that traverses media platforms, genres, art forms and situations. It is materialized as digital poetry, as a print book, art installation and theatrical performance, which was staged at the Royal Dramatic Theater in Stockholm. Furthermore, the work is constantly expanding, since it is part of new media-ecological relations. Various parts of the work

---

[1] See @astroecology.

Figs. 5 and 6: Two screenshots from the digital part of Johannes Heldén's *Astroecology* (2016a). Figure 5 shows the opening scene, while figure 6 depicts the end of the work, with one of six poems below the image.

have been shown and read from a number of times. Moreover, new installations based on the work's subject matter have been produced which include both Heldén and Håkan Jonson's print work and installation *Encyclopedia* (2015) and Heldén's Instagram account @astroecology. In the latter, Heldén describes his ongoing artistic project as "field recordings from the future." *Astroecology* bears the mark of thematic and audio-visual aesthetics that we can recognize in many of Heldén's earlier works, such as *Entropy* (2010) and *New New Hampshire & Clouds* (2017). Still, *Astroecology* differs somewhat from Heldén's previous works: while earlier works like *Elect* (2008), *The Prime Directive* (2006), *Entropy* (2010) and *The Fabric* (2013) depict an unrecognizable future world from the beginning on, *Astroecology* begins in a familiar world only to move into one that can only be characterized as dystopian, unfamiliar and unfriendly.

The transgression of media is, as I have argued in the previous chapter, the DNA of Heldén's poetic-artistic practice. Multimedia and composite expressions characterize individual works, as he combines words, music, graphics and photographs. For example, the print book *Astroecology* (2016b) contains photographs, drawings, poems, captions and footnotes with narrative, non-fiction and poetic texts. Likewise, the digital part of *Astroecology* is constituted by a dynamic image in the background that interacts with narrative texts, poems, photographs, encyclopedic texts and ambient music. All together, the interaction between genres and media creates performative events that present a possible future, a future scenario in which the world as we know it ends, that is, a world in which all known biological life seems to have been erased and the eco- or astroecological system has broken down.

In this chapter, I explore what *Astroecology* can tell us about the situation of poetry in the twenty-first century. In other words, I am interested in how poetry in the computational network environment contributes to knowledge about the Anthropocene and engages in the question of imagined futures. In this way, we find that poetry serves as an exploratory mode towards one or more horizon. I put the question of the Anthropocene and the notion of a future planet without human beings or other organisms at the center of my attention. Despite the fact that *Astroecology* is an intermedial and media-ecological work, I mainly concentrate on the digital part of the work, only intermittently drawing attention to the print book *Astroecology* when it is necessary for the sake of analysis and argumentation. I argue that Heldén's work is an attempt to develop poetry that contributes to the defining of the media-ecological environment. Therefore, *Astroecology* represents both a response to the Anthropocene as well as a way to think poetically and astroecologically about a future that is disconnected from human consciousness. Heldén makes visible the coexistence of nature as an ongoing evolutionary process and technological medializations as prefiguring the process of archiving and memorializing the past. *Astroecology* depicts the entropy of an imagined future in the Anthropocene. My claim is simply that *Astroecology* explores a particularly ecological way of thinking and presents a past, present and future within the framework of the Anthropocene, where evolution relentlessly moves towards an end that simultaneously implies the end of human beings and other organisms.

Reading *Astroecology*

Before going further into the work, it is important for the sake of the analysis to clarify the premises, partly set by the digital medium, for reading *Astroecology*. The work calls upon a different mode of reading than much other poetry does, including poetry in digital media. Most noteworthy is the fact that the reader must click on the screen in order to proceed in the work. Without the reader's interaction, poems, photographs and encyclopedic texts simply do not appear. Likewise, it is up to the reader to either complete the appearances of each poem or move forward in the work before the respective poem is completed.

Aesthetic and semiotic elements do not become objects for the reader's sensations and analysis unless he or she makes sure they all appear. In other words, unless the reader calls these elements forward, either by accident or by intention, they will not become part of the text that is read and analyzed. Similarly, the evolution and development of the world of the work are conditional, since the reader needs to click on the figure of a jackdaw that is flying over the landscape on the screen. Hitting the figure of the bird with the mouse cursor, the world on the screen jumps ten years into the future. Here, two aspects are imperative for methodological reflections. One is that even though this activity imposes a chronological narrative to the work, it is still experienced and explored in multilinear and anachronic sequences. The graphic visualization of the world on the large screen is organized in a linear fashion, and there is no way for the reader to skip ahead a decade or rearrange the order of the appearance. Still, the order of the poetic phrases and the photographs appear randomly. This non-linear order of the phases and photographs are not in themselves significant for the interpretation; however, whether or not the reader brings forward all the photographs and all the poetic phrases are, of course, vital for the experience and interpretation of the complete work. This process is significant for the reading of the work. The reader can jump from one decade to another without activating any of the photographs or phrases, by engaging only some of these elements or by fully completing each stage. The latter means that readers make sure that they have seen all photographs, completed the poem and made it available as a whole, before they, as if playing a computer game, try to hit the figure of the bird moving restlessly and playfully over the screen and thereby proceeding to the next decade.

On the one hand, this activity demonstrates how the poem can be regarded as an event and how the reader needs to perform in order to develop the poem, materialize the photographs, if only for a second, and make the work proceed. The act of reading becomes a performance that is necessary for conducting the analysis. This combination of performance and analysis is relevant for interactive works in general. Still, in *Astroecology*, readers are put in a situation in which they more or less search for the hidden photographs and poetic phrases at random. This interactive aspect of *Astroecology* might be associated with hypertext fictions like Michael Joyce's *afternoon, a story* (1989) or Megan Heyward's *Of Day, Of Night* (2002). Nonetheless, this mode of searching is close to a mode of playing, corresponding with what I have called elsewhere the "explorative mode of reading." (Rustad 2009) This kind of reading implies that the reader either feels satisfied by the search itself, that is, in finding elements in the work or where the explorative mode is replaced by a mode of close reading, that is, where the reader finds pleasure in the meaning making process. In the reading of the work, this ergodic activity might take time and require persistence. In other words, there is an aspect of patience in both the close and deep reading of the work and in the explorative and performative aspect in which the "material" for close reading is brought to the screen, comprising the sensory world of the reader. It almost goes without saying that in analyzing *Astroecology*, one must repeat the above-mentioned action several times in order to be able to grasp how the work behaves, the significance of its behavior and the meaning of the combination of art forms and genres in the work.

"Landscape elevated"

Astroecology can be regarded as an experimental laboratory, or perhaps as a modern version of Noah's ark, where, according to one of the poems, the landscape and organisms are lifted into a spaceship. At one point, this action is observed on a monitor:

> The landscape elevated and placed in the cargo hold of an unmanned spaceship. The vegetation spreads through the ventilation, forming forests, swamps, fields, a cloud (shadows). (#2036)[2]

The poem describes the elevation of a particular landscape that contains organisms removed from their natural habitats. Likewise, in other texts in the work, organic species are mentioned as candidates chosen for a non-identified experimental project. One text refers to the blue whale as "a candidate for uplift, along with jackdaw and bottlenose dolphin," (#2026) while another says that the vascular plant (a fern) has been re-programmed: "Due to this mutation one subspecies was the first plant to be re-programmed in 2024." (#2046)

In a dictionary section of the print book *Astroecology*, the term "uplift" is described: "In science fiction, uplift is the terraforming of a planet's biosphere, so as

---

[2] There is no pagination in the digital work. Hence, I refer to the sections by using the respective year in which the quotations appear.

to artificially nurture native and/or alien life-forms. It also implies the development or transformation of animals into intelligent, Type-I races using biological engineering or evolutionary intervention." (2016b, up) The technical term "terraforming" refers to a process, common in science fiction, where one reshapes a planet in order to make it inhabitable for humankind. In *Astroecology*, the object of terraforming appears to be the planet Earth and, more specifically, a landscape on the planet Earth. Therefore, the work might be regarded as a laboratory for exploring and responding to the Anthropocene, where the purpose is to try to preserve organisms and reshape the landscape in order to make it a friendly place for humans and non-humans, and to explore the future of the landscape and the planet to predict the outcome of evolution. In this respect, *Astroecology* stages a process towards an imagined future in the Anthropocene. This future and its impact on human beings are reflected in such contemporary book titles as *The Sixth Extinction: An Unnatural History* (Kolberg 2014), *Learning to Die in the Anthropocene* (Scranton 2015) and *The Uninhabitable Earth* (Wallace-Wells 2019).

In the English version of *Astroecology*, the poem quoted above lacks a line that is included in the digital Swedish-language version. In Swedish, the poem ends with the line "Här *medvetandets slut, mellanrummens kollaps* eller *årstidernas logik.*" This line is also reprinted in the book version of *Astroecology*, where it reads: "Here the end of consciousness, the collapse of spaces, or the logic of the seasons." (2016b, n.p.) The word "here" is a spatial and a temporal deixis. It points to both the landscape that is present in the visual representation on the monitor and a certain moment in time. It might be a subject's evaluation of the project to elevate the landscape, an elevation that at some point in the experiment leads to a collapse in the ecosystem, and, subsequently, it might refer to the moment when human and technological interventions in the process of evolution got out of hand.

The house and the cultivated garden that is centered on one of the monitors at the beginning of the work slowly fade away. Moreover, the once civilized and domestic location is gradually reclaimed by nature. Bit by bit, the house and garden disappear from sight and are replaced by trees. However, this replacement is also only temporary, since evolution never rests and makes no distinctions. Progressively, the vegetation likewise fades away and leaves us with a wasteland. From 2016 (Fig. 5) till the end of the work in 2156 (Fig. 6), we witness how the location is transformed from what seems to be a familiar, friendly and domesticated place into a non-biological and non-recognizable time-space.

Images of the house with the garden, verbal descriptions of events, animals, flowers and plants, indeed also the ambient music, are what we could call, using Heldén's motto, field-recordings from a future. These are either documentations of the past or archives from a future yet to come. The house serves both as symbol and indexical sign. It appears at once as what it is, a house, a home, and as a symbolic representation of the planet as the home for all organic life. The framed image can be related to the origin of the word "eco-" in the Greek *"oikos,"* meaning house and community. While Aristotle, for instance, uses the term *"oikos"* to refer to those living in a house and within a particular hierarchical structure (see Aristotle 1986, 14), *Astroecology* presents this local dimension of "eco-" as a metonymic trope for a larger egalitarian ecology – *"oikos"* as planetary and "astro-ary."

Evolution is presented as it is. It is a force that cannot be controlled by humans or technology. Both civilization and cultivated nature disappear in a process that, from a human perspective, may appear to be dystopic but that, from a non-anthropocentric perspective, is merely "natural." This process is presented through animation, sound, encyclopedic texts and poems. Thematically, this multifaceted presentation is obviously not unique in contemporary culture. Rather, it can be understood as "a cultural dominant" (Jameson 1991) and as part of a particular trend in contemporary literature (see i.e. Vermeulen 2020) and poetry (see i.e. Larsen 2018, 55–126). A number of contemporary literary works in digital media explore the relationship between human beings and their environment within an apocalyptic framework. We need only think of a work like *Toxi City: A Climate Change Narrative* (2016), by Roderick Coover and Scott Rettberg or more poetic and philosophical-explorative works such as J.R. Carpenter's *The Gathering Cloud* (2017) and *This is a Picture of Wind* (2017b, 2017c, 2020). Similar to Coover, Rettberg and Carpenter, Heldén adds the discourse of technology to this exploration and cultural dominant, offering a special way of presenting evolution and the imagined futures it brings with it. More to the point, we might say that the digital part of *Astroecology*, through the experimental framework and the media-ecological work as such, makes poetry a space and an art form for imagining a future through eco- and astroecological thought.

Astroecological thinking and imagination

Astroecology is a response to the Anthropocene, in which the fate of humankind, organisms and the world as we know it has already been decided. While the ecocritical perspective is only vaguely articulated in the digital part of *Astroecology*, the printed book makes this perspective more explicit. Here, we can read about humans' over-consumption of natural resources and the development of artificial intelligence. The work has previously been read in the framework of ecocriticism. Gitte Mose claims that *Astroecology* represents the missing link between the novel and digital literature (Mose 2020). It has been approached as an artwork that presents evolution as a natural, non-anthropocentric force of which only goal seems to be development, not conservation (Rustad 2020). Technological development is seen here as an acceleration of destructive evolution (Roberg 2019).

According to Alexa Weik von Mossner, ecocritical narratives belong to a genre that includes "any type of narrative in any media that foregrounds ecological issues and human-nature relationships, often but not always with the openly stated intention of bringing about social change." (Mossner 2017, 3) Heldén expands on this open-ended definition offered by Mossner. Heldén's poetic work combines narrative and poetic modes, including poems, photographs, visual narratives, encyclopedic texts and ambient music, and exists simultaneously and in egalitarian fashion on different media platforms. This approach, offered by Heldén, seizes the environmental changes that have and may come, changes that human progress and technological inventions have forced upon nature.

The title, *Astroecology*, composed of the cosmological term "astro-" and the biological term "ecology," denotes the study of the interaction between organisms and their local, global, planetary and astrological environment, i.e. an environment that also includes the universe. Sofia Roberg further comments on the title of the work, writing that it refers to "the interaction between living organisms and space environment, as well as the scientific study of other planets and celestial bodies." (Roberg 2019, 6) With the prefix "astro-", the title points to a spatial expansion of a conventional conception of ecology. It is a version of an ecology that includes planets other than Earth. Stars, asteroids and comets are also taken into account in order to reflect on possible futures. With such an expansion, the term reflects a time and place that transcends human time and the Earth as the planet for humans and human-known species. In this respect, the title reflects a kind of transcendental thinking, a thinking that transcends both an anthropocentric perspective and earthbound ecology.

The work encourages reflections and explorations that exceed the future of humankind and the planet earth. Such a transcendental ecology resonates with Timothy Morton's ecological thinking. In *The Ecological Thought* (2010), Morton claims that "in the West, we think of ecology as earthbound. Not only earthbound: we want ecology to be about location, location, location." (Morton 2010, 27) According to Morton, location reflects an anthropocentric worldview and represents a narrow interest in the domestic sphere. Such thinking is limited to the "here and now, not the there and then." (Morton 2010, 27) Morton's proposal is, therefore, a form of ecological thinking oriented towards "dislocation, dislocation, dislocation." (Morton 2010, 28) In other words, Morton believes that we have to change our engagement with the question of ecology and the climate situation, moving beyond our own situation and time. Consequently, Morton calls for an ecological thinking that points towards something greater than us, where humans are neither the center – the goal, the meaning – nor constitute the center of attention for reflections on politics and science. Likewise, the term "astroecology" transgresses knowledge of the planet's ecosystems in a human world and human scientific thinking. Astroecology is a concept that encourages thinking that goes beyond thinking – to think the unthinkable, to use Morton's words. This kind of thinking would include another of Morton's widely used terms, "mesh", i.e. the idea that all organisms and objects are completely interdependent and interconnected in time-space. Mesh can be described as a non-hierarchical network, a rhizome, organized without center or periphery as a principle of structure and without beginning or end. This structure supports the unsentimental and subversive mode of Morton's "dark ecology". Closely linked to such thinking, in which the understanding of humankind and nature framed through subject-object relations is brought to an end, is Morton's concept of "strange strangers." This is the idea that we cannot, and should not, try to overcome that which is strange to us. According to Morton, we should instead cultivate the strangeness of the other, avoid controlling it and thus counteract inherited ideas of hierarchies with regard to humanity's relationship to its environment. According to Morton, this is the way to recognize the strangeness of the stranger.

In the development and presentation of an ecological thinking that is transcendental, Morton highlights, among other things, the role and value of experimental art and literature as forms capable of performing such thinking. In this context, Morton points out that the shape of the works and performances for an ecological thinking are just as important as the content of the thinking: "It's not simply a matter of what you're thinking about. It's a matter of how you think." (Morton 2010, 4) Furthermore, he emphasizes how art can create a radical openness to an ecological thinking: "Along with the ecological crisis goes an equally powerful and urgent opening up of our view of who we are and where we are. What, therefore, is environmental art? If what we inadequately call the environment entails a radical openness, how does this appear in art forms?" (Morton 2010, 10) For instance, we can imagine, as is the case with Heldén's artworks, that poetry and the arts reflect an openness to alternative ways of thinking by moving across institutional frameworks and media borders, by combining art forms and genres and by making use of the affordances of digital media, including their programmability and network organization. Whether this is a radical openness in the computational network environment can, of course, be questioned, but at least it is fair to say that artworks like Heldén's *Astroecology* reflect a way of thinking that converges with an ecological or, more precisely, astroecological thinking.

In what follows, I argue that Heldén presents evolution as a force that brings the history of the planet beyond the history of humankind and known organisms, beyond a local ecology towards an astroecology. There is, in fact, no subjective evaluation of or subjective feelings related to the processes and consequences of evolution. Actually, human and non-human subjectivity are questioned. Although the title of the work refers to an ecology that transcends planet Earth as a place, embracing an ecology of the universe, Heldén's multimedia works are limited to the planetary and take local and domestic spaces as their points of departure. This place is, as mentioned above, both concrete and metonymic. Nevertheless, *Astroecology* demonstrates a shift in thinking from a local ecology to a planetary and astroecological one. Astroecological thinking is reflected through the perspective of the local, the house, the domestic and the familiar. Heldén offers an image of how the world becomes uninhabitable and how species other than humans evolve – and this is a point I will have to return to – in a way that allows us once again to question the distinction between human and non-human animals. As I show, *Astroecology* involves an exploration not only of a possible future but also of a possible future relationship between the human and the non-human, the organic and the non-organic and the technological and natural. In the following, I examine how the different forms and modes of expression employed by Heldén (poems, images, pictures, animations and encyclopedic texts) create an image of an astroecological collapse and contribute to an astroecological thinking.

Poetry and the astroecological collapse

Astroecology contains six poems. They appear in a separate frame at the lower part of the screen. They emerge as events and have a prominent, performative role throughout the process. A post-catastrophic world is present from the beginning on and is presented in the first poem with elements of destruction, flooding and vegetation that overtakes the human world.

> The illuminated trail, 8:30 pm. Low cloud cover, no stars, high levels of oxygen. The few intact lightbulbs dimmed by thousands of waterdrops. sections passing through, the swamp flooded – the water could be waist-deep in the next step. Over the course of several years the asparagus plot transforms. Covered by weed, turning into meadow, into brushwood, the beginnings of a forest. The slow rush of vegetation up towards the garage. So the clouds came closer to the ground. (#2016)

The poem adds voice, mood, sensation, intensity and new dimensions of time to the visual presentation that, at each step, runs in a loop to signify shifts between day and night. It is descriptive: the speaker's observation is situated in a present now and is marked, at turns, by quantifiable time ("8:30 p.m."), experienced time ("sections passing through") and narrative time ("[o]ver the course of several years"). This now is poetic; it is a poetic utterance filled with multiple time structures. The poem goes back in time in order to describe how the landscape, covered with fields of asparagus, has been transformed. Simultaneously, the poem directs its attention towards a future. The rain, which in the present is "thousands of waterdrops," will become an imagined and possible future: "could be waist-deep." The modal verb "could" here expresses a possibility, inscribing an uncertainty into the scientific world. Just like experienced time, this possible future-effect is measured and presented as an embodied experience. Similarly, the transformation of the asparagus plot appears as if it is an observation made by a human being. Moreover, this transformation seems to move from the poetic now, specified as "8:30 p.m.", into an unknown future, "several years." The sentence "the beginnings of a forest" continues in this reflective mode, anticipating what is to come.

In the last sentence of the first poem, the phrase "the clouds came" reflects a shift from present to past tense. This shift represents a change in perspective from a prophetic point of view, where a speaker imagines a future, to one in which the speaker is rendered a witness to past events. Further, the sentence "[s]o the clouds came closer to the ground" introduces an element of horror that underlines the dystopian dimension and atmosphere that are present throughout the work. Here, the coordinating conjunction "so" is crucial. This conjunction brings together the two sentences in question, but it also functions as a spatial coordinator since it connects "vegetation" to "clouds" or, in other words, earth to sky. The conjunction "so" brings earth and sky physically closer to one another. This action creates a sensation of claustrophobia and indicates the urgency of the situation. Additionally, the melding of earth and sky initiates a transformation of the poetic now, a transformation that was predicted in the first line with "low cloud cover" and "no stars". These phrases correspond with the transformations that are presented in the graphic representation of the world from 2016 to 2026, only that in the poem, the changes are sudden and dramatic because they appear in a now, that is, in the moment of the poetic utterance and not over the course of a decade.

The poems are significant for experiencing and understanding both the astroecological evolution and collapse that take place. The poems fill the graphic representations that are organized in intervals of ten years with emotions and events. Further, the poems reinforce the representation of a world in which never-ending changes have already happened and continue to happen. As the second poem tells us: "The vegetation spread through the ventilation, forming forests, swamps, fields, a cloud (shadows)."

As mentioned earlier, the local and quotidian levels function as visual metonymies for astroecological thinking. The house and the surrounding vegetation slowly disappear. In 2056 (Fig. 7), the house has nearly become invisible while the forest that once appeared dense, strong and vigorous, is now dying, as if it had become diseased.

Evolutionary forces have transformed the *oikos*, the home, into a visual trace, an indexical sign of the past existence of human beings and other organisms. As

Fig. 7: A screenshot from *Astroecology*. In the year 2056, the house that once stood there is almost gone and so is the once strong and vigorous forest.

one of the poems recounts, the empty house – empty either because the former owners have left it, expelled by evolution or because humankind was not one of the "uplifted" species – has become a shelter for other animals. In the poem that appears for the year 2036, a speaker says: "The birds moved into the piano. When they land the strings vibrate from the draft, a silent tone fills the room, the light from the screens fainter and fainter." (#2036) It is imperative to note the ambivalence in the poem's preferentiality here. The narrative of the birds' action and the silent tone they make are important for the poem's diegetic world, a world that corresponds with that depicted on the screen. The line "the light from the screens fainter and fainter," nevertheless, could refer either to this same diegetic world where light from the house grows weaker and weaker as both evolution and reading progress or, alternatively, to the observatory space where the world is depicted on computer monitors.

The poem's narrative mode draws attention to the physical changes in the world, while the poetic mode, which is typical for Heldén's poetry, provides the poem with sound and tactility and helps to create a particular atmosphere. Rather than emphasizing narrative questions, such as who lived in the house, why they moved out or what happened to them, the poem is a pure description of the sounds the birds make on the piano. The "silent tone" that "fills the room" heightens the atmosphere that is created and represents both a shift from a past to present tense and from a narrative to poetic mode.

The poems are structured around the sensations mentioned above and make use of what can be regarded as classic topoi from dystopian literature and film, such as the image of soot from burnt-out stars and "smoke rising from the hollows":

> Before the weather turns. Ashes trapped in the raindrops bound to the world above the treetops. Trying to make brick from iron-rich clay from the river. Burning the formless blocks in the abandoned fox-burrow below the old hotbeds, rerouting water from the drainpipes. The whole plot is undermined, smoke rising from the hollows. Later, the cat sits on the windowsill looking out purring quietly. Water dripping everywhere. Soot from burnt-out stars falling slowly to the ground. (#2076)

This poem demonstrates a form of time-space. It is temporally divided into a before and after. Past and future are thus brought together in the poetic now, which, along with the choice of motifs, makes the poem cohere. The soot in the last sentence is already introduced in the first line as "ashes" and reappears in the middle of the poem with the word "smoke" as vehicle. Similarly, water is a central motif that is established in the first line with "raindrops." It is then repeated in the second line as "the river" and in the third and fifth lines as "water." Furthermore, it is worth noting that the poem uses verbs to underline the way in which natural elements serve as containers. In fact, these should be read both literally and metaphorically. The concepts in question are presented with an inside and outside. In the first line, we read that ashes are *trapped* and that raindrops are *bound*. Both ashes and raindrops are stuck in other materials, as if there is another world above the landscape with vegetation that grows on the garage wall.

Temporal and spatial structures are central to the poem. Moreover, these two dimensions are intertwined. The preposition "above" tells us that the world of the poem is divided in two. The sky and the clouds belong to a different world than the one with vegetation. This world above is definitely physical, not metaphysical. "Above" simply means the world of clouds, as the first poem indicates. In this way, the structuring of the poem in terms of time and space is interesting because the preposition "above" also makes this world a container of the "before" and "after." The space already includes elements that will later become signs of ecological and astroecological collapse. The "after," described at the end of the poem, is already present in the "before" in the "world above."

The poem refers to changes in weather conditions, and it is in itself a transformation from one time and world to another time and world. The former world includes pre-modern techniques, while, in the latter, the poem describes a scene with a domesticated cat sitting in a window watching ashes fall from the sky. The verbs that are used, "make", "burning," "rerouting" and "sits", are significant for defining the before and after. While the first three of these verbs describe the kinds of everyday work necessary to survive, the cat simply sits, shockingly calm – "quietly," in the words of the poem. This shift is particularly violent because the quotidian scene of the cat is combined with a depiction of the "end of the world".

Potentially, both before and after include a wide time-span. The work that is conducted, is, according to the poem accomplished with pre-modern techniques, and the iron-rich clay that the subjects are burning, itself a technique that can be dated to 7000 BC, is formed through natural and evolutionary processes over millions of years. Likewise, the cat transcends the moment described. Similar to the non-identified speaker, the cat is a witness, existing outside of time. Perhaps the speaker sees the past shining in the eyes of the cat, a situation reminiscent of what the "you" does in Rainer Maria Rilke's poem "Schwarze Katze" (1908):

> Doch auf einmal kehrt sie, wie geweckt,
> ihr Gesicht und mitten in das deine:
> und da triffst du deinen Blick im geelen
> Amber ihrer runden Augensteine
> unerwartet wieder: eingeschlossen
> wie ein ausgestorbenes Insekt.[3]

In Rilke's poem, the cat is an archive, a container that holds everything it has seen, so that a spectator can later see what it has seen. In the poetic moment, these visions become available to the one who sees, who, in this moment, finds herself placed outside of time. In Heldén's poem, a subject collects and stores what has been seen in this elevated now. The poem is different in style and tenor from Rilke's. Heldén's is calmer, more homogeneous and without the epiphany that is significant for Rilke's poem. Nevertheless, in both poems the cat serves as a mythical figure and as a historical witness. The cat functions as an external archive of memories of events that exceed the duration of the ordinary lifespan of an individual cat. There is no human "you" mirrored in the cat's eyes. Rather, "later" denotes the post-catastrophic and, most likely, the post-anthropocentric world.

The figure of the cat appears in two other poems. In one of the poems, a cat's presence is materialized as footprints on an image of a digital book: "An image spread online: across the pages of a richly illustrated, handwritten book from the 1300s, the paw prints of a cat in ink." (#2116) The footprints are indexical signs that remind us of the cat's long-lasting presence in the world of literature, from the fourteenth century's book culture into the digital culture of the twenty-first century. This description imbues the cat and the poem with a mystical dimension. In the sixth and final poem, the speaker calls out to a cat: "The dream-like sequences from Tokyo, the

---

[3] "Black Cat": "As if awakened, she turns her face to yours; /and with a shock, you see yourself, tiny, / inside the golden amber of her eyeballs /suspended, like a prehistoric fly." An English translation of the poem can be found here: https://www.poets.org/poetsorg/poem/black-cat (15 December 2022).

hollow wooden synthesizer sounds, *Cat, wherever you are, peace be with you.*" (#2136) The apostrophe in italics is a quote from the experimental art house film *Sans soleil* (1983) by Chris Marker, taken from a ceremony for a lost cat. It is a common belief that *Sans soleil* was inspired by T.S. Eliot's long poem *Ash Wednesday* (1930), which expresses a hope for the salvation of humanity in a secularized society. Such a hope for humankind is not present in Heldén's *Astroecology*. Nevertheless, the reference to *Sans soleil* is interesting because the movie can be understood as an exploration of the relationship between images and memories. In this respect, the poems in *Astroecology* can be read as field notes and dream sequences, complex images from a memory bank of subjects that have been witnessing the changes in dystopian landscapes over decades, towards a future that is given at the end. This aspect opens the question of who the speaker in these poems is, a question that I will address later in this chapter.

Both the end of the world and the final astroecological collapse are depicted as images of a ruined, cold and lifeless world. This moment of death is described with intensity in the sixth and final poem through the image of a dying giraffe and an ecological chain reaction:

> The giraffe, blood pulsating from its throat. Someone said that all animals grow calm in the moment before death. You can't change your mind. It's strange. Like when a game gets out of hand, when you are a kid, you want to say hold on. I don't want to play anymore. When the music falls silent you hear the engines roar. When the roar falls silent you hear the fans drone, when the drone falls silent you hear the wind. When the wind falls silent – (#2156)

Could it be that the cat, sitting on the windowsill and watching the world around it collapse, is calm because "all animals" – according to someone that the poem refers to – are calm "in the moment before death"? Here, the image of the giraffe and the blood that pulsates is grotesque. It is at once a concrete image of a giraffe in the moment before its death and an allegory of the silence that will occur in the moment before the cessation of all organic life. This poem includes a simile, a figure of speech that is rarely used by Heldén. This comparison is embedded in the "like", strengthening the allegory in the poem because the human "you" is like a child who plays a game. The combination of allegory and simile, read within the framework of the Anthropocene, implicitly expresses the fact that humankind has treated its surroundings like how a child behaves in a game, as if human exploitation of natural resources was a game. The Anthropocene is a reflection of the irreversible changes that humanity has brought to the earth through limited ecological thinking and action. Therefore, the Anthropocene also signifies the arc of evolution, an arc caused by humans and technology, from which it is now too late to reverse or withdraw. As a human being, you cannot withdraw or say you do not want to be part of evolution, whatever its course and causes may be.

The allegory and simile, the meanings of which are depth-oriented, are replaced in the last three lines of the poem by a figure of heterophony. Here, the world appears with multiple sounds like a cacophony and, as each sound peels away, a frightening announcement of silence becomes louder. The wind, the last sound on earth, falls silent. It is the image and sound of the final death. When the wind no longer makes a sound, it is because it no longer meets resistance from geological or organic objects. Frictions and intensities are absent, because there are no longer differences in air pressure and temperature, the meteorological conditions for moving air, and because the earth has stopped turning around the sun and its own axes. The beginning of this collapse is also mentioned in the poem from the year 2096. Here, the absence of wind is caught in the image of unmoving clouds: "Above the horizon: the clouds unmoving". Taking into consideration the fact that wind is an astroecological phenomenon, the silence of wind might indicate not only an earth-bound collapse but also a collapse in the solar system, *sans soleil*, a world without the sun.

Evolution and time cease, along with the wind and all known life forms. At this point, the poem also ends, marked by a dash, which coincides with the visual representation of the world, depicted almost like a dash, at the end of the work. As a metapoetic element, the poem is silenced, the only way it could possibly end, in which the prolonged postponement of a union between sound and meaning, semantics and semiotics, dissolves.

Collective memories and archived knowledge

As I have argued already, *Astroecology* is science fiction poetry; it stages an imagined future. The poems combine past, present and future, condensing the nowness of the poems into a single moment. Further, the work also functions as an archive of the past. The poems are complex images from a memory bank, representing sensations and experiences associated with the effects of evolution on the landscape. The work also contains other sources of collective memories along with other types of memory technology. These technologies include photographs of landscapes and organisms and encyclopedic texts about species that have become extinct and therefore only exist as representations of collective memories.

Photographs of nature appear on the screen in short moments of time. They are made visible due to the reader's action and appear as if they are sense-memories, short and sudden glimpses of things previously seen. In short, they intensify the feeling of absence and the loss of past time and nature. These memories are neither place- nor time-specific, nor are they oriented towards the planetary, the national or the local, as is the case with the graphic representation of the house in the woods. They are also not linked to a specific sense-subject, enhancing the possibility of reading them as collective memories of a world that has always already been in the process of disappearing.

Encyclopedic texts appear on the screen in the transition between each period. While the photographs are not contextualized or combined with captions that explain what we see, these encyclopedic texts include both visual and textual representations. They present future loss in the world. They function as threshold texts, both because they appear in between a shift from one decade to another and because they provide information about how various species have evolved and died out from 2026 onward. That is, they constitute stages and transitions in the Anthropocene towards the end of ecology where everything becomes static and soundless, as is shown in the last graphic representation (Fig. 6) and recalled in the two last poems.

The word encyclopedia (from Latin, *encyclopaedia*) can be explained literally as a cycle or branches of knowledge in a particular field that is presented in a comprehensive manner. In the *Cambridge Encyclopedia of Language*, "encyclopedia" is defined as "a book or set of books containing many articles arranged in alphabetical order that deal either with the whole of human knowledge or with a particular part of it, or a similar set of articles on the internet."[4] In this sense, the texts in *Astroecology* perform a different function in the work's presentation and exploration of the evolutionary process towards the astroecological collapse than the graphic representation and the poems. Further, this definition of encyclopedia underlines the fact that the texts are representations of human epistemology in print media. I will briefly focus on this specification of a particular media, "book" or "books," and the production of knowledge specified as "human knowledge."

Books and "articles on the internet" are involved in determining the conditions for knowledge production; and both reveal a rather conventional epistemology. Moreover, "books" denote knowledge production (and the production of humankind) in the "Gutenberg galaxy" (McLuhan 1962). Jonas Ingvarsson, amongst others, has argued that in the digital era, print books are no longer regarded as the main media for the production and distribution of knowledge (Ingvarsson 2020). Rather, books have become one medium among many. The *Cambridge Encyclopedia of Language*, for instance, is an online encyclopedia, which means that it serves as proof of the need for an alternative definition and a movement away from a book-centered understanding of the genre. Similarly, *Astroecology* is an online work; but it is also a media-ecological work. The encyclopedic texts are materialized in several

---

4 https://dictionary.cambridge.org/dictionary/english/encyclopedia (13 December 2022).

medializations of the work, including as print, index cards in an art installation and digital texts. In other words, the encyclopedic texts underscore the media-ecological situation of poetic projects like *Astroecology*. Even though it is a poetic work, it plays with the genre of the encyclopedia as a non-media-specific genre.

Relevant in this context is also the idea that encyclopedic texts represent *human* knowledge. In this respect, encyclopedic texts are anthropocentric in origin. They are, or were, written by and for humans; they reflect a human culture and the human way of organizing knowledge about the world; and they participate in producing and confirming the world as a human world. To some extent, these criteria also hold true for *Astroecology*.

Astroecology's encyclopedic texts are conventional in form. Each article is organized as if it were an article in a print book. In other words, the articles follow conventions that are developed in print culture. An illustration is shown on the left-hand side, while the text is on the right-hand side. The articles contain names of relevant species in Latin and in Swedish – or English or Danish, depending on in which language one choses to read the work. Furthermore, the articles include information about each species' distinct qualities. There are short stories that explain how the species in question became extinct. Parts of the information are scientific. For example, it is said about the blue whale, which appears on the screen on the threshold between the year 2026 and 2036 (see Fig. 8), that it is the largest animal that has ever lived on the planet and that it has a known lifespan of over 80 years. This is factual knowledge about the species, knowledge that is developed through an anthropocentric worldview, i.e. the species as humans see and know it. This non-fictional information about the blue whale is combined with a fictional staging of a possible future: "The last blue whale was hunted into a shallow bay in the Arctic in 2026, where she beached and expired after several hours struggle to return to deep waters."

This encyclopedic text is interesting for several reasons. First, it contains a description of a death struggle that could have happened but where the dating of the event to the year 2026 is fictitious. The image of the struggling blue whale trapped in a shallow bay finds its parallel in the fate of a mouse that, according to one of the poems, was found stuck inside of a bottle: "a plastic bottle with a dead hazel mouse in it. It had found its way through the opening but could not get out." (#2066) Neither of the two animals was able to find its way out. The blue whale's struggle is both an imagined description of the whale attempting to free itself and an allegory of the situation faced by all human and non-human animals in the Anthropocene. Secondly, the text says that a non-identified subject or force hunted the blue whale. It is likely that this force is an effect of changes in the whale's natural habitat, represented here through the technique of personification. Third, the

Fig. 8: One example of an encyclopedic text in the digital part of *Astroecology*.

information about the last blue whale is interesting because it reinforces *Astroecology* as a work that assesses and presents tragic future scenarios, that is, as a form of a "risk society" (cf. Beck 1992). *Astroecology*'s structure can be thought of in terms of "what if" and "as if." It is likely that the blue whale will die out at some point in the future, which means that the story remains a possibility, a form of (science) fiction that, because of evolution, will at some point turn into fact. Still, there is no proof that suggests that blue whales will die out in the year 2026. And yet, this scenario *feels* true. The epistemological change that is brought forward when fiction feels like it is true occurs because it is not the exact year of the last blue whale's death that matters but rather the very idea that blue whales will die out, that the blue whale's final struggle will take place, just as if it had already taken place. Fourth, it is worth mentioning that the text is written from an imagined future perspective, where 2026 is already in the past, hence, the temporal form of verbs like "was hunted". Nevertheless, the text puts the future, the year 2026 and the extinction of the blue whale, into a present now and shows how our knowledge of and feelings in the present are filled with expected future events. Whether one read the work in 2023 or 2033, it offers a space in which to experience the feeling of a possible future and possible loss.

While the blue whale is presented as somewhat passive with respect to the changing environment, another text endows *Vulpes vulpes* with human-like agency. This text also begins with a classifying definition of the fox as species, before it reveals that the fox has developed the ability to think systematically and act relationally towards its surroundings. The presentation establishes a parallel to early civilizations in human history:

> fox, *Vulpes vulpes*, four-legged animate object. In 2028 they began to construct simple bridges across ditches and streams. A few years later they were extinct. Afterwards intricately woven straws were found in their burrows, signs of handicraft or art; in the field they dug a shallow network of canals, perhaps a replica or map of the archipelago in a nearby lake. (2036)

Temporal phrases such as "in 2028" and "a few years later," as well as the adverb "afterwards" refer to a historical chronology. Together with the positioning of the event in the year 2036, this aspect serves as an archived micro-narrative that fills the gap between two decades in the macro-narrative. The text explains that the fox has developed characteristics and qualities that we usually associate with abstract and complex thinking, and that it performs actions that we would associate with actions performed by humans in previous civilizations. The notion of a non-human world and a civilization created by animals challenges the inherited understanding of encyclopedic texts as anthropocentric knowledge.

In contrast to the text about the blue whale, this text does not provide information about why or how *Vulpes vulpes* became extinct or how it evolved into an advanced species that constructed complex systems and made arts and maps of archipelagos in nearby areas. Perhaps future evolution is the only explanation for this development, where the text presents a narrative parallel to human history, as if the fox had taken the place of humans in a social, cognitive and artistic hierarchy. The fox strengthens its position in the ecosystem and utilizes its natural habitat to reinforce its ability to survive. It develops a sense for aesthetics and has an urge to discover new lands, systematize the knowledge of these lands and, perhaps, in the absence of humans, colonize the land (and planet). The position that the fox has conquered, makes it dominant and gives it the ability to develop knowledge that, in the history of humankind, is defined as anthropocentric – knowledge of the world from the human point of view. Still, despite or indeed because of its ability to make its species stronger, the fox also disappears.

In *Astroecology*, the fox and other non-human species develop human-like features. Still, they are not anthropomorphized. Rather, we can read these texts as explorations of how evolution would go if, or when, humankind disappears and leaves the planet to animals and other organisms. One consequence of such an exploration is that *Astroecology* raises questions about the relationship of all species to their environment and the validity of our cultural distinction between human and non-human animals. Moreover, the world of *Astroecology* appears as a more-than-human world. In Morton's concept of the mesh, the distinction between nature and culture, humans and other organisms, is blurred and questioned. Similarly, Giorgio Agamben argues in *The Open: Man and Animal* (2002) that human history views human beings as separated from other animals. This argument provides the foundation for one of Agamben's central concepts, "the anthropological machine." According to Agamben, we have now reached the point where the distinction between humans and other animals is being called into question. Or, in Agamben's words, this distinction is now "in the open." We find a similar eco-philosophical position in Heldén's *Astroecology*. The work proposes a future where some animals, due to evolution and their own conditions, have developed characteristics that enable them to make crafts and art and to mime structures discovered in landscapes distant from their natural habitat. In this way, we can regard the work as a representation not only of a possible future but also of a future in which the anthropological machine has been replaced by an evolution that shows the species' existence and its behavior, skills and final destiny in a non-human world.

Observations out of time and place

While the poems represent observations and embodied experiences of changes in the landscape, the photographs and encyclopedic texts could be mediated observations, field notes made from someone or something positioned outside of the landscape. As I have mentioned, in *Astroecology* different species and a landscape, possibly the whole planet, are "uplifted" into a spaceship, only to be observed by one or several subjects. The work does not say anything about who these subjects might be. There is no information about who has taken the photographs, written the encyclopedic texts, archived them, explored and experienced the landscape and written the poems. Neither does it say for whom the photographs, encyclopedic texts and poems are meant, nor is there any information revealing who – if anyone or anything at all – is watching the monitors on the wooden desk.

This situation reflects various levels of mediation. One can imagine the reader positioned behind her computer screen, the computer placed on a wooden desk perhaps, watching the image of the two monitors on the wooden desk. One of the monitors shows the appearance of the poems, the appearance of which reflects a process of mediation. The poems appear on the surface of the screen because of the action conducted by the reader on her computer and because someone, or something, perhaps a computer, has written them. Likewise, on the other monitor, the world appears mediated and remediated through a surveillance system, as photographs, and through the writing and graphic illustrations in the encyclopedic texts.

These layers of mediation and remediation emphasize the process of creating, of representing and of viewing. We might call this a situation of hypermediacy. According to Jay Bolter and Richard Grusin, hypermediacy reminds the reader of the media involved in the work (Bolter and Grusin 1999, 272) and, therefore, makes the reader conscious of the act of seeing. In *Astroecology*, we are immediately made aware of the presence and the position of an observer. The reader is not told who this observer is but can see and read what the non-identified observer can see and read. This position is anachronic, outside of history and outside or beyond the time and place of evolution. It could be the position of the narrator looking into the diegetic world. Nevertheless, it is a "supernatural" time-place, which allows one or more subjects to experience the development without being part of it. It is a time-place out of joint, we might say, to paraphrase Hamlet, after being haunted by the ghost of his father. Philip K. Dick uses the phrase as a title in his novel from 1959 to refer to how events in the narrative are supernatural. We also might recall Derrida who uses the phrase to signify anachronism, how the past, and more to the point, the ghost of Marx, haunts our present (Derrida 2006). In *Astroecology*, a ghost from the past and future haunts the present.

With the monitor space, Heldén creates a framework for mediations and establishes a mixture of materiality: the imitation of wood combined with electronic devices. He puts into play traditional and "new" materials and media, a reflexive use of materials that is also recognizable in his other works. The opening page in Heldén's *The Prime Directive* (2006), for example, shows an image of two books circling around their own axis. They are of course not books but digital images of books, which in *The Prime Directive* constitute entrances into the work's two sections. Rather than being understood as opposites or competitors, the combination reflects a desire to create connections across material, medial and cultural lines. In *Astroecology*, the monitor position highlights the media event as a process towards the collapse, and it emphasizes that what is shown is an experiment. Still, just as much as the position could be the position of scientist, conducting the experiment, the desk could be the author's. The image reflects a widely used rhetorical topos, the author's desk. However, in science fiction and in a technopoetic worldview and the computational network environment the scientist and the author could just likely be a computer.

In one of the print poems in the book *Astroecology*, we read: "We built an AI, its purpose was to replace me." (2016b, no. 34) The statement can be read as an intratextual reference to the work *Evolution* (2014), where Heldén and Håkan Jonson developed a poetry machine with the intention of replacing the poet Johannes Heldén (cf. Chapter 2), but it may as well be meant for the work and world of *Astroecology*. In the latter case, it is fair to interpret "me" as a human being that has been replaced by AI as the one who monitors the elevated landscape on the screen, who writes the future encyclopedic texts and collects and archives the photographs of the past. The pronoun "me" might refer then to the last human speaker.

Further, it is likely that the AI is involved in the production of the poems. In her article about *Astroecology*, Roberg writes that the work establishes an uncertainty as to whether the poems were created by a human or a machine (see also Roberg 2019, 11). Nevertheless, artificial intelligence and algorithm as co-authors of the poetic texts are less prominent than in *Evolution*, in favor of a representation of post-anthropocentrism and the thematization of nature and evolution in the Anthropocene.

Astroecology is a technogenetic work, a collaborative work by humans and non-humans. The text thematizes this collaboration. The observation post looks like a human space, the encyclopedic texts create a continuum between the human and the non-human, and the photographs might be taken by a human or a non-human and archived by the AI. Further on, in most poems, a grammatical subject is missing. It says, for instance, "The landscape elevated", "The vegetation spreads", "Here the end of consciousness, the collapse of spaces, or the logic of the seasons," "Trying to make brick," and "Burning the formless blocks." One of the few exceptions from this is found in a poem that refers to an "I" who found "a plastic bottle with a dead hazel dormouse inside it." The dead hazel mouse is, as I discussed earlier, an emblem of the fate of humans and other organisms in the Anthropocene. They are trapped in evolution, an evolution that takes place within a closed ecological system; they cannot find a way out of the linear development of evolution.

Other poems emphasize an embodied presence that makes visible sensations and an affective and cognitive subject. In one of the poems, it says "[d]own below, heavy footsteps head home" (#2096) and in another "[t]he raindrops leave black trails on the forearms" (#2126). The reference to the sound of what could be a human body moving downstairs, presumably in a house, and the visual trace rain on a forearm is surprising since elsewhere the poems and the work depict a world without human beings. Nevertheless, from a technogenetic perspective, the subject is both human and non-human. A poetic subject observes and writes down what it sees; it hears and feels. In this respect, what I call a technogenetic subject appears as open, explorative and prophetic, one who simultaneously sees what has happened and knows what is going to happen.

Field recordings and technogenetic subjects

Astroecology is a response to the Anthropocene and represents an alternative strategy for dealing with the experience of evolution. There is a sense throughout the work that the future is already present. The work displays and performs knowledge of our past, present and future through multiple temporalities. The work moves linearly towards an imagined future by an interval of ten years, from 2016, which is the starting point of the work, till its ends in the year 2156. In this way, a geological time is reflected as the dramatic changes in the landscape slowly take over and erase traces of human activities: the house, the garden, the fence and the path that went through the forest. In this respect, the linear organization and progression serve a particular purpose. Textual, visual and audio representations are predetermined in the work, and the reader cannot interfere with the outcome, as if the future is already destined. The reader can only, less intentionally, decide the order of the appearances of words in the poems, photographs and texts. This lack of the reader's ability to interfere has its analogy in the narrative about evolution and the astroecological collapse in the work. The work encourages, or should we say forces, the reader to engage in the narrative, even though the reader has no influence over the progression of the evolution of the world. This creates an interactive engagement that does not contradict the presentation of evolution and the Anthropocene as phenomena and conditions that have put humans as subjects on the sidelines. Rather, it emphasizes that human actions have intervened in evolution and continue to do so, even after human subjects have disappeared from the planet. To this linear presentation of evolution, the work adds a circular rhythm as the world shifts between day and night. Furthermore, poems, photographs and encyclopedic texts add past, present and future times. They appear as punctual elements and as archival documentation, establishing how the history of the planet, i.e. the planet as it was, may develop in the future. Additionally, the poems present a dense and heterochronic now, which in itself brings together past, present and future sensations.

According to Bruno Latour, linear time is the time of the Anthropocene (Latour 2018). He argues that the Anthropocene has affected our conception of time and, not least, future prospects. It seems, Latour writes, that it seems as if in the Anthropocene we have become more aware of how human activities have affected our perception of the temporal structures on the planet and that we by that have entered a time-space where multiple temporalities have no epistemological value. Furthermore, Latour claims that the Anthropocene calls for a collective metanarrative that brings together temporal diversity. As Ann-Louise Sandahl puts it in her critical presentation of Latour's notion: "now all people on earth are forced to live at the same time, whether they want to or not." (Sandahl 2016, 37) Sandahl shares Latour's view that every entity on earth, humans, organisms and objects are incorporated into this new time scenario of the Anthropocene. However, she argues against the idea that the time of multiple temporalities in the arts is over. *Astroecology* has a fluid timeless time, where the past, present and future are intertwined and exist simultaneously. Rather than a disruption of the linear development in ten-year intervals, these heterochronies supplement the linear narrative that human and non-human animals share. They fill the linear time with other conceptions of time. Overall, they imply an ecological thinking that transgresses conventional temporal conceptions.

Astroecology demonstrates how poetry in the computational and network environment can respond to the Anthropocene as a time-space where both past and future are present whether we like it or not. Heldén and *Astroecology* implicitly present an argument about the necessity of temporalities other than linear time in order to understand and fill with meaning the geological narrative that transcends the time of humankind. In the world of *Astroecology*, the observatory space, the world on the monitor, the poems, the photographs and the encyclopedic texts are all results of a collaboration of subjects that cannot be traced back to either humans or non-humans alone. For instance, the poems bring together not only sensations, experiences, events, intensities and knowledge in the evolutionary process that takes place on one of the monitors but also a larger timespan and a more complex, heterochronic structure in which future sensations are not only produced by humans. Therefore, *Astroecology* is a world and a work of ecological relationships. This is a relationship that includes humans and non-humans but one in which the distinction between human and non-human animals, other organisms and artificial intelligence is no longer of any epistemological value.

Chapter 5
Instagram Poetry and the Logic of Media Platforms: Sabina Store-Ashkari, Alexander Fallo and Trygve Skaug

Fig. 9: Screenshot of a poem by the Norwegian Instagram poet Sabina Store-Ashkari: "one day / I decided / that from now on / I will forgive / myself / for everything/ I accepted / because I thought / it should be like that" (my translation).

The poem above (Fig. 9) is by the Norwegian Instagram poet Sabina Store-Ashkari. It is an Instagram poem and was published on Store-Ashkari's Instagram profile, @ingentingusagt on 12 November 2020.[1] By now, the post has received 561 likes and 31 comments, a response somewhat higher than what Store-Ashkari usually receives.[2]

---

[1] https://www.instagram.com/p/CHgM8k6LnsQ/ (5 December 2022).
[2] Per 5 December 2022.

ථ Open Access. © 2023 the author(s), published by De Gruyter. [CC BY-NC-ND] This work is licensed under the Creative Commons Attribution-NonCommercial-NoDerivatives 4.0 International License.
https://doi.org/10.1515/9783111004075-005

The comments contain emojis with hearts and clapping hands, as well as affirmative phrases like "Åh. Sukk. Ja" ("Oh. Sigh. Yes"), "Akkurat sånn!" ("Just like that!") and "Helt riktig" ("Absolutely right"). The responses confirm that the poem is appreciated, that its motif and message are familiar and representative to many and that it is useful: it can provide comfort and hope and even offer a solution.

Instagram poems are poems written with the intention of being published and distributed on the platform Instagram. In a relatively short time span, Instagram poetry has become a popular form of poetry; and, given the number of followers, it is a type of literature that has become impossible to ignore. For example, Instagram writer Rupi Kaur, who I referred to in Chapter 1, has nearly four and a half million followers on Instagram.[3] R.M. Drake has just over two and a half million,[4] while Atticus has more than one and a half million,[5] and Yrsa Daley-Ward just over two hundred thousand.[6] In Norway, Trygve Skaug, Alexander Fallo and Sabina Store-Ashkari have about two hundred thousand, twenty-two thousand and seven thousand followers, respectively.[7] Compared to the first group of poets, the Norwegian poets' number of followers is relatively small. However, given the fact that Norwegian has far fewer speakers than English and that most Norwegian readers of Instagram poetry likely also follow and read English-language poems on Instagram, these numbers are high. These three poets can therefore be said to be representative in the Norwegian context.

In this chapter, I discuss some aspects of the interaction between Instagram poems and the platform Instagram as well as between the literary form and the medium of distribution, Moreover, I show how the content, form and function of Instagram poems are, to a great extent, determined by the logic of the media platform, that is, by the way the platform functions. In this context, I trace some key media-technological aspects that frame the poetic activity on the platform. This discussion is then followed by close readings of a small selection of poems by Norway's most popular Instagram poet, Trygve Skaug. By calling attention to Norwegian Instagram poetry in this way, I also briefly mention how this poetry differs from better-known Instagram poetry in English, a difference that is all the more striking since Instagram as such is typically thought of as a global platform with few national differences.

As elsewhere in this book, my approach is based on an understanding of the medium, in this case Instagram, as a non-neutral platform. José van Dijck and Thomas Poell advance this perspective in an article from 2013, arguing for the need to examine

---

3 https://www.instagram.com/rupikaur_/ (13 December 2022).
4 https://www.instagram.com/rmdrk/ (13 December 2022).
5 https://www.instagram.com/atticuspoetry/ (13 December 2022).
6 https://www.instagram.com/yrsadaleyward/ (13 December 2022).
7 https://www.instagram.com/trygveskaug/?hl=nb, https://www.instagram.com/alexanderfallo/?hl=nb, https://www.instagram.com/ingentingusagt/?hl=nb (13 December 2022).

the logic that governs platforms: "Far from being neutral platforms, social media are affecting the conditions and rules of social interaction. Therefore, their sustaining logic deserves to be scrutinized in detail to better understand its impact in various domains." (van Dijck and Poell 2013, 5) If it is true that the logic of Instagram, as they claim, influences the social interaction that takes place on the platform, and thus does not merely function as a neutral channel for sharing content, then it is also reasonable to assume that this logic affects the poems that are written to be published, distributed and read on Instagram. Previous research has shown how, to varying degrees, both analogue and digital media affect or interact with the form and distribution of a poem. This observation also applies to Instagram. The platform's logic, including actions by its owners and programmers (such as redefining algorithms and the platform's interfaces), thus influences how it is used; in other words, the platform's logic affects how Instagram poets write, what they write about and when they publish.

Reception and research – the situation in Norway

In recent years, Instagram poems have, with increasing frequency and intensity, been discussed in the daily press, on podcasts and in popular science journals (Thomas 2020, 88). Admittedly, the reception has been diverse. Generally, the poems are considered to be of poor poetic quality. Some critics even claim that these texts are worthless as poetry. One well-known example of such a critique is by the British poet Rebecca Watts, who, in an essay in the journal *Poetry Nation Review*, describes Instagram poems as "artless poetry" and as an expression of "the complete stagnation of the poet's mind." (Watts 2018; also see Korecka 2021) A similar critique has been made by the Norwegian literary critic and scholar Frode Helmich Pedersen, who, in the *Morgenbladet* on 31 January 2020, writes rather bluntly that "Trygve Skaug's enormously popular poems are not good." (Pedersen 2020a)[8] In a dispute in *Bokvennen litterære avis* from 24 February 2020, Pederson furthers his initial claim: "If anyone can show me an Instagram poem of high-quality, I am all ears." (Pedersen 2020b)[9] These reviews, though, neither reflect on the role of the played by the media platform, on media conditions, nor on how media actually function. In contradistinction to these writers, the Norwegian literary critic Ingunn Økland alerts readers to these perspectives in a review of another Norwegian Instagram poet, Alexander Fallo and his print collection of

---

[8] My translation. The original Norwegian reads: "Trygve Skaugs enormt populære dikt er ikke gode."
[9] My translation. The original Norwegian reads: "Hvis noen kan vise meg et instadikt av høy kvalitet, er jeg lutter øre."

poems *du fucker med hjertet mitt nå* (2020). In the review, Økland highlights the vulnerability that occurs as a consequence of transferring Instagram poems to a book format: "Alexander Fallo falls for the temptation to include single sentences that have a certain charm on Instagram but that are far too flimsy on a white book page." (Økland 2020)[10] Økland suggests that poems that are appreciated on Instagram are not necessarily as easily cherished when they are printed in a book. There are many possible reasons for this difference in reception. We read and write differently in different media (Hayles 2012; Mangen, Walgermo and Brønnick 2013) and in different situations (Drucker 2020). Moreover, media are used for different purposes. Different media logics work differently. This is also true of poetry. Consequently, the media environment, the way media work and the logic of media are all important for our understanding and evaluation of Instagram poems.

For the last years, research on Instagram poetry has accelerated as the poems have grown in number and popularity. A few years ago, hardly any academic attention was given to Instagram poetry. Similarly, few literary critics showed interest. This should not come as a surprise if we account for the fact that this poetic media genre is still in a relatively early phase: Instagram was first launched in 2010, primarily as a photo-sharing program. Only later did users begin to publish poetry on the platform. Still, it is probably fair to claim, as do Magdalena Korecka and creative writing researcher Lili Pâquet, that Instagram poetry has long been considered to belong to a popular cultural field with "little literary merit." (Pâquet 2019, 296; Korecka 2021, 8) This evaluation may also explain why many of the researchers who have taken an interest in the genre are relatively young and come from research fields other than traditional literary studies. Examples of research conducted on Instagram poetry include Bronwen Thomas' book, *Literature and Social Media* (Thomas 2020). Here, Thomas incorporates Instagram poetry as a significant part of the material. Further on, in her overview of the research, Korecka mentions among others analyzes of Instagram poetry's pedagogical potential for literacy across media (Kovalik and Curwood 2019; Korecka 2019); Pâquet, who argues for the influence of self-help literature on Instagram poetry (Pâquet 2019); and Shweta Khilnani who focuses on affective and aesthetic aspects of Instagram poetry (Khilnani 2021). Jeneen Naji approaches Instagram poetry from the perspective of posthumanism (Naji 2021). Camilla Holm Soelseth has researched the genre with methods developed from digital

---

10 My translation. In Norwegian, the quote reads: "Alexander Fallo faller for fristelsen til å inkludere enkeltsetninger som har en viss sjarm på Instagram, men som blir altfor spinkle på en hvit bokside."

humanities (Soelseth 2022). Kathi Inman Berens discusses Instagram poetry as a form of electronic literature (Berens 2019). Both Kristin L. Matthews and Magdalena Korecka explore Instagram poetry within the framework of political and activist literature, in particular struggles against racism and oppression (Matthews 2019; Korecka 2021). Korecka investigates contemporary audio-visual poetry on social media platforms such as Instagram, Twitter, TikTok and YouTube.[11] She highlights political and activist dimensions of this poetry, dimensions that give legitimacy to these genres. In this regard, Korecka expands on Rosa Crepax's notion that Instagram poetry is essentially digital feminist activism, written by young female feminists (Crepax 2020, 75; Korecka 2021, 4). In addition, some research on Instagram poetry has focused on particular authors. Due to Rupi Kaur's enormous popularity, it is not surprising that she has received significant attention from researchers. Several of the publications already mentioned draw attention to Kaur's poems.

In light of this brief overview, two features in particular should be emphasized. First, we find that the research has explored Instagram poetry along three main lines: Instagram poetry has been examined as a media phenomenon, as a genre and as a cultural-political phenomenon. To varying degrees, this research engages with the question of the relationship between Instagram poetry and the rest of the literary field, including literary genres and the history of poetry. In this respect, the research is divided between those who regard Instagram poetry as more "popular" than other poetry (Penke 2019, 451) and those who, like Matthews, emphasize the innovative aspects of the poems and how these aspects contribute to making us question literary conventions and reading habits in other media. Thomas also touches on these innovative aspects. She points to the crucial interaction between Instagram poetry and its respective platform, claiming that Instagram poems share two common features: first, Instagram poems are a form of platform poetry; and second, that readers' participation in a community is established in the intersection between the platform and the poems (Thomas 2020, 87). Other scholars define Instagram poetry through repetitive motifs, whether they emphasize the poems' orientation towards everyday motifs or pursue the hypothesis that the poems function as literary activism (Korecka 2021).

The second key feature that emerges from this review of the research literature is that scholarship on Instagram poetry is, to a certain extent, colored by fascination and enthusiasm. This research has arisen from a number of academic fields, including literary studies, media studies, sociology, anthropology and creative

---

11 https://www.poetry-digital-age.uni-hamburg.de/en/forschung/laufend/social-media-poetry.html (5 December 2022).

writing, and it has tended to be conducted by young researchers in an early stage of their academic careers. This latter characterization is not a devaluation of either the researchers or their publications but is rather meant as an observation that provides insight into who these researchers are. In other words, it is important to understand who contributes to knowledge in the field and hence sets the premises for many of the discussions that have taken place so far. To a certain extent, one might say that the lack of interest from more established poetry researchers underscores the point made by both Pâquet and Korecka, that the field of Instagram poetry has been regarded as "popular culture." (see Pâquet 2019, 296; Korecka 2021, 8) Nevertheless, a potential methodological challenge needs to be mentioned in this respect. The lack of temporal distance, i.e. the short timespan between the publication of the poems and the research conducted on them, makes it difficult to identify significant trends and patterns. Moreover, enthusiasm and temporal proximity can lead to overly simplistic claims about what Instagram poetry can do. Crepax, for example, writes that poetry on social media such as Instagram is suitable for thematizing the exploration and negotiation of identities among marginalized subjects (Crepax 2020, 79). Apart from the fact that one can claim that literature and art in general open spaces for negotiating marginalized identities, Crepax's characterization is simply too schematic. It is by no means given that the community that provides the context of Instagram poetry is representative of those with a particular marginalized identity. Social media is as likely to limit as to open negotiations about marginalized identities.

Another example of how some of the research on Instagram poetry jumps to conclusions that are not representative or is based on limited material, is Thomas' claim that critics and academics have rejected Instagram poetry because the poems are largely by young female poets of color (also see Korecka 2021, 6). She reads the reception of the poems into a tradition where young female writers are considered too private and melodramatic (Thomas 2020, 90), which from a sociological perspective is an interesting contextualization. Still, Thomas fails to examine the extent to which the poems themselves might be at least part of the reason why literary studies in Europe and the US has, until recently, taken little interest in Instagram poetry. For example, it is by no means obvious how a well-known poet like Rupi Kaur could be considered a victim of negligence. Further, regarding Instagram poetry in languages other than English, the situation might be quite different. In Norway, for instance, the two most well-known Instagram poets are men, Trygve Skaug and Alexander Fallo. It is these male poets, and not young female poets, who have been criticized for writing bad poetry.

As far as I can tell, little attention has been paid to the function that Instagram as a media platform might have in the encounter between poetry and the poems' "what" and "how," that is, what the poems are about and how the poets write them. One crucial exception is Korecka, who points out that Instagram poetry is "a kind of poetry that connects social media affordances (e.g., the use of hyperlinks), visual strategies and aesthetics with socio-political issues." (Korecka 2021, 1) Furthermore, Korecka investigates social media poetry with a media-specific approach. For example, she includes platform studies and analyzes social media affordances in relation to hashtags and algorithms (Korecka, *forthcoming*).[12] However, how such strategies and socio-political thematizations are related to the media conditions of Instagram, as well as what these media conditions consist of, must still be further clarified. In the following, I discuss three key components relevant for Instagram as a social media platform. I argue that these three components are important for understanding the role of the platform and Instagram poetry as a media-specific form of poetry.

Programmability, connectivity and popularity

All forms of communication on social media are characterized by norms, strategies, mechanisms and economic conditions that are partly outside and partly revealed on the social media platforms. The function and dominance of these platforms in many areas of communication lead van Dijck and Poell to claim that social media have "changed the conditions and rules of social interaction." (van Dijck and Poell 2013, 2) In "Understanding Social Media Logic" (2013), van Dijk and Poell explore some of the key conditions that are manifested on social media platforms in order to describe how social media works and to identify what they term social media logic. According to van Dijck and Poell, "social media logic refers to the processes, principles, and practices through which these platforms process information, news, and communication, and more generally, how they channel social traffic." (van Dijck and Poell 2013, 5) These key conditions for social media logic are defined as programmability, connectivity, popularity and datafication. In what follows, I will be most concerned with the first three of these conditions.

"Programmability" refers to social media as code-based and computational in the sense that it includes both arithmetical and non-arithmetical processes, both algorithmic and non-algorithmic events. Because digital media are based on codes, they can easily be modified. Likewise, the form and content on the surface of the media platform can also be easily amended. Therefore, the term deals with

---

[12] It should be mentioned that Korecka takes a more media-specific approach in her ongoing dissertation on social media poetry, "Visual Poetry on Social Media Platforms: New Media Aesthetic" (working title) within the context of the ERC project "Poetry in the Digital Age" at Universität Hamburg.

computers and its software facilities and includes codes, background data, algorithms, protocols and interfaces. These aspects of social media constitute various functions on a platform. For instance, they might motivate and control what users write and publish. Additionally, as van Dijck and Poell write, these aspects outline "how social media platforms shape all kinds of relational activities, such as liking, favoring, recommending, sharing and so on." (van Dijck and Poell 2013, 5) Programmability allows human and non-human actors to suggest posts, content, networks and users that you may know or that the algorithms think you want to know because you like the same things or have common connections on social media. As I will return to later, it is reasonable to claim that programmability also affects Instagram poems, including how they are shaped and what they represent.

A second aspect of social media logic is "connectivity". The concept of connectivity describes how social media is networked: users are connected to other users, machines and platforms are connected to other machines and platforms, and users are connected to machines. In a sense, network connectivity can be regarded as the meaning of social media. According to Mark B. Hansen, what is mediated in social media is first and foremost connectivity on a large scale: "[W]hat is mediated by Web 2.0 is less the content that users upload than the sheer connectivity, the simple capacity to reach myriad like-minded users, that is afforded by the act of uploading content." (Hansen 2010, 180) Similarly, Henry Jenkins, Sam Ford and Joshua Green emphasize the affiliation between connectivity and dissemination (2013). They put forward how interconnection and distribution work together and strengthen each other, even in cases in which this is not in itself an intention or goal. On the one hand, the individual user has the freedom to choose "friends" and to create networks. On the other hand, connections and, consequently, the distribution of content, are generated automatically. The former, according to van Dijck and Poell, typically reflects an individual and private initiative; the latter is often motivated by commercial intentions: "a strategic tactic that effectively enables human connectedness while pushing automated connectivity." (van Dijck and Poell 2013, 5) In this manner, connectivity depends on and reaches its full potential because of programmability.

In research on Instagram poetry, scholars often emphasize that the poems contribute to establishing or confirming online communities because they highlight topics that appeal to many users and that can easily be engaged with. This strategy, in turn, generates likes, comments and regramming. These responses can be considered as both communicative and phatic, that is, communicative actions that are ritualistic and perform the function of establishing or maintaining social contact (Jakobson 2014, 238–242). Likes, comments and regramming that have a phatic function can occur in both small, private networks and in large, commercially based communities on social media. Van Dijck and Poell argue that connectivity should be considered as an "advanced strategy of algorithmically connecting users to content, users to users, platforms to users, users to advertisers, and platforms to platforms." (van Dijck and Poell 2013, 5) Media technology gives users the ability to search for and select whom they want to follow and be connected to, while algorithms highlight and recommend users, content and networks based on a variety of criteria. This process entails what van Dijck and Poell call "automated personalization" and implies that content that is presented on platforms is calibrated for specific users. The users know some of the criteria for the automated pairing, while other criteria are not accessible. This means that processes concerning sociological community-building on platforms are doubled and that they are configured and distorted by algorithm-driven processes, processes that are conditioned both by users' preferences and needs and by the platform owners' interests and commercial purposes.

In addition to programmability and connectivity, van Dijck and Poell discuss "popularity". Popularity is perceived in sociological research as a complex concept. To simplify somewhat, popularity can be explained as processes concerning different practices of ranking based on criteria for hierarchies and status. The number of followers, likes and regramming can quantify popularity on social media, while positive comments reflect popularity in a qualitative manner. They both signify what Instagram users think is important. Still, according to van Dijck and Poell, popularity is determined by both algorithmic and socioeconomic mechanisms. This means that an Instagram user's background affects the number of followers and that popularity will vary depending on the extent to which algorithms can direct users to a specific Instagram account (van Dijck and Poell 2013, 7). In this sense, the logic of Instagram highlights some users and content over others.

Parameters for popularity such as likes, regramming and comments are part of a "like economy". Caroline Gerlitz and Anne Helmond describe this economy as an infrastructure for the exchange of data, traffic, affects, contacts and money. The exchange of these commodities has been facilitated and strengthened as a result of features that make it possible to like, comment, share and save posts, to access an Instagram group via a link from a web page or from an email or to upload an Instagram post, photo or video to a web page and link it to the relevant Instagram account. Of these social plugins, Gerlitz and Helmond highlight the "likes" button as the most important for the like economy (Gerlitz and Helmond 2013, 1353). Likewise, van Dijck and Poell point out that likes are regarded as the strongest indicator of popularity.

It should come as no surprise that Instagram poems are part of a larger popularity context and contest, a like economy, as described above. Instagram is programmed to reward those users who have many followers. Instagram poetry is no exception. It is characterized by this environment, from which it gets its fuel, engagement and political potential. Because of popularity, poets with many followers dominate the field. Indeed, the platform gives Instagram poets an opportunity to actively attract more readers. In addition to the poets' effort to write poems that are similar in form or content to the type of poems that previously received many likes, were extensively shared and received many comments, they can also choose to create a business account and access services that provide information about their readers and that even recognizes the readers' patterns on Instagram. By analyzing this information, Instagram poets can target the literary form as well as the time the poems are publish in order both to satisfy established followers and to reach new readers through networks.

With regard to popularity, it is also necessary to mention how Instagram promotes popularity through rankings. For example, hashtags like #poetry and #poems are used to draw attention to the most read or popular poems.[13] Thus, Instagram leads the flow of readers in the direction of the poems and poets with the highest rankings. In other words, Instagram is programmed to reward popularity and, obviously, many of the poets on Instagram want to reach as many readers as possible. Therefore, it is fair to say that the poets not only seek connectivity but also popularity. In this sense, popularity becomes a goal that Instagram poets relate to, whether that goal is to create a greater impact or to earn money within a "like-economy". Poets choose Instagram as a platform for their poems because the platform has proven to be well suited to their poetry, but in terms of the argument sketched above, we can also assume that they choose Instagram because it is the most adequate platform for satisfying personal ambitions. If you do not become famous, then you can at least increase the possibility of being read and seen. The latter is a further example of the importance of the phatic function of Instagram poetry. Indeed, we should not lose sight of the fact that with this kind of poetry, we are dealing with a particular aesthetic dimension that is linked to the specific interface of Instagram. This is an interface that Instagram poets may want to explore and use for purposes other than reaching a wide audience and gaining popularity.

The last aspect of social media logic that van Dijck and Poell elaborate on is "datafication". This term denotes the possibilities that a platform have for collecting information about its users and for converting this information into data and new (commercial and financial) value. This is information that, in turn, can be used to make predictions and estimates and to control and anticipate what users prefer to read, as well as to direct personalized advertising. Datafication is part of

---

13 See e.g. https://www.instagram.com/explore/tags/poets/. This overview contains poems that have been marked #poets. This means that it includes both Instagram poets and other poets (such as e.g. Robert Frost). The latter group cannot be considered Instagram poets since they do not write poems that fall under the definition of Instagram poetry given at the beginning of this chapter.

what Shoshana Zuboff describes as a relatively new global-social economy where users are put under massive surveillance (Zuboff 2019). Even though this aspect is crucial in all activities online, I consider it to be less relevant in the discussion of the media conditions for Instagram poetry. Still, I briefly mention datafication here because the concept is reminiscent of an aspect and economy of social media. Instagram poems are inevitably a part of this economy. Furthermore, the concept emphasizes that such a seemingly simple act as "liking" a poem on Instagram contributes to a larger economy that goes far beyond the popularity of a poem and poet. This is the reason behind Berens rhetorical statement:

> Perhaps we could agree that a "like" is "trivial" engagement. But what about the terabytes of data shed by and then harvested from Instapoetry fans? It cannot be "trivial" when 160,000 people "touching" just one Instapoem leave behind so much information that is quite literally out of their hands – is, in fact, a loss they can neither feel nor tally? (Berens 2019)

The discussion of van Dijckand Poell's model shows how the logic of social media is part of the media situation of Instagram poetry. Social media matters – even for Instagram poetry; it affects the production and the development of Instagram poetry. Social media also affects how the poems are distributed, read and responded to. For example, algorithms and hashtags are central to connectivity and popularity because they enable the poems to reach a larger network of readers. The poets write their poems, but they do so in a resonant space where the aspects I have been discussing play a crucial role because the logic of social media influences what poets write, how they write, how the poems reach an audience and how they are received. The various processes that take place "below" the surface of the platform, that is, the deeper layers that constitute important premises for the production, distribution and reading of Instagram poems, make it challenging but no less imperative, to understand the relationship between the poems, the publishing platform and the readers' response to the poems.

Instagram poetry and its technological situation

So far in this chapter, I have claimed that Instagram's poets and poems are, to some extent, subordinate to the media-technical affordances of the platform. With its logic, Instagram is the situation of and the environment for the poems, a partly deterministic situation and environment which are reflected in the fact that the poet, by publishing his or hers poetry on Instagram, accepts both the technical affordances and the context that constitute the platform and the way it works. To publish a poem on Instagram does not require much technical skill. It is easy to publish a poem, and it is almost impossible for the poet to change or to have an impact on the technical conditions that predispose publications. The poems are usually written in a writing and text-editing program and then published on Instagram. They can appear solely as a written poem, with no visual framework other than the platform's interface, from which the poet cannot escape. Furthermore, they can appear together with illustrations, where the illustrations are part of the poems' visual expression as the example below from @trygveskaug show (see Fig. 10). Finally, a poem can appear on

Fig. 10: The poem by Trygve Skaug was published on 11 June 2022, during Pride month. The photograph contains more information than the poem alone, including a shadow text that is partly present but impossible to read. "Oh / I am pretty slow then / hope she catches / the kindest guy in the world / I thought / about both of the girls / because they were so good / but then it was of course / not at all a guy / it was both the girls / like, each other" (my translation).[14]

---

14 https://www.instagram.com/p/CeqJotbMgdW/ (5 December 2022).

Instagram as a photographed book page or as a text written in the field that is reserved for comments. The variation and combination of these strategies for publication may be regarded with both aesthetic and media technology reasons. Either way, the different strategies represent a variety of ways that the poems become visible, readable and searchable.

The relationship between Instagram poetry and its platform technology is different from how many digital-poetic genres are related to their platforms. In other genres, media technology is often used in a surprising and frequently experimental way. The poet develops and challenges media-technological solutions, adapting the media platform to the poetic expression, or, alone or in collaboration with a programmer, makes conscious choices about which code language the digital poem should emerge through. The latter is, for instance, the case with code poetry where code language and poetic language are often thought of as a whole (see e.g. Marino 2020; Vorrath 2022). Such a holistic approach means that programming codes are being included in the idea of the poems. For Instagram poetry, the media and the poems also must be regarded as intimately related but the table has been turned. Rather than adapting the medium and its interface to the poetic idea and expression, as we saw was the case in Johannes Heldén and Håkan Jonson's *Evolution* and in Heldén's *Astroecology* (see Chapters 3 and 4), the poems are adapted to the platform's interface, to the mobile media and their small display and to the logic of the platform. As mentioned above, the poet chooses to publish her poems on Instagram and thereby accepts the possibilities and limitations of Instagram.

The fact that Instagram poetry does not represent an aesthetic whose goal is to change the platform through literary and technological experiments, does not necessarily suggest that poets are indifferent to the medium. Rather, they are engaged in the medium in a different way than authors of most other kinds of digital poetry. They take advantage of the functionality and infrastructure offered by the platform, including social plugins that condition the interactions with readers, like comments and other forms of feeback, and broad distribution in networks. The information that readers leave in form of likes, regramming and comments is part of a feedback loop that poets can use to evaluate whether the poems work and, if they work, how they work. Consequently, this feedback might have an impact on how poets write and what they write about.

Most obviously, Instagram affects the visual form of the poems since the visual aesthetic of an Instagram profile becomes part of the visual expression of the poems. This implies, as Naji also contends, that the poetics of Instagram poetry includes the interface of the platform. Naji claims that both the visual design of Instagram and the functions associated with the interface are part of the poems' form. Moreover, these aspects have a productive impact on the way the poems work. The interface of Instagram comprises the poems' visual framework and includes information like the time of publication and the number of likes and comments. With regard to connectivity and popularity, the interface is designed to encourage participation by leaving a comment, thereby creating a sense of community. By considering the interface as part of the poetics of Instagram poetry, I reinforce the claim that the platform matters. As a result, in order to understand Instagram poetry as a genre, one must explore the media conditions that determine the poems, that provide them with a function and that make them work the way they do.

Fig. 11: Screenshot of a poem by the Norwegian Instagram poet Alexander Fallo: "the Uber Driver / knows where we are going / I have no clue / your head on my lap / just follow the gut feeling" (my translation).

The poem above (Fig. 11) is by the Norwegian Instagram poet Alexander Fallo and is entitled "ubersjåføren" ("the Uber Driver"). It lacks punctuation, and it is written without the use of capital letters. The absence of punctuation and capital letters are well known from modernism and can, for this poem, be considered both as a marker of modernism, i.e. as a graphic cliché, and as an example of how a media platform partly influences how one writes. This is the language of Instagram poetry, i.e. where basic grammar rules are broken or ignored in order to give the impression that the poem is an "instant" expression of a subjective experience. Furthermore, the group of lines is formed in a way that creates a smooth diagonal line on the right margin. However, this graphic element does not turn the poem into a figurative poem where the poem's visual shape is imitating that which it represents. The visual shape does not contribute to the poem's interpretative potential, which is the case for visual and figurative poetry. Regarding the question of the role of social media logic, the above-mentioned features in the poem represent choices made and techniques performed by the poet Fallo. Likewise, Store-Ashkari, whose poem I referred to in the beginning of this chapter, uses italics in her poem, a choice that is obviously hers and not Instagram's. Nevertheless, both of these poems can serve as examples of how Instagram poems, although they vary in content and form, have a number of similarities due to the media platform and its logic.

The poems by Fallo and Store-Ashkari are typical Instagram poems: short texts, most often only one stanza per slide, with short lines, usually a few words or less on each line, and with uneven line breaks. In this manner, they look like any print poem that could have been published in a book. For this reason, they can easily be adapted into print. Thus, these poems differ from much digital poetry, such as the kinetic poetry of which bpNichol and Ottar Ormstad are two prominent exponents, Jason Nelson's "game poetry" or Johannes Heldén's algorithm-based poems. These examples of poetry in digital media are more experimental in form, and they challenge the understanding of what poetry can be and what it can look like. This is not typically the case for Instagram poetry. Nevertheless, it is important to remember that Instagram poems can also be more experimental in form. Tyler Knott Gregson (@tylerknott) publishes video recordings of himself reading his poems. One reading per day.[15] Gregson follows a ritual where he greets his audience in a way that establishes an imagined community: "This is one of my favorites, ever, so please listen up. I love this one." The greetings usually include humorous comments: "What's up you beefcake pantyhose?" He continues by holding up the written poem he will read to the camera, i.e. "here's typewriter series 55". The poem simultaneously appears on the screen. Most of Nikita Gill's (@nikita_gill) Instagram poems appear as photographs of print poems, but she also posts poems that are handwritten and that include drawings.[16] This way of combining several layers of media is also common for the poems on @kaitdoes, who also applies a technique of erasure poetry in some of her poems.[17] While Gregson makes use of his Instagram account in order to perform and distribute his poems in a form of poetry reading, @kaitdoes is, I claim, one of the most interesting contemporary

---

[15] https://www.instagram.com/tylerknott/ (13 December 2022).
[16] https://www.instagram.com/nikita_gill/?hl=en (5 December 2022).
[17] https://www.instagram.com/p/CUupTwWrA82/ (5 December 2022).

Instagram poets because her poems appear as an amalgam of poetry and visual media arts and, therefore, challenges established distinctions between the two art forms.[18]

Still, it is fair to say that neither the three examples given above nor the poems by Fallo and Store-Ashkari make substantial use of poetic techniques associated with poetry as an art form. For example, the potential of enjambment as a poetic technique that creates ambiguities, delays perception and meaning making and directs the reader's attention to metapoetic qualities are largely absent. Although enjambments in the poems break up the sentences, they do not create extra meaning or open space for ambiguous readings. Of course, for other poems, and for other Instagram poets, the enjambment can provide the poem with meaning. The term "Instagram poetry" does not denote dysfunctional line breaks. However, as I will return to later in the chapter, some of the characteristics of the poems, including the lack of ambiguity, can be linked to the logic of Instagram, as well as to the medium on which and the situations in which the poems are often read.

Platform-specific poetry

The claim made above touches upon a crucial aspect regarding the meaning of Instagram and its logic for Instagram poetry as a genre, that is, its form, content and function. Instagram poetry is platform poetry because of the poems' special affiliation with one or more platforms.[19] As platform poetry, the poems are adapted to the technical media on which they are primarily read, including the possibilities for connectivity and network distribution that are offered by the platform. Matthew Kirschenbaum writes that literature on social media is oriented towards what the platforms can offer in terms of functionality and infrastructure. Furthermore, he claims that this literature is characterized by the fact that it is designed to be shared and read on a medium with a small reading surface, such as a mobile phone or tablet (Kirschenbaum 2018, 34). Furthermore, both Magdalena Korecka and Niels Penke point out that the poems need to be adapted to the photo format of Instagram (Penke 2019, 461; Korecka 2021, 7). Penke even states that short Instagram poems often get more likes and are shared more often than longer poems, and he argues that this is due to the fact that short poems are better adapted to the platform and to the mobile medium on which the poems are

---

18 See Chapter 2 for a brief discussion of poetry and media art.
19 Obviously, Instagram poetry can also be published on other media platforms, such as on Facebook, on a coffee mug or on a t-shirt. An exploration of how Instagram poems wander across media and materializations is interesting, but will not be pursued further in this chapter.

often read (Penke 2019, 473; 303). In other words, because of the media platform and because the poems must be readable on a small screen, the poems contain a limited number of words and characters.

Moreover, the situation in which the poems are most often read might also affect the length of the poems. In fact, when Gregson reads one of his longer poems on @tylerknott, he prepares his listeners and emphasizes that this is an exception: "It's a long one. Let's go." According to Johanna Drucker, the place where one reads will affect how one reads. She highlights the concept of "sight-reading" and writes that *"where* we read is as fundamental to the way the meaning of written language is produced and contributes materially to how we understand *what* we are reading." (Drucker 2020, 167) In this respect, in a discussion on the relationships between media and the form, content and function of Instagram poetry, one should include the places where the mobile medium and the application are used and where the poems are read. It is reasonable to assume that Instagram poems are read in other places and in other situations than one usually reads print poetry. A possible reading situation for Instagram poetry could be as follows: one reads a poem quickly, clicks on the like button and perhaps leaves an emoji with a short comment, before one scroll through one's feed, likes another poem, checks the latest news on the phone and reads a Facebook post. This could take place during a lunch break or while one is waiting in a station of the metro.[20] Drucker's concept of sight-reading is useful for understanding how we read Instagram poems. She includes the role of the medium in her model. By adding medium to the concept of sight-reading, she highlights that reading and meaning making are also media-sensitive events. With regard to the definition of Instagram poetry as poetry written to be published, distributed and read on Instagram, the logic of the platform, such as popularity, and where and in which situations the poems are read will have an effect on the poems. In other words, the poems not only need to be adapted to the application and the screen of the mobile device but also to the place and situation of reading. In this sense, we might slightly revise Drucker's claim and argue that '*where* we read and on which *medium* or *media* we read are as fundamental to the way the meaning of written language is produced and contributes materially to how we understand *what* we are reading.'

The reading situation of Instagram poetry is "unclean." It is a mixture where the reader performs a sight-reading of texts in different genres, applying both aesthetic and efferent reading. The reader's feed and the Instagram poets' account are

---

[20] The description serves as a point of reference to Ezra Pound's imagist poem "In a Station of a Metro," "The apparition of these faces in the crowd: / Petals on a wet, black bough.", to emphasize my claim that Instagram poetry uses some of the trappings of a modernist aesthetic without actually doing anything of substance or transforming it in any way.

also not "pure" but might contain a combination of poems, photographs, videos and self-promotion. Daley-Ward, for instance, acts as a poet, model and actor on her Instagram account. Her profile includes both poems and photographs of herself. The photographs look like fashion photographs in which Daley-Ward appears posed and well dressed, and most of the photographs are of high visual and technical quality. Thus, it is fair to say that the poems are part of a broader visual culture of self-presentation. She and other Instagram poets demonstrate how poets' profiles appear as hybrid where the boundaries between poetry, self-promotion and influential material are blurred and where the common feature is that the various posts serve purposes that, in light of van Dijck and Poell's observations, can be understood as part of Instagram's logic. The different genres and discourses that the poems are part of are entwined and feed each other, increasing popularity and connectivity across diverse networks.

The fact that the poems are written in order to be read on an application on a mobile phone is relevant for understanding Instagram poetry as platform-specific. On the one hand, both the application and the technical medium affect individual poems. Obviously, long poems would not adapt well to the platform, a mobile screen or the various reading situations. On the other hand, the application and its design are of importance in the organization of the poems. A book, with its principle of organization and its conventions for writing and reading, encourages a poet to explore a theme or a motif in a linear or sequential order and to let a story unfold through several poems. In contrast, Instagram serves as a publishing platform and archive that invites and facilitates a different organization of the poems and, hence, a different relationship between the poems. Because of the logic of the feed on Instagram, single poems without any coherence to other poems by the same poet, appear frequently. The network organization – the connectivity of Instagram – makes it just as easy and conventional to link one's poem to a poem by another Instagram poet. Further, a poet can mark a coherence between poems by using specific hashtags, by collecting several poems under one entry, so that readers have to scroll left or right in order to read them, or, as many Instagram poets do, by creating a narrative sequence between poems. Nevertheless, the poems do not necessarily appear in the readers' Instagram feed in the order in which the poet publishes the poems, which they (most often) do as print poems in a book.

Gebrauchslyrik and application technology

Because the platform is part of the poems' poetics, and because it offers functionality and infrastructure that make literature on social media designed to be shared, I will stress the practical dimension of Instagram poetry and the genre as a form of contemporary *Gebrauchslyrik*. The term *Gebrauchslyrik* was coined by Bertolt Brecht in 1927 and is a genre that according to Fabian Otto can relate both to choices of everyday subject matter and the poems' style of language. Elaborating on *Gebrauchslyrik*, Otto continues: "vorrangig die beim Lesen leicht zugängliche und vielfach in irgendeiner Weise (gesellschafts-)politisch ambitionierte Lyrik gemeint." (Otto 2003, 4)[21] In Scandinavia, the term has been associated in particular with the political poetry of the 1960s and 1970s.

The practical and everyday dimensions of Instagram poetry are reflected both in the platform and poems. The poems are written to be read on a platform where connectivity and popularity serve, among other things, as governing mechanisms; the poems are predisposed to use, response and popularity markers. Kirschenbaum too suggests that there is an obvious connection between social media as a platform used in everyday life and Instagram poems as utility poetry with everyday themes. He claims that literature in social media prioritizes "the ordinary, the everyday, and the plain as opposed to the exceptional or the surprising or the dense." (Kirschenbaum 2018, 34) As I described in the beginning of this chapter, Instagram poetry is often political. The poems use motifs from everyday life to describe, in an accessible language, identity and exclusion, to overcome the feeling of shame and to strengthen self-esteem. In fact, these topics are considered so important that many researchers include them in the definition of Instagram poetry. Kathi Berens claims that Instagram poems are sentimental and ordinary (Berens 2019), while Thomas suggests that social media such as Instagram offer the opportunity to observe other people's everyday lives, "getting closer to the dailiness of life." Thomas 2020, 19) She emphasizes with precision how poems dealing with the topic of self-care coincide with the poems' linguistic everyday language: "The tone and vocabulary of this poetry is distinctive, reminiscent of the language of self-help and self-improvement that provides such an important outlet for young people struggling with issues of identity and self-worth." (Thomas 2020, 91) Poems about identity, love and feelings of vulnerability are attractive to many readers. These topics engage readers; and readers express this sense of engagement through likes, comments and regramming. In this way, the emotional aspects of everyday life in Instagram poems reflect an orientation towards popularity. Moreover, van Dijck and Poell point out that social media algorithms are set up to detect and reinforce trends by distributing posts to many:

> [P]latforms claim they can track instantaneous movements of individual user behavior, aggregate these data, analyze them, and subsequently translate the results into valuable

---

[21] "primarily meant for poetry that is easily accessible and that often in some way has (societally) politically ambitious" (my translation).

information about individuals, groups, or society at large. Social media logic of detecting representative trends based on real-time analytics is increasingly mingling with polling strategies established by mass media logic. (van Dijck and Poell 2013, 10)

Instagram can collect information about how Instagram poetry is used as well as about popular trends and the topics that attract the most readers. Following van Dijck and Poell, moreover, we might claim that the platform's mechanisms not only "measure" expressions and opinions but actually help to shape them. In this way, the platform significantly contributes to the mediation of the poems and their meaning – despite the fact that the poems often give the impression that they are expressions of spontaneous feelings and opinions

The platform – including readerly feedback facilitated by the platform's social plugins – contains structures and information that helps form the poems. In this respect, Instagram poetry can be regarded as part of what Fredrik Tygstrup has called the "Culture Industry 2.0." Tygstrup describes how twenty-first-century digital media have changed the production of culture: "An insight into the users' concrete purchase and consumption behavior – what is emphasized, shared, skipped, returned to, etc. – opens up for a new microengineering of market-oriented works." (Tygstrup 2016, 24)[22] According to Tygstrup, this means that the experimentation that structures the experience of surprise and defamiliarization is replaced by products and works that are familiar and easily recognizable.

Tygstrup's analysis is useful for understanding the relationship between Instagram and its poetry. Moreover, Tygstrup helps us understand how the poems, whether intentional or unintentional, are written to meet expectations from readers and a market. The poems function within a sphere that no longer resembles the traditional literary industry. The popularity of the poems, whether they work or not, is measured in the number of likes. At the same time, algorithms affect how the poems are distributed, where and how they are read, as well as which poems are liked. Thus, the algorithms help to create and mediate feedback. Therefore, it is also reasonable to claim that, rather than advanced technological expertise, Instagram poets need to know how to build a network of "followers" through Instagram and other social media. To gain popularity, they must write poems that meet the expectations of old and new followers. They should not write poems that surprise their readers, because such poems do not fit the market economy and the media logic of Instagram. Rather, the poems must be adapted to the conditions set by the platform's interface, algoritms and the platform owners.

---

22 "Indsigt i brugernes konkrete konsumvaner – hvad der understreges, deles, springes over, vendes tilbage til osv. – åbner for en ny microengineering af markedsrættede værker" (my translation from Danish).

A short reading: Everyday life, sentimental formula poetry and familiarization

Topics explored in Instagram poetry are, as I have pointed out, taken from everyday life. The poems participate in the construction of the contemporary situation, in which classic themes in the lyric tradition are inscribed. In one of the examples mentioned above, Fallo refers to an American company that provides services for mobility and uses the situation as a motif in order to encourage readers to follow their desires and, in a clichéd register of "carpe diem", to risk something in order to experience romance and love. In the example from Store-Ashkari that I referred to at the beginning of this chapter, the poem stages a speaker who frees herself from feelings of guilt and shame. This poem too includes an encouragement meant to inspire others to do the same, that is, to no longer be controlled and oppressed by expectations from others. Likewise, in the poems by the most prominent Instagram poet in Norway, Trygve Skaug, these topics and strategies are easily recognizable.

Many of Skaug's poems can be described as formula poetry. He makes a claim, followed by a twist where the claim is anchored to a speaker's or addressee's concrete quotidian situation. This might come in the form of a couplet, such as "Grip dagen / (og hold den nede til jeg kommer)" ("Seize the day / (and hold it down until I arrive))",[23] or in the form of a standard poem about the relationship between an "I" and a "you":

> Du vet
> hvor du har meg
> for det var du
> som satte meg
> her
>
> You know
> where you got me
> because it was you
> who put me
> here[24]

This poem was published on 26 February 2019. It is organized into short lines.[25] The line breaks in the poem are, as in the other poems I have referred to, frequent but

---

[23] 20 May 2020. Here: https://www.instagram.com/p/CHNvYPTlT6j/c/18071067946245105/ (5 December 2022).
[24] My translation.
[25] https://www.instagram.com/p/BR_2OIpAW9w/ (5 December 2022).

do not provide the poem with extra meaning. They function only insofar as they adapt the poem to the interface of the platform and medium on which it most likely is to be read – a mobile phone. The line breaks do create short pauses, i.e. perceptual breaks that make the reader turn her gaze from one line to the next. However, such strategies of postponement do not establish tension or ambiguity in the poems. Polemically, we might say that the line breaks make the texts look like poems even though they could just as well be prose or aphorisms.

The responses to the poems quoted above are, as is typically the case with the responses to Skaug's poetry on Instagram, positive. The latter poem, "Du vet" ("You know"), has received 3693 likes, while the two-line poem has received 2191.[26] It is easy to see why Skaug's poems reach so many readers. The poems are affirmative: they include topics that affirm and confirm a sense of a community.

Skaug's poems are often interpersonal, and they are, with very few exceptions, sentimental. They are sensitive and convey the thoughts and feelings associated with love, the loss of love and the sense of falling in love.

> Når du oppdager
> at du er så slepphendt
> at du klarer
> å miste
> noe du aldri
> har hatt
>
> When you discover
> that you are so sloppy
> that you manage
> to lose
> the thing you never
> had[27]

This poem, published on 6 July 2018, has received 4179 likes.[28] It consists of a single adverbial clause and pretends to work as a slightly long hashtag à la "#thatfeeling". Skaug himself has put "#densiste" ("#thefinalone") as a hashtag on the poem, a hashtag that could serve as a title for the poem and that potentially gives an indication as to how the poem should be interpreted.

Poems with temporal clause-linking constructions are well known in the history of poetry. In this sense, Skaug places himself in a long tradition of poetry that uses this technique. The temporal adverbial clause functions by modifying

---

26 1 June 2021.
27 My translation.
28 https://www.instagram.com/p/Bk5TO1ZlKYF/?hl=nb (1 June 2021).

something or by expressing a relation to something or someone. The temporal adverbial clause in Skaug's poem cannot reach its semantic meaning as a grammatical whole unless the meaning is fulfilled by a subsequent verb and sentence. The "when" correlates with a "then", but this "then" is absent. The feeling that the temporal adverbial clause hints at is made present through this absence.

The poem is syntactically incomplete. Likewise, as a correlation, it reflects the sense of being incomplete when one is lacking or missing something or someone. Yet the lines "å miste / noe du aldri / har hatt" ("to lose / the thing you never / had") become nothing more than a seemingly paradoxical comment on being sloppy. The poem is affirmative. As an aphorism, it contains words to which everyone can relate. The paradox does not invite a more in-depth interpretation. The insight is immediate, thus it adapts to the reading on a mobile phone in situations that do not invite wonder or lingering.

Like other Instagram poets, Skaug too engages with specific political issues. In the context of the Black Lives Matter movement in 2020, he published several activist poems that reflect the power of love and community:[29]

> Ingen flodbølge
> er bare
> de få dråpene i front alene
> derfor er det akkurat vi
> som ikke kjenner ham personlig
> som ikke bor i det landet
> som ikke føler det kneet rett på kroppen
> som skal være alle de dråpene bak
> vi er milliarder av liter
> med kraft og kjærlighet
> som skyller inn
> og knuser rasismen til pinneved
> hvis vi en og en og en dytter sammen
>
> No tidal wave
> is just
> the few drops alone in front
> therefore it is us
> who do not know him personally
> who do not live in that country
> who do not feel that knee on the body
> who shall be all those drops behind
> we are billions of liters
> with power and love

---

29 https://www.instagram.com/p/CBEITHgFkNB/ (5 December 2022).

> that washes over
> and smashes racism to pieces
> if we one and one and one push together[30]

The poem appears as an inscription on a photograph that shows turbulent seas and waves crashing against land, not unlike the photograph used by Nikita Gill for one of her activist poems.[31] The photograph in Skaug's poem has a redundant effect and serves a purely illustrative function. Compared to the other poems by Skaug that I have commented on here, this is a somewhat longer poem, a poem where superfluous words and lines are not eradicated in the editing process. One could argue that the poem should have stopped with the line "which should be all the drops behind" and that the pronoun "de" ("they") in this line could have been omitted. This would have made the address to a "we" even more open, and the drops would have gained a non-specific reference. The poem is an encouragement based on causality. The subjunctive "derfor" ("therefore") acts as an initiator for this encouragement, but the temporal form of the verb in line eight, "som skal være" ("which shall be"), does not follow in a logical way. Rather, the line should follow up on the verb "er" ("is") in the second line, so that "we", as consequence, are the drops behind. This temporal coincidence would have created a double activist performance: the poem as an event creates an event.

Skaug has tagged the poem with the hashtags "equality", "justiceforgeorgefloyd," "blacklivesmatter" and "antirasisme" ("anti-racism"). Thus, he connects the poem to a network of poems with the same theme and engagement, an interconnection that increases the number of potential readers. It has received 5056 likes and 113 comments, all positive responses with emojis and thanks, expressed in verbal text such as "FLOTT!" ("GREAT!") and "Du setter så fint ord på det de fleste av oss ikke klarer og [sic] uttrykke" ("You put it so nicely what most of us can't express").[32] Some tag the response by others or comment on comments, and several of the comments have received likes. The readers' actions express a sense of community; their comments represent a consensus regarding both the importance of the poem's theme and the poem's quality as *Gebrauchslyrik*. The number of likes and the many comments tell us that this, in terms of the logic of what Tygstrup calls the Culture Industry 2.0, is a good poem. It works for the readers, in the readers' situation and in the political context in which it is published.[33]

---

30 My translation.
31 https://www.instagram.com/p/CXJTQPho6O4/ (5 December 2022).
32 1 June 2021.
33 The poem is also published on Facebook, where it has received 1300 likes and 24 comments and where it has been shared 372 times (21 September 2021).

The poems are how they are due to the way Skaug wanted them to be and to his assessments and poetic abilities. However, the poems also are a product, as I have argued, of the logic of Instagram. It is obvious that the media platform, the technical medium on which the poem is typically read and the reading situation do not facilitate poems that require a greater degree of cognitive work to be "decoded" or enjoyed. The simple message of the poems indicates that as many readers as possible should immediately understand them and equally immediately like and share them. In addition, perhaps the poems are meant to create good feelings and therefore invite forms of communication that serve a phatic function and reflect a sense of community rather than critical reflection. Here, Skaug's poems differ from, for example, Yrsa Daley-Ward, who also publishes anti-racist poems in connection to Black Lives Matter. One of her poems is short and is written over a photograph of a branch: "I do not see a problem // wait am I the problem?"[34] The poem was published on 5 June 2020, the same day that Skaug published his poem. Where Skaug's poem somewhat naively is oriented towards a "we", Daley-Ward draws attention to the speaker, and she questions the position of this speaker and herself. In contrast to this self-reflective poem, the collective "we" that Skaug tries to establish, appears without critical self-reflection.

The differences between the two poems are many and reflect both strategic choices and dissimilarities in the two poets' individual styles. Also, it is fair to say that Instagram poems that are self-reflective appear less frequently. Therefore, it is relevant to ask why and how Instagram's logic and the reading situation of Instagram poems invite or are adapted to such a poetic orientation. It might be more uncomfortable to read a line where readers are forced to look at and think of themselves and their position and where they are forced to ask themselves if they are part of the problem. Van Dijck and Poell argue that social media algorithms provide the users with more of what they have already enjoyed. Skaug does the same. He writes poems in which the quality is measured in terms of recognition and through which the readers can feel a sense of unity. In this respect, Skaug's collective "we" fails to take notice of the individual, religious, cultural or socio-economic differences. Still, Skaug's poems express something readers can relate to. This is the poem in the Culture Industry 2.0, where Instagram establishes the conditions for the poems, including how they are written, what they are about, how they are distributed and how they are received.

---

34 https://www.instagram.com/p/CBDyzf1nSGm (5 December 2022).

The poems, the situation and the media logic

Instagram is not a neutral medium: there is nothing to suggest that Instagram poetry is not touched by the logic of Instagram. Instagram poems, like all other poems, can in principle be about anything, and they can take a variety of forms. Nevertheless, both the previous reception of Instagram poetry and the analyses in this chapter show that Instagram poems largely deal with only a few topics, that they are oriented towards everyday life, that they are made to be used or immediately useful and that the most popular Instagram poets in Norway refrain from experimenting with poetic forms. One reason for this is that the poems work within the framework of media conditions that are set among others by Instagram.[35]

That the poems are written to be read on an application on a mobile phone is part of the understanding of Instagram poems as platform-specific. In this chapter, the ways in which Instagram poems are media-specific has been discussed through a conceptual framework developed by van Dijck and Poell. This framework contributes in substantiating how Instagram affects the poems form, content and function, the distribution of the poems and the interaction between the poems and the readers, including activities such as likes and regramming. Furthermore, the research shows that some topics are prioritized by algorithms while other topics are less visible and less distributed, and that activities on social media are part of a media culture partly controlled by popularity and "like-economy".

The dimension of everyday life in Instagram poems fits well with Instagram, a platform that long since and independent of its content, according to van Dijck and Poell, has "penetrated deeply into the mechanics of everyday life." (van Dijck and Poell 2013, 3) Among others, van Dijck and Poell aim at how the media platform is used in a number of quotidian situations and that this use have an impact on the contents that are produced, contents that in various ways are adapted to the situations where the platform is often used. Instagram poetry is one example of this adaptation of a genre. The poems refer to a recognizable everyday life situation, in which familiarity is confirmed by comments such as "Så sant," "Amen" and "Tror det blir slik etter hvert som livet leves" ("So true," "Amen" and "Think

---

[35] Here, it is important to remember that Instagram is a network medium connected to other platforms in a network. This implies that the platform is continually under pressure from other social media platforms and, consequently, that it follows trends and gains new technological features through such platforms as Snapchat and TikTok. In this way, it can offer many of the same possibilities as other platforms. In other words, it is not only Instagram that dictates its own terms.

it will be so as life goes on").³⁶ Furthermore, the everyday motifs emphasize the nature of the use of Instagram poems, i.e. the poems are written to be used on certain occasions, whether it is for a political cause, for comfort or to create a sense of community – or all at once. The everyday dimension represents some of the qualities of the poems in a more conventional sense. That is, the poems, despite their poetic limitations, have an aesthetic and efferent value for the readers. This value has to do with recognition and repetition: the poems give more of what the readers have already read. Still, the usefulness of the poems goes beyond this. The poems are not necessarily singular, beautiful and original, but they have an effect on a specific media platform in specific situations.

As a form of *Gebrauchslyrik*, Instagram poems are most often without ambiguity; they do not offer interpretative resistance but are, nevertheless, or perhaps precisely because of this reason, poems that reach many people. In addition, with connectivity and popularity, including the like-economy, as some of the driving forces, Instagram poetry is to be regarded as a kind of market-oriented, media-specific poetry. In this respect, it is tempting to recall the distinction established by Roland Barthes between "readable texts" (*texte lisible*) and "writable texts" (*texte scriptible*) (Barthes 1974). Readable texts are easily accessible and do not require a particular effort or interpretation to be understood. Contrary to writable texts, readable texts lack ambiguous meaning, and they do not engage readers as cocreators (Barthes 1974, 5). According to Barthes, readable texts evade joy, diversity of opinion, delay and uncertainty that lie in interpretations and in re-readings. The texts are closed and do not open up for other performances and moments through new readings. Therefore, according to Barthes, readers become consumers and, more than that, they are products not producers of texts.

It might be the case that ambiguous or less accessible texts counteract interconnection and popularity and intimidate rather than attract new readers. If so, Instagram is barely made for "writable texts", that is, complex and ambiguous poems. Rather, Instagram's feed, hashtags, algorithms, networks, the reading situation and the implied mode of reading fast all require poems that one does not have to dwell on, which do not have to be read several times to be understood and enjoyed. Moreover, Instagram poems are not the kind of texts where one discovers new meaning through the process of rereading. In short, the poems are not made for rereading. Many of the poems are characterized by empty phrases, and they try to evoke certain emotions in the reader, emotions that seem to optimize interconnection, whether the

---

36 These three examples are found in comment fields related to Trygve Skaug's calendar poems in 2021. See https://www.instagram.com/p/CW7oUm2sYsj/?utm_medium=copy_link and https://www.instagram.com/p/CW97H0vqIFE/?utm_medium=copy_link (5 December 2022).

interconnection occurs because readers express opinions about the poem or because they ritually push the like icon in order to create a sense of contact with the poet and a community.

Still, even though readers are made for consumers, they also partly fill the function as producers. To like a poem and to regram it increases the value of the poem. Van Dijck and Poell point out that many users of social media have an interest in maintaining a large number of followers for the sake of market value and, we might add, to increase the possibility of publishing the poems in print at a publishing house (van Dijck and Poell 2013). Likewise, both Berens and Thomas highlight Instagram as a commercialized system where literature is included. Thomas states that this type of literature is "already always implicated in commercial systems," (Thomas 2020, 2) while Berens writes that "[r]eposts, likes and comments are the currency of social media." (Berens 2019) The like-economy is part of a larger ecology and economy. For example, Skaug, on his Instagram account, promotes his own shop and sells tickets to his own concerts. This is, of course, not surprising, but it is one of many examples of how Instagram poets are engaged in different activities, where poems are mixed with the seemingly private and the commercial, a mixture that implies that different networks and environments on social media are intertwined.

With its orientation towards interconnection and popularity, Instagram facilitates a type of commercial consumer culture reminiscent of what Barthes once described as a culture "which would have us 'throw away' the story once it has been consumed ('devoured'), so that we can move on to another story, buy another book." (Barthes 1974, 16) Barthes developed his concepts in relation to print literature. Still, in the contemporary literary environment that I have called the computational network environment, Instagram and print books cannot be kept separate. The logic of Instagram also affects print literature. Instagram can have a direct impact, for instance by the fact that an Instagram poem is published in a print collection of poems, or the impact can be indirectly, as in how the Instagram style of writing affects the writing of print poetry. All the Instagram poets that I have referred to in this chapter have published print poems after they became popular as Instagram poets. In this way, the logic of Instagram directly affects literary institutions and the book market, as well as the understanding of what poetry can be. In this literary media environment, literary institutions cannot ignore the way social media work and what social media represent. Literary institutions are already involved in the literary media culture in which Instagram plays a part. It is a culture in which the distinctions between analogue and digital are becoming more and more blurred and where books of poetry, publishers and readers are infiltrated by a media logic that is still relatively new and that we must assume is still evolving.

Chapter 6
Unfinished Poetry: Nils-Øivind Haagensen from Facebook to Book

Fig. 12: Screenshot from the Norwegian poet Nils-Øivind Haagensen's Facebook profil with the poem "Detnorskearbeiderpartiet." "Photo by Nils-Øivind Haagensen."

On 11 February 2019 at 9:46 p.m., the Norwegian poet Nils-Øivind Haagensen published the poem "Detnorskearbeiderpartidiktet" ("The Poem for the Norwegian Labour Party") on his private Facebook profile (see Fig. 12).[1] In a short message following the post, he writes that he has just performed the poem from a stage at The House of Literature in the Norwegian city Fredrikstad. The poem was later printed in Haagensen's collection *Det uregjerlige* (*The Unruly*, 2020), a collection of poems on political and social issues.

This is not an unusual situation for the birth of a poem in the media-ecological situation of poetry: a poem might be written on a piece of paper, in a notebook or on a mobile phone, perhaps for a particular occasion or because something has happened in the world that has caught the poet's attention, prompting her to write a

---

[1] https://www.facebook.com/people/Nils-%C3%98ivind-Haagensen/624120737 (5 December 2022).

Open Access. © 2023 the author(s), published by De Gruyter. This work is licensed under the Creative Commons Attribution-NonCommercial-NoDerivatives 4.0 International License.
https://doi.org/10.1515/9783111004075-006

poem about it. Just think of many of Dmitij Strotsev's recent collection of poems, *Беларусь опрокинута* (2021; *Belarus Overturned*) that are written in a style he calls "poetic reportage" as a response to the political events that took place in Belarus in 2020, in the wake of the presidential election on 9 august 2020. Strotsev published his activist poems on social media and later in the book *Belarus Overturned*. These too are examples of poems in progress; they are performed or published online, then further changed and improved before being published in print, digitally, or in both formats. For the last decade, social media has become another situation and place for performing unfinished poems. Indeed, contemporary poems are distributed through different networks and exist in many situations and on multiple media platforms. They are written for and presented in different situations, situations in which the respective media involved set some of the premises for the performance, publication and/or distribution of poetry, including how the poet thinks and writes.

The poem "Detnorskearbeiderpartidiktet" involves at least three situations and medializations: the poem read on a stage, the poem published on Facebook and the poem published in a print collection. In this chapter, I examine closely two poems by Haagensen, both of which were published on his Facebook profile and in his collection *Det uregjerlige*. In particular, I pay attention both to how travelling between these two situations and media and the role of the two platforms impact the poems respectively. The purpose is to explore how the media in question and the journey of the poems through media environments have an impact on form, content and function. By closely reading Haagensen's "Detnorskearbeiderpartidiktet", I will show how the situation for poetry on Facebook is different from the situation of Instagram poetry, complicating the various claims and conclusions made in Chapter 5 concerning Instagram poetry and Instagram as a platform and culture for writing[2] and reading. Haagensen's poem is interesting not only because it represents a poetic practice in which the poet uses Facebook as a platform for testing the poem as a work in process, as unfinished but also because it explores a national trauma, namely the terrorist attack on the Government's building in Oslo and the Labor Party's youth camp on the small island of Utøya on 22 July 2011.

Unfinished poetry

Nils-Øivind Haagensen is a well-known poet, author and publisher in Norway, who, since his debut in 1995, has published 11 books of poetry, 4 novels and 2 collections of essays. Moreover, he has edited several anthologies and has translated

---

[2] In total, 77 people were killed during the attack.

10 books of poetry. For his work, he has received significant literary prices and, in 2013, he was nominated to the Nordic Council Literature Prize, generally regarded as the highest award for literature written by a Nordic author. Haagensen frequently publishes his poems on his Facebook profile. Many of these poems are likely to find their way into print. In this regard, Haagensen is one of several established "print poets" who uses Facebook as a test platform for poems in progress – for unfinished poems.

To view poetry through the lens of the "unfinished" can be engaged on at least three levels. First, the potential to be different is embedded in poetry as an art form; second, the unfinished can be viewed as a cultural, political and/or aesthetic strategy; and third, the unfinished can be considered a media-determined phenomenon. I call these different levels of the unfinished. This term implies the fact that all three may be applied to the same poem, even though the driving force for the unfinished-ness is dissimilar. For instance, a poem always has the potential to be revised from one print edition to another, or a poem performed during a reading will not necessarily be identical to the print poem, which the poem read is based on.[3] Further, because poetry (as well as other art forms) perhaps more than ever, travels across cultural, geographical and language borders, unfinished-ness is a cultural and aesthetic aspect of contemporary poetry and art. Nicolas Bourriaud argues that with globalization, artworks not only travel more, but the very idea of artworks as less site-specific and more "globetrotting" is embedded in the concept of contemporary art. Therefore, he conceptualizes contemporary artwork through metaphors like "radicant" and "wanderer", and he claims that once artworks are set in motion, they take a "journey-form" and are staged in "heterogeneous contexts and formats": these works subvert the notion of a defined identity, translate ideas and have a "transplanetary" behavior (Bourriaud 2009, 22).

The two levels mentioned above are both included in the environment of programmable and network media and can be applied to how poetry works and behaves in the computational network environment. In his study of digital media aesthetics, Peter Lunenfeld identifies what he calls "unfinished business" and claims that "unfinished" is what defines the aesthetic of digital media (Lunenfeld 1999, 7). Lunenfeld argues that texts in digital media continually change, claiming that this reflects that they are never finished. His study includes, inter alia, how websites and stories change in our time but can even be applied to the relationship of software. "Software is never finished", Lunenfeld claims (Lunenfeld 1999, 11), because there are always new difficulties that arise. Updates appear; "old"

---

[3] Here, I follow the argument of Peter Middleton who claims that a poem performed on a stage can be regarded as another materialization of the poem, equalized with the same poem in print.

software becomes defunct. Likewise, a text or website may look different from one day to the next. Still, it is perceived as the same text or website. Similarly, in my reading of Heldén's *Evolution* (see Chapter 3), I regard the text as one poem, even though, or exactly because, the poem continually changes.

Lunenfeld relates the idea of an unfinished aesthetic to the ontology of digital media. Due to the programmability of digital media, there is never a fixed or finished digital object but only electronic events on the screen. This is what Hayles call "flickering signifiers" which turn digital texts into events (Hayles 2005, 39; 167).[4] Lunenfeld's point is that digital media technologies simplify and encourage the violation of linear processes of production and distribution (Lunenfeld 1999, 20). He therefore calls for "an open-ended aesthetic for digital media, an aesthetic that accepts the limitations, and perhaps naïveté, of inherited concepts of 'finishing' a work." (Lunenfeld 1999, 3) Therefore, unfinished aesthetics can be regarded as a media-specific phenomenon, as Lunenfeld does. Still, the idea that we only see and read partial poems in the network of medializations of the same poem is, as I have argued above, also a cultural and aesthetic phenomenon.

In some cases, it might be appropriate to regard the travel of poetry across media as a media-specific unfinished poetics. Indeed, I will consider digital media's programmability and network orientation as an invitation to and reflection on the possibility of considering poetry in digital culture as a process that not only concerns a particular materialization of a poem but also concerns the migration of a poem across media.[5] In *Evolution*, Johannes Heldén and Håkan Jonson explore the idea of how the unfinished is embedded in a work and in poetry as such (see Chapter 3). Further, we might also argue that network media, the connectivity of different media platforms, also inspires a poet to follow an aesthetic where texts can and will often be transformed. Again, Heldén's *Astroecology* would serve as an example of this. It is a media-ecological work in which new medializations of the project have appeared and will most likely appear in the future (see Chapter 4). Due to programmable media, a poem can be easily modularized and changed because of its underlying codes, and network media have demonstrated the ability to connect texts and people in new ways. Therefore, rather than developing in a predictable and linear journey, digital poetry moves and changes in a network of processes and media. Poems can be adaptations of previous poems, move from multimedia to monomedial poetry, contain intermedial references to other materializations or be

---

4 I also present the concept flickering signifiers in Chapter 2.
5 It should be mentioned that digital media technology is not a prerequisite for regarding poetry as unfinished. Numerous of poets across time have altered their poems between publications and republications.

part of a multiple poetic artwork, one in which poetic and medial components contribute to a multi-aesthetic effect.

As I will argue in this chapter, Facebook is one site where poetry can be published in an unfinished state. While the number of scholarly works produced on Instagram poetry over the last few years is impressive (see Chapter 5), research on poetry on Facebook is still modest. There are many reasons for this. One is that Instagram poetry has shown itself to be a powerful genre, a genre that is impossible to overlook and, for that reason, has received much attention and enthusiasm. Further, regardless of the many variances, Instagram poetry seems to work well as a genre, which is not the case with poetry on Facebook. Indeed, to grasp poetry on Facebook as a genre, as "Facebook poems", as for instance Fuad Azzam attempts to do (Azzam 2019), is problematic, if not impossible. I will here refrain from trying to define poetry on Facebook, beyond stating the obvious fact that Facebook poem appear inside the framework of the interface of the platform, that they utilize some of the affordances of the platform and that the media environment of Facebook has some impact on the poems.

Even though Facebook is a social media platform and therefore shares many of the same features with other platforms, such as "content sharing, public communication, and interpersonal connection," (Burgess, Marwick and Poell 2018, 1) it seems to fit better for some purposes than others. José van Dijck and Thomas Poell (2013), for instance, suggest that Facebook is more of a social networking site than Youtube, which, according to van Dijck and Poell is more of a user-generated content site (van Dijck and Poell 2013, 5). For this reason, Facebook might work well as a platform for distributing poetry through social networks, including testing unfinished poems for an audience of "friends" and "followers," either as an alternative to poetry reading or as a supplement to it.

A poem and a national trauma

Haagensen's poem "Detnorskearbeiderpartidiktet" is a poem about a national trauma, the terrorist attack on 22 July 2011. By drawing on memories from the past, the poem is an attempt to restore or establish an order for the speaker and society. It is a fairly long poem with short lines and consists of four parts numbered from 1 to 4. It is structured upon sequences of memories, and the speaker's memory is given a chronological order. Part 1 starts with "det første jeg husker" ("the first thing I remember"); the second part includes both a sequence that starts with "det neste / jeg husker" ("the next thing / I remember") and one that is introduced with the line "men jeg husker" ("but I remember"); finally, part 4, the shortest of the sections, includes memories that are closest in time ("last summer"). The poem does not end in a new order or sense of the world but rather by questioning whether the poem and the arts in general are capable of holding the world together: "og jeg tenkte: ble jeg hel igjen nå?" ("and I thought: now, did I become whole again?")

The poem has an additive structure that gives form to the chronology in the poem and fills the temporal sections with memories. The additive style is reflected in the use of lists and in the frequent use of the conjunction "and," suggesting how memories both create a chronology and are juxtaposed. A long list of names of famous politicians in the Labor Party is followed by and juxtaposed with names of victims from the terrorist attack at the Labor Party's youth camp on Utøya. This list of names is again followed by and juxtaposed with the speaker's memories of a telephone conversation he had with his mother the day after the attack.

The first two parts of the poem create an affective space of nostalgia and despair. The poem directs its attention to the past, blending the history of the Labor party with individual memories from the speaker's childhood: "det første jeg husker / fra da jeg var liten av det norske arbeiderpartiet" ("the first thing I remember / from the Norwegian Labor Party when I was little") and "det neste / jeg husker / av det norske arbeiderpartiet" ("the next / I remember / of the Norwegian Labor Party").[6] These memories are represented in fragments rather than as a coherent story. This progressive layering of memories represents an attempt to create a coherent whole, to patch together the identity of the speaker and the world.

These first two parts are organized through parallelisms, where lists of names are arranged in order to balance one another. Here, Haagensen combines names of famous politicians from the Norwegian Labor Party with the names of the lesser-known, politically engaged young people who were killed during the attack on Utøya. In the first part, Haagensen lists the names of Labor Party leaders. This list ends in an ironic, potentially pathos-filled voice: "Thorbjørn Berntsen / herregud, Thorbjørn Berntsen / og så Thorvald / Thorvald Stoltenberg // som navn på norske elever" (Thorbjørn Berntsen / Oh my God, Thorbjørn Berntsen / and then Thorvald / Thorvald Stoltenberg // as if names of Norwegian students").[7] In the second part, the names of the politicians have been replaced by the names of some of the victims of the attack. The list contains ten names before it suddenly ends in a burst of the speaker's voice:

---

6 My translation.
7 My translation.

[. . .]
barn

som
Tore Eikeland
og Håvard Vederhus
og Lene Maria Bergum
og Guro Vartdal Håvoll
og Thomas Margido Antonsen
og Victoria Stenberg
og Ronja Søttar Johansen
og Margrethe Bøyum Kløven
og Sharidyn Svebakk-Bøhn på bare fjorten
og –
nei –
jeg orker ikke mer

[. . .]
children

as
Tore Eikeland
and Håvard Vederhus
and Lene Maria Bergum
and Guro Vartdal Håvoll
and Thomas Margido Antonsen
and Victoria Stenberg
and Ronja Søttar Johansen
and Margrethe Bøyum Kløven
and Sharidyn Svebakk-Bøhn only fourteen
and –
and –
I cannot stand it[8]

The lists are chronotopes. Sequence of names makes a particular time and space present, helps to constitute the speaker's identity and the identity of the Labor Party, two identities that are constantly negotiated throughout the poem. The famous names from the history of the Labor Party are listed to evoke the past, to create a nostalgic feeling, so that they will be remembered as national heroes and for their achievements for Norway. The names of the young victims of the attack at Utøya are listed so that these too will be remembered. They are heroes too, even though they were deprived of the chance to make a change in society. In the poem, they still matter and still make a difference.

---

[8] My translation.

The collapse of the voice in the middle of the list of names of the victims is an inscription of an embodied experience. It is an experience that makes the speaker visible or, rather, hearable. The response is the outcome of the attempt to say the unsayable, to say the names that must be mentioned in an attempt to make them present. Because it is impossible and because the list of names of innocent victims is unbearable and too long, the speaker breaks the chain of names and bursts out in affection. The response represents a turn from the objectivity of reading a list of names to a subjective voice, an affective move revealing an emotional reaction.

Furthermore, the turn is also temporal: it moves from the past towards what could have been a future, from one generation to another, that is, from the old politicians to the young people who could have but will now never become a new generation of politicians. It is noteworthy that the poem, by reciting the names, attempts to create a continuum between the old men and the young men and women. However, just as the potential historical continuum was broken on 22 July 2011, the continuum in the chain of names in the poem is broken too. With the rupture at the end of the quote above, the speaker draws attention to himself and his physical and mental reaction and to what he finds intolerable. The poem does not say that the people who the speaker names are dead. However, the fact that the speaker cannot continue and that most of the names of the victims will not be present in the poem, turn the attention towards the absence, those who are not here anymore. Finally, this affective break turns absence to presence, the past to the present; the moment of speech, or writing, that is, the speaker who recollects the break, the wound, and who tries to create meaning by patching together an epideictic speech and poem.

The poem constitutes an emotional space in which the ironic and the sincere, as well as the public and the private are blended, and within these, there are various private voices and memories. In the lines that follow, the speaker recalls a conversation he had with his mother the day after 22 July: "men jeg husker / moren min har bursdag 23 juli / og jeg husker jeg ringte henne på dagen / dagen etter / for å gratulere / og hun sa å, nei / nei, nei, nei / nå er alt ødelagt / for alltid" ("but I remember / my mother's birthday is 23 July / and I remember I called her that day / the day after / to congratulate / and she said oh, no / no, no, no / now everything is ruined / forever").[9] Here, the speaker's mother erupts in affection. In the speaker's recollection, there is a sequence of three events: a memory of his mother's birthday on 23 July, a memory of the speaker calling his mother and a memory of his mother's reaction to the terrorist attack the day after it happened. The first two memories are bound together by a partial repetition of "jeg husker"

---

9 My translation.

("I remember"), with the important change in the conjunctions from "men" ("but"), which is a grammatical response to the line above, "jeg orker ikke mer "("I cannot stand it") to "og" ("and"). The frequent use of conjunctions structures the poem as an additive poem, a poem that is characterized by the continual addition of information, memories, names and events. "Men" ("but") marks a turn from the list of victims of terror to the mother's birthday but also an emotional and cognitive turn from something the speaker cannot complete to an attempt to re-establish self-control, and by that, to save the poem. Still, the memory of the distant, mediated conversation, the phone call, cannot make the attack absent because his mother's emotional response makes it present.

Here, the repetition of "dagen" ("day") in the utterance "på dagen / dagen etter / for" ("that day / the day after / to") and the position of the enjambment after "etter" ("after") strengthen the presence of the terrorist attack. His mother's birthday is on 23 July but is referred to as "the day after." In other words, 23 July will never be the same, that is, it will never merely be the 23 July or only his mother's birthday. Therefore, the poem makes clear that the act of terror is an act from which the speaker (and we) cannot escape, neither emotionally nor cognitively, as time and memories will forever be present. Further, it shows that neither private life nor something as trivial as a phone call to his mother is a space free from contemporary disasters. Moreover, not even the voice of the mother, the *voix elle-même*, as Marcel Proust writes in *À la recherché du temps perdu* (Proust 1919, 164), would ever be the same in the speaker's memory.

From the individual to the collective

The statement made by the mother as well as the speaker's memory of her voice both testify to the fact that no one can escape the events of 22 July. The changes that have occurred as a result of the attack are not reversible; a prior order cannot be restored. These changes persist throughout the poem, simultaneously haunting the speaker and the Norwegian society as a whole. The speaker appears in the poem as an individual Norwegian citizen born in the early 1970s, a period of social-democratic decade in Norway, which was followed by the liberal 1980s. The speaker, though, is also a collective, social-democratic voice, representative of Norway in the late-modern and contemporary period.

Memories of the terrorist attack evoke feelings of fear and persecution. In the first part of the poem, a subject-object relationship is established between the speaker and the Labor Party. As a child, the speaker's image of Labor Party members was of "voksne menn / så mange voksne menn / i dress og slips / i tv-ruta / så mange navn / på så mange men" ("grown up men / so many grown up men / in suits and with ties / on the TV screen / so many names / of so many men").[10] He remembers these men, twelve in total, with honor and pride. As previously mentioned, this list of names ends with "Thorbjørn Bentsen / herregud, Thorbjørn Berntsen / også Thorvald / Thorvald Stoltenberg" ("Thorbjørn Berntsen / Oh my God, Torbjørn Berntsen / and then Thorvald / Thorvald Stoltenberg").[11] These and other politicians of the Labor Party are well known and represent the social situation in Norway in the 1970s, 1980s and 1990s. Therefore, these men have formed the social-democratic society of Norway, as the speaker once knew it.

The expression "herregud" ("Oh my God") connotes the greatness of these people; it confirms the important role they played *in the media* for the construction of an image and feeling of Norway's social-democratic society. Further, the expression "herregud" can also represent a sudden realization of the time that has passed or an articulation of a shock, yet another affective response to the difference between the situation in the past, when the world appeared safe and predicable, and the situation in the present in which one is forced to recognize the fact that nothing can ever be the same.

Within this affective space, Haagensen also makes use of humor. The politicians that are named are, or were, his heroes, as if they were football heroes that he would name his children after, if he, according to him, had had a son. With a list of names that is hilarious in its length and that seems subversive (as another form of turn or revolt in the poem), it reads:

> Hadde jeg
> fått en sønn
> på sytti og åttitallet
> skulle han hett
> Gunnar Trygve Bjartmar Guttorm Ronald Reiulf Torbjørn Thorvald Odvar (med en d)
> Nakken
>
> Haagensen[12]

> If I
> had had a son
> in the 1970s or 1980s
> he should have been named

---

10 My translation.
11 My translation.
12 The names mentioned in the fourth line are the first names of various famous Labor Party politicians from the 1970s, 1980s and, in some cases, 1990s. The single names mentioned in line six and seven are the birth names of the poet Nils-Øivind Nakken Haagensen.

> Gunnar Trygve Bjartmar Guttorm Ronald Reiulf Torbjørn Thorvald Odvar (with one d) Nakken
>
> Haagensen[13]

While other lists of names in the poem are organized in a vertical order, the names here appear in a horizontal sequence. They have changed from appearing as memories of past politicians to now function as an imagined possible past and present. While the other lists represent what has been, this list represents what could have been. Further, while the list of names given in vertical structure appears objective and contains names of politicians and young adults that the speaker only knew through various media ("on the TV screen"), the imagined scenario of naming a child after all of them becomes an attempt to imbue the names with a personal dimension. The people named have made an impression on the speaker: they have all, in different ways, done something to him, shaping him as a subject. Therefore, to imagine naming his son after so many different people is a symbolic act, though still humoristic. It is a way of saying that he and his imagined son, just like the victims of the attack on Utøya, are children of these men, the incarnations of a social-democratic Norway.

Of course, when the names are listed in a horizontal structure, it is because this is how we write our first names, whether there are one or two or, as in the poem, nine of them. They are all the first names of his imagined son, but the structure and change from memories of the past to an imagined and fictive past, both reflect the additive style as an attempt to constitute a new whole. The paradigmatic releationship has been dissolved as none of the names can replace each other. The speaker imagines a way of patching together a broken contemporary reality, a reality that neither he nor his mother seems to understand. To name something or someone is to confirm a subject-object relationship between the speaker and those who are named. To name a child after someone is to connect past and present. In the poem, the suggestion of naming the speaker's imagined son after these great men is a way to present a past that never was and a future that never will be. Just as the poem, the imagined son becomes a container where these names are provided with new contexts. Because "[e]verything is ruined", as his mother says, the speaker (and the society) must find a new way to give meaning to the world, to the way in which we imagine the past and present as well as the public and private. This is precisely what the poem and the speaker attempt to do.

In the third and fourth parts of the poem, a new and re-constituted speaker appears. The third part begins as follows:

---

[13] My translation.

en gang
var de kjedelige og uforståelige
arbeiderpartiet
nå er de dødelige
og engstelige
som deg
og meg
hver gang

once
they were boring and beyond comprehensible
the labor party
now they are mortal
and anxious
like you
and me
every time

Part three includes a temporal change from "once" to "now" and "every time". The change concerns the impact of the terrorist attack on how people perceive the Labor Party. While they were once tedious and incomprehensible, as if they were out of reach, perhaps even too dull for a poem, they are now like you and me, and, therefore, worth poetic attention. The temporal and cognitive distance reflected in the first three lines above have changed into an engagement and a relation in which the speaker invests time, private memories, events, anticipation and imaginations.

Indeed, part three is focused on the present, a temporality that is both thickened and extended because of "hver gang" ("every time"). "Hver gang" is important here because it refers to repetitions of feelings, reflecting a claim of identity and representation: "er jeg arbeiderpartiet" ("I am the labor party"). Moreover, it also refers to itself as a repetition or a non-progressive present. Here, the poem takes on a quality that we tend to associate with the lyric poem and its simple present. Jonathan Culler writes about the simple present in lyric poem: "lyrics use a special non-progressive present with verbs of action to incorporate events [. . .] and increasing their ritualistic feel." (Culler 2017, 128) "Hver gang" appears as an anaphoric repetition three times in this third section. In addition, the repetition of "og" ("and") and "og jeg" ("and I") are repeated nine times, and "er jeg arbeiderpartiet" ("I am the labor party") appears three times in this section.

The "once" has ended up in a "now," though not the "now" of a split second but "now" as expanding and non-progressive, a duration of time that does not stop but continues. In this extended now, the speaker claims to identify himself with the Labor Party. The many names of politicians from the Labor Party have been replaced by a slogan: "I am the labor party". This claim resonates with the sentiment expressed by so many Norwegians after the terrorist attack: "I dag er vi alle AUF-ere" ("Today, we are all the AUFs"),[14] a version of the now famous response heard in the wake of the attack on *Charlie Hebdo* on 7 January 2015: "Je suis Charlie."

The repeated claim or slogan, "I am the labor party", is a rhetorical move that makes the poem reminiscent of an epideictic speech. This is by no means a random association. Several scholars, including Culler (2015, 130), make this connection between the lyric poem and the epideictic speech. Also, since the poem is written in memory of great men, women, boys and girls, the connection to the epideictic speech and its rhetorical features is to be expected. "I am the labor party" is an attempt, through speech, to reconstruct what has been destroyed. It gives hope and, consequently, can be read as a response to the mother's statement of despair. The poem is an attempt. It can do nothing but try to make a difference. Therefore, the poem ends with a question about whether the speaker – and by speaker we must also read "the Labor Party" – and the society as a whole have been restored:

> sist sommer
> i Stratford-upon-Avon
> William Shakespeares fødeby
> så jeg en svane i kveldsmørket
>
> det så ut som et halvt hjerte
> et halvt lysende, skimrende
> hjerte
>
> og jeg kjente mitt eget begynne å slå
> og jeg tenke: ble jeg hel igjen nå?
>
> last summer
> in Stratford-upon-Avon
> the birthplace of William Shakespeare
> at nightfall, I saw a swan
>
> it looked like half a heart
> half a shining, shimmering
> heart
>
> and I felt my own start beating
> and I thought: now, did I become whole again?[15]

---

14 AUF is the youth organization of the Labor Party, the member of which were the direct victims of the terrorist attack on Utøya.
15 My translation.

The reference to Shakespeare and the intertextual relation to Ben Jonson's poem at the end are perhaps attempts to emphasize and unite the beauty and political function of poetry. The speaker may have seen something similar to what Ben Jonson saw when he wrote a poem to Shakespeare after his death, a poem in which Jonson turns Shakespeare into a swan on the river of Avon: "Sweet Swan of Avon! What a sight it were / to see thee in our water yet appear" (Jonson 1618). Shakespeare himself uses the swan as a motif in some of his plays. In *Othello*, for example, Emilia says: "I will play the swan / and die in music." (Shakespeare 1979, 1011) Besides the fact that Haagensen's swan is exactly what it is, a swan that this poet and other poets have seen before, it is also a symbol, as in the two literary examples, of beauty, loyalty and strength. "And die in music", as Emilia puts it, is a manifestation of how art can unite beauty and death, either, like in *Othello*, as an expression of the desire to aestheticize death or, like in Haagensen's poem, as an attempt to re-establish the beautiful after an act of terror.

The occasional and instant-ness of Facebook

Haagensen's poem demonstrates that, in contrast to poetry on Instagram, longer poems (perhaps even long poems) can work well on Facebook. Further, the network environment of Facebook seems to welcome complex poems, poems that require a different way of reading than Instagram poetry. As my analysis of the poem so far demonstrates, the poem is complex, and even though it is an affective poem, which invites a post-critical reading, it takes time and requires a close reading to reveal the fuller meaning potential of the poem.

The form and style of Haagensen's poem is not unique to Facebook. Rather, we find this form and style in many of his poems, such as "(hva gjør du med dagen, / hva gjør du med natta)" ("(what do you do with the day, / what do you do with the night)") from the collection *God morgen og god natt* (2012; *Good morning and good night*). Still, differences and similarities between the poem on Facebook and the print poem can be identified on a number of levels. Some differences are simply the result of material confinements. For instance, the fact that a long list of forenames in the poem on Facebook is split into two lines in the print poem is because the space is dictated by the page's margins. Other differences are related to the platform's interface. Moreover, we also must take into account the editorial or poetic choices made by the poet and his editor. When published on Facebook, the poem appears in the context of the standardized interface of the platform. The visual context for the poem is in part provided by Facebook's standards and in part by the information that is specific to Haagensen's profile, such as profile photos, the presentation of biographical facts, recent posts, photos that have been uploaded, his network of friends, etc. Most of this information is not directly related to the poem but can still have an impact on how the poem is read. In addition, the connectability that is offered by the social media platform is of importance and is also most likely a significant source of motivation for publishing the poem on Facebook. By now, the poem has been read more than 200,000 times, it has received 183 likes and 18 comments and been shared 18 times.[16] The comments are positive and confirm that the poem is appreciated and that the readers recognize some of the functions of the poem: it prompts reflection and emotion.

"Detnorskearbeiderpartidiktet" is occasional poetry, that is, poetry that is written for a particular event and that describes or comments upon this event. Occasional poetry is often meant to be read as part of the same event for which it was composed. This is the case for "Detnorskearbeiderpartidiktet". Haagensen's comment on his Facebook profile confirms the poem as an occasional poem: "Just performed at Litteraturhuset i Fredrikstad's first event, The Great Conversation. About the Labor Party."[17] As part of the standard information in each post on Facebook, the post and the poem is dated, "11.02.2019". This date also appears on the print poem, though with no further contextual information.

On Facebook, the poem appears alongside a photograph taken immediately after the event where Haagensen read the poem. It is an instant photograph. It is not stylized, and it shows a few known politicians. Shabana Rehman Gaarder, a Norwegian stand-up comedian and public debater, stands casually on the stage, looking at the audience. The editor and politician from the Red Party, Mimir Kristjánsson stands next to Gaarder and checks his mobile phone; in the back, Hadia Tajik from the Labor Party talks to someone. In other words, the photograph leaves us with information about the situation in which the poem was performed, including about which people also participated in the event.

The photograph documents the event, strengthening the poem as an occasional poem. It situates the poet, who is now also the photographer, in the present, thereby becoming – in contrast to the print poem – part of the visual expression of the poem on Facebook. It is an indexical sign, a photographic deixis, pointing towards a time and place that have been and therefore are absent, only present as a photograph as Roland Barthes may have put it. As a deixis, the photograph makes this time and place of the occasional poem present for the reader and viewer on Facebook. Still, it needs to be contextualized. In fact, on Facebook, both the photograph and the poem need contextualization.

---

16 As of 7 April 2022.
17 "Nettopp framført på Litteraturhuset i Fredrikstads første Den store samtalen-arrangement. Om Arbeiderpartiet." (My translation from Norwegian to English.)

The comment that contextualized the poem and photograph is rather typical for Facebook and connects the poem both to the photography and the situation it represents. Further, the two words "just" and "performed" are of relevance for the poem. The word "performed" tells us that the poem is not only a poem written and published on Facebook but that it also exists in another materiality and situation. It reminds us of the fact that the poem exists in the here and now, as one reads it on Facebook, as well as in the there and then, on the stage in Fredrikstad. This is how the ecological situation of poetry can be. The word "just" connects the two situations together. It gives the impression that Haagensen has barely received the applause and left the stage before he posts the poem on Facebook. The word "just" contributes to the instantness of the situation, not that of the poem but of the situation of the distribution of the poem.

In terms of the form of the poem, there is little that separates the Facebook poem from the print poem. The changes that have been made are mostly the result of the editorial process. Still, these changes and the word "just" in Haagensen's comment confirm that social media involve instantness, even for poets: one writes something and publishes it without paying too much attention to misspellings or following grammatical rules. Haagensen has, of course, written the poem in advance, but the situation where he, there and then, in the moment, a few minutes after he has read it, at 9:46 p.m., chooses to publish the poem underlines the differences in publishing it in print form and on Facebook, in the instant and oral culture of social media. The oral nature of communication on social media is referred to as "digital orality," that is, "the osmosis between the textual and oral spheres in chats or texting (Soffer 2016, 1).[18] Although Haagensen obviously is a more language-conscious and language-sensitive writer than the average Facebook user, he too writes in an environment where the present situation, the software and the communication culture of Facebook have an impact on the writing.

Although the poem in print largely has retained the same form and structure as the poem on Facebook, some changes do appear. Considered as text editing work, these are minor. Still, as poetic editing work these minor changes are significant. One change is the structure of the stanzas. For instance, the poem on Facebook includes an extra line break between the list of names of major politicians of the Labor Party and the following analogy to Norwegian nature.

---

18 In her article "The Oral Environment of Snapchat", Oren Soffer is primarily concerned with Snapchat as a dominant platform of digital orality. Still, Soffer's arguments regarding the technological impact of changes in communication are of relevance to all social media platforms.

og så Thorvald
Thorvald Stoltenberg

som navn på norske elver
norske fjorder
og norske
fjell

and then Thorvald
Thorvald Stoltenberg

as names on Norwegian rivers
Norwegian fjords
and Norwegian
mountains[19]

In the print poem, this extra space between "Stoltenberg" and "as names on" is not included. It may be that in the poem on Facebook, the extra line break is a note of instruction to the poet himself on how he should perform the poem, that when read aloud, Haagensen should put in an extra pause before "as names". It is possible that Haagensen has considered the fact that the extra line break would not be necessary in the print poem. If the purpose of the line break is, in fact, to highlight the name "Thorvald Stoltenberg", then it would be redundant since his name is repeated and therefore underlined anyway. Another possible explanation is that Haagensen, in editing the print poem, found the extra line break to be too much. Because the poem contains short lines and many line breaks, the poem is already filled with several potential small pauses, pauses that occur when we move our gaze from the end of one line to the beginning of the next.

Obviously, a single rather than a double line break will minimize the space between the two lines, bringing them closer visually and in sound pattern and, consequently, strengthening the connections that constitute the analogy. However, the analogy works inside a section of the poem, rather than across two sections. In other words, the list does not end with "Thorvald Stoltenberg" but continues with romantic national images of Norway. The word "mountains" ends the section, which implies that it is more vigorous than "rivers" and "fjords". The three topoi, "rivers", "fjords" and "mountains," contribute to the image of Norwegian nature, while it is only "mountains" that makes the analogy really work. It would not make sense to compare a politician to a Norwegian river alone, at least it would hardly be a flattering comparison. The politicians mentioned are often portrayed as solid in the development of the social democracy in Norway after World War II.

---

19 My translation.

Therefore, the analogy needs the mountain to fulfill the comparison of these great politicians with national-romantic motifs.

Another, perhaps merely technical but nonetheless significant change between the poem on Facebook and in the book is in the use of italics. Words that occur in the print poem in italic letters appear without italics on Facebook. A mechanical media-deterministic causality for the lack of italics in the poem on Facebook, is that if one copy-pastes from a word processing software on which one writes a poem, like in Word or Pages, to Facebook, then calligraphic qualities like italics will be left out. Another simple explanation is the situation of the poem as it has just been performed. When the poem is read, the audience will, of course, not hear whether a word is put in italics, but the poet can use other characteristics with his voice and body that approximate the function of italics to signify the value of words. Regardless of what the reasons might be, the difference occurs and is significant for the question of the role of media.

In one line of the print poem, "som Emil in *Emil*" ("like Emil in *Emil*") (Haagensen 2019, 17), the personal name "Emil" is printed in italics in order to denote that the speaker is not referring to any Emil but to a specific Emil. It could be to Emilia in Shakespeare's *Othello* or to the Swedish author Astrid Lindgren and her stories about Emil from Lönneberga. Or it could be both references. The former interpretation is strengthened by the Shakespeare reference at the end of the poem; the latter is supported by the fact that, later in the poem, the speaker says "du og jeg, Gro" ("you and I, Gro").[20] A famous catchphrase from the stories about Emil from Lönneberga is "du och jag, Alfred" ("you and I, Alfred"), uttered by the main character Emil to confirm the personal connection he feels with Alfred, a worker on his father's farm. In Haagensen's poem, the "you and I" refers to the speaker and another famous politician from the Labor Party, Gro Harlem Brundtland, as an attempt to establish a similar feeling of community, to bridge the gap between the speaker and Brundtland, who, because of her authority, is often spoken of as the mother of modern Norway.

One can imagine that the migration of a poem from Facebook to print, from a social media environment to a literary environment that includes other processes, actors and networks embedded in the book publishing system, potentially entails radical changes. This is not the case for "Detnorskearbeiderpartidiktet". It is striking that the two versions, the print and the Facebook poem, are so similar. No words or lines have been omitted. Nor has the poem undergone any major

---

20 Gro is the first name of Gro Harlem Brundtland, the first female prime minister of Norway, who served as prime minister in three periods in the 1980s and 1990s. For this reason, she is often called "landsmoder", the mother of modern Norway.

changes from the transition to the book, implying that the poem, with the exception of a few minor changes, was largely finished when it was read on the stage in Fredrikstad and published on Facebook. Therefore, the medium, in this case Facebook, appears more as a platform for distribution than as a medium and a creative agent for the poem through which the poet thinks and writes with and through.

Then again, other poems in *Det uregjerlige*, which have also been published on Haagensen's Facebook profile, have undergone major changes before they were published in print. One example of this trend is the poem "Poverty and inequality" (Haagensen 2020, 10–15), published on Facebook on 29 July 2019.

"Poverty and inequality"

The poem "Fattigdom og ulikhet" ("Poverty and Inequality") consists of four parts and explores, as the title implies, issues of poverty and inequality in contemporary Norwegian society. The form of the poem is mainly the same in the two media in question. A major difference, however, is that the poem on Facebook makes use of several double spaces, while the print poem includes none. Therefore, the print poem appears visually tighter, more cohesive and as an uninterrupted piece of rhetoric or train of thoughts within each of the four parts. Further, single words have been left out from or added to the print poem, while some of the verbs are used in a different tense. Changes in verb tenses seem mainly to be editorial. In addition, sentences and phrases in the poem on Facebook have been removed from the print poem. In the beginning of the poem, we read:[21]

> det er 30 pluss
> i Oslo, vinduene i leiligheta
> står åpne, vidt gap, verandadøra også[, nytt]
> [vidt gap,]ei stillegående vifte på nattbordet og jeg
> (p. 10)

> it is 30 plus
> in Oslo, the windows in the apartment
> are open, wide open, the porch door too[, new]
> [wide open,]a quiet fan on the bedside table and I

---

[21] Words and phrases that are included in the Facebook poem but left out in the print poem have been placed in brackets.

This is just one of several places in the poem where words have been erased before the poem was turned into print or, alternatively, where words have changed positions. The latter does not necessarily effect the meaning of the poem; nevertheless, in some cases, it changes the function of the line breaks and, hence, the structure of the sentences. In the example above, the erasure of "new / wide open" actually eliminates the enjambment, since the clause in line four is no longer a continuation of the clause in line three. This creates an interesting break because the first two lines end in enjambment. The cessation of the enjambment at the end of line three underlines the contrast between the first three lines and the last one, between the visible and the less visible and between the apartment, that is only described with the open window and porch door, and the bedroom, that is more described in detail with a fan, a bedside table, a bed (metonymically represented with the beside table) and the speaker. Because of the open windows, porch door and noise from the city, the apartment is not empty unlike the bedroom that, despite its furniture, appears empty. In other words, the lack of continuation between lines three and four in the quote correlates to the speaker's detachment from the world, the feeling of loneliness, which is nevertheless reflected in the silence and quiet fan in the bedroom.

In addition, the four lines are ekphrastic. They can be read as a verbal representation of a visual representation, whether this apartment exists visually or not.[22] With the phrase " new / wide open" intact, the ekphrastic description would have been broken, since this phrase is not a description of a window or door. Rather, the phrase appears as an interpretation of the fourth line, as it is obvious to the world, or "wide open" as the poem says, that the speaker is lonely. Hence, with the erasure of "new / wide open", the ekphrastic description remains intact.

In this poem, there are also changes other than those mentioned above between the two medializations of the poem. One significant difference concerns the print poem, which has gone through a rather significant and thorough editing process that again has led to a more concentrated poem, where less robust metaphors have been altered or removed. One example of this is in the beginning of the fourth part of the poem, which on Facebook looks like this:

vi var flyktninger, skrev
jeg, men
det er ikke sant, det
var ikke sant heller, vi

---

[22] James Heffernan famously defined ekphrases as verbal representations of visual representations (Heffernan 1993, 3). Claus Clüver argues that the verbal ekphrasis's other can be "a real or fictitious text" (Clüver 1997, 26).

> var fire små og to store ålesundere
> uten formell utdanning
>
> we were refugees, I
> wrote, but
> that is not true, that
> was not true either, we
> were four small and two big Aalesunders
> without formal education[23]

In the print poem, the first four lines in the quote above have been erased and replaced with one new sentence in one line. Moreover, the word "refugees", which might be meant to function as a metaphor or an analogy, has been replaced by an adjective:

> Vi var fattige mennesker
> vi var fire små og to store ålesundere
> uten formell utdanning
> (s. 14)
>
> We were poor people
> were four small and two big Aalesunders
> without formal education[24]

The poem in print is not necessarily finished, but it seems more finished than the poem on Facebook. Again, the poem on Facebook carries traces of spontaneity, as if Facebook is treated as a platform where the poet, safe and with less caution, can try out tropes and figures and other poetic techniques before he continues to work on the poems in the print medium as the final end of the process of making the unfinished finished.

A platform for unfinished poems

In my discussion of these two poems as unfinished poems on Facebook, I have demonstrated how Facebook might work as a platform for testing out poems in progress, where the poet reveals an unfinished strategy and aesthetic. Here, Facebook, in contrast to Instagram, proves itself to fit and nurture such poetic practices.

Some social platforms, such as Twitter, restrict the number of characters one can use for each message (or tweet). Such a restriction obviously constrains the

---

[23] My translation. The word "Aalesunders" refers to people from the city of Ålesund, Norway. In addition, Ålesund is Haagensen's place of birth.
[24] My translation.

length of a Twitter poem. As I explained in Chapter 5, Instagram poetry also involves many restrictions. The poems, or stanzas, need to be short in order to fit the screen on the mobile phone, the interface of Instagram and the most likely reading situation. However, Facebook does not operate with these kinds of regulations. Therefore, the platform seems to work somewhat better for longer poems than what is the case for both Twitter and Instagram. Facebook does not seem to determine the form and length of the poems, which opens it up for longer and more complex poems. In contrast to Instagram poetry, for example, there are few if any cultural conventions established for poetry on Facebook. Further, because the platform is used to publish poems in progress – again in contrast to Instagram poetry, where the platform is used for "finished" poems – the poet does not need, at least not to the same extent, to take into consideration the reading situation and the technical media for reading poems on Facebook.

Here, it is worth mentioning that Haagensen's poems in *Det uregjerlige* have received some critical reviews. The literary critic Bernhard Ellefsen reviewed *Det uregjerlige* in the weekend journal *Morgenbladet* on 28 February 2020, suggesting that Haagensen is "the original insta poet." With rather unflattering words, Ellefsen writes:

> Here, politics is a matter of voting (light red) in elections, dreaming of a time when social democracy had not lost its grip, making fun of the political opponents that his "friends" too dislike and whipping themselves like white men, all in a language that shows that Haagensen is the original insta poet. The epigone Trygve Skaug, for instance, has continued with the same, clammy form of "we" that Haagensen uses to flatter his readers.[25]

As my close reading above has shown, Haagensen's poems are more complex than what Ellefsen's review acknowledges. Perhaps Facebook, from which the poems are derived, determines Ellefsen's reading. He reads the poems superficially, too fast and not closely enough and with prejudice, perhaps because the poems have been published on Facebook (though not Instagram). He does not recognize the power that lies in the combination of irony and sincerity as well as the sense of public and private, which dissolves the potential nostalgia that lies on the surface of the poems. Thus, Ellefsen misses how the poems constitute a more complex "we". For instance, in the "detnorskearbeiderpartidiktet" this "we" is

---

25 My translation. In Norwegian, the quote reads: "Her er politikk et spørsmål om å stemme (lyserødt) ved valg, drømme om en tid da sosialdemokratiet ikke hadde mistet grepet, gjøre til latter akkurat de politiske meningsmotstanderne som 'vennene' også misliker, piske seg selv som hvit mann, og alt sammen i et språk som viser at Haagensen er den opprinnelige *instapoeten*. Epigonen Trygve Skaug har for eksempel overtatt den samme, klamme 'vi'-formen som Haagensen bruker på sitt mest innsmigrende." (Morgenbladet 28 February 2020).

dissolved and, rather than being re-established, is ultimately questioned. For this reason, it is not "clammy" and it does not "flatter readers." In this sense, the "we" is radically different from the "we" in many Instagram poems (see Chapter 5). Further, Haagensen's prosodic poetry differs from the everyday language of the Instagram poems that I analyzed in the previous chapter. His poems would never make it on Instagram: they are simply too long, too complex and too demanding. They are more immersive and, because of the line breaks, lists, additive style and temporality, they slow down the reading process and put the reader in a different reading mode than the one minute hyper-reading of Instagram poems, which one perhaps does inbetween e-mails checks and news updates on one's mobile phone.

With Instagram poetry, poets write in accordance with the logic of Instagram. In Haagensen's poems, there are only a few traces of the tentative distribution platform Facebook. Rather, Haagensen writes poems ment to be published in print, but publishes them on Facebook as one of several locations and situations for poetry, perhaps to test the poems or to get occasional poetry out there in its situation, in the political debate and, in doing so, to contribute to the exploration of a national trauma. This is, I will argue, the case with "detnorskearbeiderpartiet" that is distributed on several platforms.

My point in the analyses and argumentation above is that the computational network environment of poetry changes our notion of a work and when or, if at all, a work is finished. Obviously, a print poem can always be changed in new print or non-print publication and performance, but the culture of an unfinished aesthetic has been strengthened, based on conditions provided by the computational network environment. This environment intensifies a poetic practice in which, rather than writing poetry for a single and exclusive medium of publication, one uses different media platforms for testing poems or for contextualizing them in a certain situation and in a specific media environment.

Facebook is, as van Dijck and Poell argue, primarily a social networking site. It fits well in a digital media situation, as the one described by Lunenfeld, in which the linear processes of production and distribution is violated (Lunenfeld 1999, 20). The two poems by Haagensen that I have analyzed in this chapter partly represent this situation. Still, it is fair to say that they follow a linear process in their production. The media-ecological history of digital works like *Evolution* and *Astroecology*, described in Chapters 3 and 4, more fully shows the potential of the violation of the linear production line. Haagensen's poems, on the contrary, do follow a linear path of different situations and media. It is likely that "print poets" like Haagensen will regard the print poems as the finished poems, but poems on Facebook are published too, and they are part of the history of publishing and reception for the print poems. We might even argue that the Facebook poems are more read than the print poems. The question is, therefore, not only one of a multilinear or linear route of production and distribution but also one of how to treat the different publications and performances of the poems and what functions the various media platforms serve. The poems are transformational. They are edited, they appear in different materializations, some are monomodal, containing only the written text, and others are multimedia poems, containing both texts and photography.

Chapter 7
Digital Poetry Reading: Podpoesi.nu and @detlillarum's #digtfix

On YouTube there is a clip of John Ashbery from 2016.[1] He is reading his poems as part of an event at Pioneer Works in New York. Ashbery is old; he is sitting on a chair, his body is a little sunken, he is breathing heavily. He begins by telling a joke that makes the audience laugh. The mood is set. Ashbery has established a relationship with the audience: he has engaged the audience and diminished a potential feeling of distance between the poet and the audience, opening a space where one feels welcome and part of a community. Ashbery's joke concerns himself, which makes him even more a man of flesh and blood, rather than an "unreachable" poet distant from the world and the audience. He is not untouched by time: "Old people always told me: 'Don't get old.' Unfortunately I did not pay attention." The joke has nothing to do with the poems that he is about to read from the chair on the stage, but it explains why Ashbery is sitting in a chair while he is reading. It takes one minute and 23 seconds from the time he sits down and gives his greetings to the person who introduced him until he starts reading. Ashbery spends the first 28 seconds on the joke, then 32 seconds where he does not say anything, flipping back and forth to find the pages with the poems that he is going to read. "I am going to read from this book," he says, and connects the print poems in the book with the poems he is about to read. Then after another 23 seconds, during which he explains the content and context of the book, he finally starts reading the first poem.

Most poetry readings have a prologue, an introductory paratext that is not part of the poem that is performed but which is nevertheless part of the poetry reading as an event (see Novak 2012, 376–377; Mønster, Rustad and Schmith 2022, 58–62). This paratext can be verbal or non-verbal. The example from Ashbery's reading above is both verbal (he talks to the audience) and non-verbal (he refers to the situation that he is sitting and includes this in the introduction). This chapter is not specifically dealing with prologues in poetry readings online, but it is worth noticing that those who published this reading on YouTube chose to include Ashbery's prologue. In digital poetry reading the inclusion of a prologue, or the absence of one, reflects a certain view of what a poetry reading is or could be, whether it should be cleaned of discourses other than the poet's reading of poems or include a mixture of discourses that feed the experience of the poetry reading. Moreover, just like most poetry readings that are performed on a stage, digital poetry readings

---

[1] https://www.youtube.com/watch?v=FptzpDSV4Ow (5 December 2022).

Open Access. © 2023 the author(s), published by De Gruyter. This work is licensed under the Creative Commons Attribution-NonCommercial-NoDerivatives 4.0 International License.
https://doi.org/10.1515/9783111004075-007

also convey a desire to create an immediate contact between the events on the screen and those watching. The prologue might serve as part of a strategy of "immediacy," which creates a sense of authenticity. Here, immediacy is used in the tradition from Jay Bolter and Richard Grusin and denotes the strategy of remediation in which one tries to make the process of mediation invisible (or inaudible), as opposed to one of "hypermediacy" in which the processes of mediation are emphasized (Bolter and Grusin 1999). The latter also involves highlighting the (new) media's specific characteristics and, thus, defending both the newness of a medium and the remediation. Bolter and Grusin emphasize that the two logics are not counterparts and refer to what can be perceived as a paradox in Western (digital) culture: "Our culture wants both to multiply its media and to erase all traces of mediation: ideally, it wants to erase its media in the very act of multiplying them." (Bolter and Grusin 1999, 5)

Poetry reading is an aesthetic practice that has found its place in digital media, be it on separate websites, as podcasts or on social media such as YouTube and Instagram. It is an art form and a practice that has been remediated. Like other poetic practices, poetry reading travels in and between digital cultures where it exists in parallel with and in order to complement non-digital poetry readings, be it poetry read live from a stage or old recordings of poetry readings. It contributes in making poetry accessible in a different way than many other genres and practices that I have explored so far in this book. In addition, digital poetry reading is interesting because the digital situation changes how a poetry reading can look and sound. For instance, there is a difference between poetry readings on a publisher's website, poetry readings on podcasts and poetry readings on social media platforms, whether they are distributed as prerecorded readings or as live streams of an event. It goes without saying that both the number of poetry readings and the variety of such readings have increased dramatically during the COVID-19 pandemic (2019–). They are all digital poetry readings, but they are different due to the poets' choice of style, the media of distribution and the way media are used. As I will discuss in what follows, these differences help to identify the significance of poetry readings and the functions they might have in the computational network environment.

Digital poetry reading

Poetry reading is a performance where poetry is read aloud. It could be the poet reading her own poetry, or it could be someone reading another person's poems. Poetry reading involves the voice and body of the one who reads, as well as the place where the reading takes place (Serup 2017; Mønster, Rustad and Schmidt

2022). Just like many other poetic practices, poetry reading has evolved. During the twentieth century, several paths in the development of the modern form of poetry reading can be identified. One is avant-garde experimentation in Europe and Russia from the 1910s. Another is the poetic development within the Harlem Renaissance in the 1920s, with poets like Langston Hughes bringing poetry closer to other performative art forms and strengthening its commitment to political activism. A third is the Black Arts Movement of the 1960s, with Sonia Sanchez and Amiri Baraka as prominent poets. A fourth is marked by the changes to the poetic scene with the rise of the Beat Generation. Poets like Dylan Thomas, Gary Snyder, Allen Ginsberg and Lawrence Ferlinghetti were central figures in the development of modern poetry reading. These and other poets read more performatively, writing poems that came close to oral language and oral performance situations. We need only think of Lawrence Ferlinghetti's poem "Populist Manifesto" from 1975, in which Ferlinghetti juxtaposes a conservative and less performative kind of poetry reading with a modern, interactive and performative poetry reading: "We have seen the best minds of our generation / destroyed by boredom at poetry readings." (Ferlinghetti 2001, 17) With a recognizable reference to Allen Ginsberg's *Howl* (1956), the speaker appeals to fellow poets and asks them to perform. In the first stanza of the poem, it famously says: "Poets, come out of your closets." (Ferlinghetti 2001, 17)

Still, in the modern form of poetry reading we might distinguish between a more text-centered form of reading and a more performative form of reading (Mønster, Rustad and Schmidt 2022). The former is what Frederick C. Stern calls a formal poetry reading, which he explains as "poetry readings in which the emphasis by the poet is less on acting and displaying than it is on reading, that is, on the text as voiced, events to which the audience comes to see the poet and hear her/him read but at which it does not expect acting, spectacle, 'performance.'" (Stern 1991, 73) In a performative poetry reading, the poet includes her body to a greater extent, creating an event that is more than "just" a reading of poems. In this respect, the body is regarded as a significant conceptual dimension of the reading, reminiscent of how the body entered art and performances in the 1970s (Bernstein 1998, 168). The distinction between a text-centered and a performance-oriented reading is by no means definitive. Rather, the two should be positioned on either side of a continuum between which a poetry reading swings like a pendulum. For instance, even though it is fair to say that the Ashbery reading that I referred to in the introduction is primarily text-centered, Ashbery does engage his body by making a point that he will be reading in a sitting position. Further on, the fact that we can see Ashbery on the screen, strengthen the necessity of including his sitting position in the analysis of the performance. In a non-visual poetry reading online, other voice-related aspects, which I will return to later, must be engaged in order to define a reading as performative.

The literary and artistic movements mentioned above revolutionized the form of poetry readings, transforming it from a genre subordinate to print poems into a self-governing art form. In other words, poetry reading was liberated from print and made into an independent poetic-performative event. On the one hand, this liberation of the poetry reading from print occurs more or less simultaneously with a change in the history of poetry, during which it partly developed in a more performative, gregarious style. On the other hand, modern poetry reading was accompanied by the expansion of sites where poetry could be performed, such as the Six Gallery in San Francisco and the Poetry Center in New York. These places made it possible for poetry reading to unfold and evolve. In short, there is, historically, an interdependence and synergy between new places, new forms of poetry reading and new forms of poetry.

It should not come as a surprise that a similar reciprocal interaction takes place between the invention of new digital media platforms and developments in poetry readings. Digital media technology both facilitates and helps to shape online poetry readings. Reading of poetry online is determined both by media-specific characteristics and by aesthetic and functional choices made by the poet or web curator. In this respect, poetry reading might involve at least five aspects: the poet, the poem, the audience, web curators and the media involved. These aspects interact with eachother and will most often be of relevance in a poetry reading, regardless of which media – digital or analog – it is performed in. The term "poet" comprises the poet's voice and body. Both are vehicles for the poem and are of semantic and aesthetic significance. How the poet uses her voice, how she reads and how she moves, stands, uses her arms etc. all matter in the poetry reading. Even though a curator is not present in the poetry reading, she is an important agent in the selection of poets (and perhaps poems) for the reading and in considerations concerning the number of poems to be read, the length of each reading and how the reading are presented and distributed online.

By "Audience", I mean the extent to which the poetry reading, whether live-streamed or recorded in the form of videos or sound clips, includes an audience that is present. In the example from Ashbery's reading, the video focuses on the poet but includes responses from the audience. We can hear the audience laughing, confirming that Ashbery's joke was well received. Further, the sound of an audience underlines the interaction between Ashbery's reading of his poems and the reaction from the audience, which, in turn, fuels Ashbery's reading. Or to put it more simply, if an audience had not been present, then Ashbery would probably not have told the joke. Moreover, without the sound of the audience, it would have been hard to tell whether he made a connection with the audience. Additionally, the "audience" here includes how a media platform facilitates connections between readers and viewers through likes, comments and hashtags that customize, as José van Dijck and Thomas Poell write, "social networks and communities." (van Dijck and Poell 2013, 8)

Digital poetry reading as a poetic art form demonstrates the role of remediation for contemporary poetry in the computational network environment. In addition to refashioning and changing the art form, remediation of poetry readings proves that there is not a question of competition between old and new media or digital and non-digital poetry reading. Rather, the goal is to reach readers and viewers and to make poetry readings appear in different situations. Concerning remediation, Bolter and Grusin write:

> The goal is not to replace the earlier forms, to which the company may own the rights but rather to spread the content over as many markets as possible. Each of those forms takes part of its meaning from the other products in a process of honorific remediation and at the same time makes a tacit claim to offer an experience that the other forms cannot. Together these products constitute a hypermediated environment in which the repurposed content is available to all the senses at once, a kind of mock Gesamtkunstwerk. (Bolter and Grusin 1999, 68)

In this respect, remediation becomes a two-way movement, directed at once backward towards poetry reading in older media and forward towards poetry reading woven into the digital media environments. Rather than competition, it is a matter of availability, speadability and complementarity. A computational network environment might include a hypermediated environment. This is an environment in which digital poetry readings, in a substantial way, have increased in number, vary in forms and are more available – in terms of period, genre and language – than ever before.

In addition to describing poetry readings in terms of remediation and as an event of interaction between media through the two strategies of immediacy and hypermediacy, digital poetry reading can be grasped as a poetic and aesthetic practice that varies between imitating a physical poetry reading and intensifying the digital poetry reading as something different from non-digital poetry reading. N. Katherine Hayles introduces imitation and intensification as two complementary strategies involved in the transition of print literature into digital literature (Hayles 2008, 162). The two strategies can also be applied to literature in other genres that wander between media platforms. Imitation and intensification refer to how digital texts imitate media, material and literary conventions and simultaneously intensify media, material and literary properties that are specific to the texts in the digital environment in which they are included. Therefore, imitation and intensification refer to a play between continuation and deviation of conventions and affordances. Intensification of the affordances of certain media platforms for the production and distribution of poetry readings, turns digital poetry readings into a media-specific practice. Still, digital poetry readings do not only differ from analog poetry readings. Because of the role played by media platforms, poetry readings will vary from one digital media platform to another and, consequently, might represent different functions and forms of aesthetic expression. Digital poetry readings will vary in degrees of imitation and intensification: it is always a result of an interplay of choices made by the poet, and sometimes a curator, and the possibilities offered by media technologies and the poem in question.

Digital poetry readings might be born digitally or digitalized, as in the example of Ashbery's reading. The obvious difference between non-digital poetry readings and digital poetry readings is that the latter is based on binary codes. As discussed in Chapter 2, Adalaide Morris highlights this crucial difference between poetry in digital and analog media: "What makes digital poetry different from poetry that takes place in the air or on the page is the coding used by the poet and / or her collaborator to prepare information for display on networked and programmable machines." (Morris 2006, 8) The digital or digitalization process inscribes poetry reading in the environment of programmable and network media. Accordingly, it becomes part of a different logic of distribution and a subject for algorithms. Mark B. Hansen recalls the role of algorithms when he points out the novelties of twenty-first-century media: "The principle governing the images' selection is not the aesthetics of the human audiovisual flux (as is the case with cinema and all previous audiovisual media) but rather the capacities embedded in the computational algorithms themselves." (Hansen 2010, 182) The selection process is partly transferred from human to machine. This means that for some of the social platforms for which poetry readings are produced to be distributed, the poetry readings are selected, organized and recommended for users by preprogrammed or self-learning algorithms. Thus, users can become acquainted with readings and types of readings that they would not otherwise see and hear. Furthermore, Hansen writes: "What does become interesting, however, is the way in which the work mediates for the human perceivers the technical logic of computational networks." (Hansen 2010, 183) Digital poetry readings are part of a network of electronically interconnected media such as computers, tablets and mobile phones. Moreover, poetry readings are not isolated online events but included in an ecology of other poetry readings as well as other types of aesthetic and non-aesthetic practices and texts. Therefore, the media ecology of poetry reading involves all the processes and actors involved in production, distribution and reception. These aspects of digital poetry reading come into play whether or not one consciously chooses to watch and listen to poetry reading online or one happens to come across a poetry reading recommended in a feed. I will not include the many contextual factors for digital poetry readings here; instead, I will leave these factors in the background until I look at a small selection of poetry readings in Scandinavia later in this chapter. As we will see, the choice of media platform is significant for the type of digital poetry reading offered to viewers.

Close and hyper listening

In the computational network environment, videos and live streamed poetry readings flourish. Nevertheless, there are many monomodal poetry readings: they seem to represent an alternative to multimedia performances that are live streamed or recorded as videos. One example of such a poetry reading that only includes the poet's voice are podcast readings, a form of digital poetry reading reminiscent of readings played on the radio. These readings appear "purified". The only basic medium that is distributed and stored is sound. With the poet's voice as the only medium for the reading, the attention is amplified towards the voice, which alone is significant for the reading. In this respect, it is fair to call poetry readings on podcasts text-centered. They are stripped-down forms of poetry reading and connote a return to poetry reading precisely as poetry *reading*.

Podcast readings and other forms of poetry readings comprised solely by the sound of the poet's voice comes close to what Charles Bernstein calls "audio text". Audio texts contribute with "sound to meaning" and, according to Bernstein, make the audience aware of themselves as listeners (Bernstein 1998, 5). The fact that, in the age of digital media, there has been a turn towards intensifying and giving presence to the sound of the poem and the poet's voice can be read as a reaction to hypermedia and the dominance and possibilities of digital multimedia. It is a turn that is both liberal and conservative. On the one hand, digital media technology enables and simplifies the archiving and distribution of monomodal poetry readings. On the other hand, the prominent visual media culture finds its counterpart in the emphasis on poetry reading as a phonetic practice that facilitates contemplative close listening in an environment that cultivates a hyper-attention. Still, rather than "close reading" and "hyper reading," both developed by Hayles, it would be more accurate to approach the situation of podcast readings and the role of audio texts in the computational network environment from the standpoint of "close listening" and "hyper listening." "Close listening" is a concept developed by Bernstein. He writes that it is a method developed for the reading situation, where one deeply concentrates on listening to the audio text. Thus, Bernstein establishes an approach to poetry reading that embraces the entirety of the audible event, that is, the reading as a meaningful oral and audio performance: "Close listening may contradict 'reading' of poems that are based exclusively on the printed text and that ignore the poet's own performances, the 'total' sound of the work, and the relation of sound to semantics." (Bernstein 1998, 4) The "total sound of the work" implies that the reading exceeds the written poem and its semantic meaning and sensory qualities and involves how the poet uses her voice, including the speed of her reading (Bernstein 1998, 6). With the attention solely on the poet's voice and the conceptualization of poetry reading as an oral and audio performance, the concept of close listening stands in opposition to the situation of a multi-sensory poetry reading in which the reading includes both visual and aural qualities and in which the audience is both listening and viewing. Hence, it is a situation for poetry reading which is closer to but not identical with reading poetry live from a stage, one in which the attention of the audience is flexible and alternates between different information streams.

Of course, this does not mean that pure audio poetry readings are new. Gramophone recordings of recitations of poems have a long history. The online magazine PennSound and its archive, facilitated by Charles Bernstein among others, is only one out of many examples of websites that offer a huge collection of voice recordings from poetry readings in public or semi-public spaces. We need only think of BBC radio's "Poems for Thought," The Poetry Programme on the Irish radio station RTÉ Radio 1, which also includes Twitter,[2] "Tämän runon haluaisin kuulla" ("This is the poem I would like to hear"), a program that has been running on the Finnish national broadcaster YLE's Radio 1 since 1967, or in Norway, "Dagens dikt" ("Poem of today") on NRK radio. Podcast readings can be regarded as the remediation of this form of poetry reading on radio. As I will show in what follows, podcast readings are closer to an imitation of a poetry reading on radio than they are to an intensification of the poetry reading as a digital poetry reading. Using the Swedish website and online archive Podpoesi as an example, I will emphasize close listening. Here, it is the poet's voice that alone comprises the poetry reading and not her body performance (the way she moves, what she is wearing, etc.), the place where she reads or the audience and community.

Pod*reading* on Podpoesi

The Swedish website and archive Podpoesi is one example of how podcasts function as a digital platform for poetry reading.[3] The Swedish publisher Podpoesi Press, a small publishing house that mainly publishes new Swedish poetry in chapbook format, established Podpoesi in 2010. The website has a collection of

---

[2] https://twitter.com/PoetryProgRTE (5 December 2022).
[3] www.podpoesi.nu.

poetry readings by more than 100 poets, mostly Swedish but also poets who have been translated into Swedish. Among those who are represented, we find such well-known and celebrated poets as Tua Forsström and Johan Jönson and Roman classics like Horace, as well as newer poetic voices like David Zimmerman and Iman Mohammed. In addition, there is a section with a collection of readings by Swedish newcomers. With the exception of the newcomers, the poets are represented on the website with a photograph and a link to their respective readings. The photographs are organized into four columns. However, the organization of the poetry reading does not seem to be of significance other than that the latest published readings are at the top of the page. In other words, the order of the photographs with links is not related to theme, style, genre, generation or other parameters. The length of the reading ranges from a few minutes to 10 minutes. They readings can also differ in style.

The Fenno-Swedish poet Tua Forsström is included with two poems. Forsström is a much-celebrated poet, the recipient of the Nordic Council Literature Prize in 1998 and the author of 12 collections of poems, of which *Anteckningar* (*Notes*) from 2018 is the latest. The poems that Forsström reads are titled with the Roman numerals "I" and "IV", are both are from *Anteckningar*. The two readings are fairly long at 8:53 and 4:44 minutes, respectively, and are suited to being heard on a digital device. The duration of the readings corresponds to what is common at live poetry readings at poetry festivals, usually lasting between 8 to 20 minutes.

Forsström reads slowly and thoughtfully, with a calm voice. Her pronunciation is clear, and she uses pauses to highlight certain words and phrases. In print, the poem "I" starts like this:

> Minns du ännu när du var ett barn
> och gick med oss samma väg dag efter dag?
> Det var en liten fors som brusade så
> starkt, och berget stupade i vattnet
> (Forsström 2018, 9)

Translated into English, this stanza reads:

> Do you still remember when you were a child
> and you walked with us, day by day, the same road?
> It was a little waterfall that roared
> so strong, and the crag dived into the water[4]

---

4 My translation from Swedish to English.

In her reading, Forsström uses pauses in a way that differs from the enjambments in the print poem:

> Minns du | ännu när du var | ett barn | och gick med oss | samma väg | dag efter dag? || Det var | en liten fors som brusade så starkt | och berget stupade i vattnet[5]

This is how Forsström typically reads her poem. It is a way of reading that fits well with the text- and voice-centered poetry reading that calls for a mode of close listening. Forsström's voice carries the poem and offers to the listeners a contemplative connection between them and the poet. She reads in a way that makes all other semiotic and aesthetic resources, including the body and place, superfluous. We are left with the sound of her voice and the images that her words evoke. Her reading is introverted, wherein her voice alone leads us into the words, sounds and rhythms of the poems and their meditative world(s). Forsström's way of reading correlates to her poems that are contemplative and apostrophic, calling upon a "you" that is absent. In the poem that I quoted above, the image of the crag, that plunges into the abyss, interrupts the innocence and harmonic event of the everyday activity of walking together along a road. This sequence demands a gentle and careful reading. A rough reading would be redundant and theatrical, and it would most likely have deafened the silence that occurs in the present, in the nowness of the poem, and that is strengthen by the awareness in the speaker's imagination of the crag that dived into water.

The silence from the absent you is further reinforced by the shift from present tense in the first line to the past tense in the rest of the poem, a shift that not only underscores that the speaker is looking back in time at something that has been and no longer is, but that a devastating change has occurred and left the speaker with this silence. The images evoked by the poem are dramatic, but the speaker's mourning is silent and, because of the absent you, meditative. In Forsström's reading, the words do not need to be further reinforced. The memory of the little child, who roared like a little waterfall before it was interrupted, destroyed by the mountain that fell, is self-sufficient.

The tenderness in Forsström's reading underlines the meditative aspect and silent mourning embedded in the poem. As such, and somewhat boldly, we might say that Forsström's reading is appropriate for the podcast medium, which cultivates sound and voice and offers a pure and single modality for listeners to experience the physical properties of language.

---

5 In accordance with quotation techniques for oral poetry, pauses between words or phrases are marked with the sign "|", not "/" as when quoting from print poems.

Other readings on Podpoesi differ from Forsström's way of reading. Anna Arvidsson, who is one of the poets who is presented as newcomer, reads the poem "Ikväll kramade jag min förövare" ("Tonight I hugged my perpetrator"). The reading is in style close to spoken word performances. She alternates in tempo and rhythm, between a soft, insecure voice and a more confident, performance-oriented voice, which, along with variations in tempo, intonation and voice inflections, presents the embodied experiences of the speaker.

The poem begins with the lines "Ikväll | kramade jag min förövare. | Vi skulle på konsert | och jag var der med en vänn som hadde en vänn som hadde en vänn och han skrek 'hej, fan, hvad lenge sen' och dom kramade honom och gjorde ryggdunkningen" ("Tonight | I hugged my perpetrator. | We were going to a concert | and I was there with a friend who had a friend who had a friend and he shouted 'hello, hell, how long ago' and they hugged him and did the back banging.")[6] Arvidsson starts by reading calmly and hesitates when she says the word "konsert" ("concert"), extending the sound "n." Meanwhile, in the more explicitly performative reading, in a spoken word style, there is the potential for the repetition and rhythm of the sequence of friends, "en vänn som hadde en vänn som hadde en vänn." This alternation in style and tempo structures the poem and Arvidsson's reading. Moreover, it underlines the paradox in the combination of "hugged" and "my perpetrator" and the relational structure in the poem between the speaker and her friend's friends. The speaker is not immediately part of this chain of connections, and, in the sequence of hugs, she becomes more and more marginalized.

Arvidsson's way of reading is reminiscent of slam poetry, a form of poetry reading that is close to the spoken word tradition and one in which the performance of the body is crucial for the experience of the reading. What is special about sound recordings, such as the poetry readings on Podpoesi, is that the body is not visually present but only present through the voice of the poet. Still, in some readings we can imagine the poet's body, whether we have seen it or not. This is due to the style of the poetry reading and the way the poet uses her voice. In fact, some parts of Arvidsson's reading evoke an intermedial dimension and the presence of a body. Through her voice, she makes a body present. Moreover, she even manages to give the body, which of course is not visually present, a function. It is as if we can perceive the poet's performative body, even though it is not part of the visual expression of the reading. The body works through the voice in a reciprocal interaction. The voice originates (obviously) from her body, but just as much as the body sets the voice in motion, the voice sets the body in

---

6 My translation from Swedish to English.

motion to the extent that we can imagine the poet's body moving to the rhythm of the words.

Thus, Podpoesi is an example of a media platform that provides access to an archive. Further, it is a distribution channel and a platform for experiencing "pure" poetry readings, where this purity provides access to synesthetic experiences. Still, as the examples from Forsström and Arvidsson demonstrate, the poetry readings on Podpoesi are not uniform but include a number of different voices, forms, genres and traditions. Nevertheless, Podpoesi mainly contains poetry readings that are less dependent on the use of video, photography, dance or other forms of visual expressions.

Podcasts as a platform for distributing and experiencing poetry readings thus operate with aspects that imitate rather than intensify reading events in other media. Still, because the media platform is part of a network of other platforms, the readings are given a framework that also makes the experience different from the poetry reading that they imitate. In the written introduction to Arvidsson, for example, one can follow the link to her Facebook profile. Additionally, the reader can easily share a reading on other social media platforms through links such as "Share the poem on Facebook" and "Share the poem on Twitter." This implies that Podpoesi is part of a larger media-ecological collaboration with other media platforms for the distribution and experience of poetry readings. In other words, poetry reading on another website or on a different social media platform is just a keystroke, an electronic link, a hashtag or an algorithmic calculation away.

Poetry readings born on social media

While all the poetry readings on Podpoesi appear as formal and edited and with high quality sound, poetry readings on Instagram, for instance, often appear as if they are recorded spontaneously; indeed, many of the poetry readings are recorded without professional equipment. Again, we are dealing with a great variety of poetry readings on social media, which include both video recordings and live streams. Still, what interests me here is how some of the poetry readings on Instagram, both with regard to technical standards and aesthetic strategies, adapt to a social media culture. Social media culture constitutes notion of "liveness", adding immediacy and intensity to the rhetorical power of words (van Dijck and Poell 2013, 4) and giving an impression of immediate communication (Leaver et al. 2020, 9). Rather than trying to imitate a poetry reading on a stage, which would often be the case for poetry readings that are live streamed, many recorded poetry readings on platforms such as Instagram intensify the immediacy and the quotidian quality of the platform.

Many of the poetry readings that are published and distributed on Instagram were born on social media, that is, they are performed and recorded in order to be published on a social media platform. This does not imply that the video recordings would lose semiotic and aesthetic features if they were removed from their social media platform. Rather, to be born on social media implies that the aesthetic expressions of the video recordings are adapted to the culture of social media, that is, social media has put its mark on the recorded poetry readings.

One example of Scandinavian poetry readings on Instagram is to be found on the Danish Instagram profile Det lilla rum (The pink room). Det lilla rum, the name of which can be read as a comment on Virgina Woolf's novel *A Room of One's Own* (1929), is both a bookstore and a café in Copenhagen. In addition, it serves as an arena for publishing and distributing poetry readings on Facebook, Instagram and YouTube. In their presentation on Facebook, they stress their feminist profile:

> DET LILLA RUM is a sustainable feminist book café, primarily run by volunteers and the love for literature. DET LILLA RUM was founded in the hope creating a free space, a liminal space, between many other busy spaces and everyday life, where you can enter and enjoy one of the many books from the bookshelf and drink an organic coffee / tea. A space where you can join in on various literary and creative happenings: events, poetry readings, presentations, talks and keep up with your own little reading club. A kind of literary salon and little literary breathing space. (see: https://www.facebook.com/detlillarum/)[7]

As a modern bookstore and café, Det lilla rum offers many activities that extend far beyond the concept of being a café, activities that encompass poetry, which once again emphasizes how poetry flows more or less seamlessly between different sites and media for its distribution. With readings of literature, including poems, novels and short stories, and with other literary activities on social media, Det lilla rum has established a variety of places for poetry and alternative means of communication outside of their physical location in Copenhagen. This demonstrates the media ecology of our contemporary world in which events and initiatives take place on several media platforms, digital and non-digital, more or less simultaneously. This is also the situation for poetry readings on social media,

---

7 "DET LILLA RUM er en bæredygtig feministisk bogcafé, der først og fremmest er drevet af frivillige kræfter og kærlighed til litteratur. DET LILLA RUM er skabt i håbet om at kunne skabe et frirum, et mellemrum, mellem mange andre hurtige rum og en travl hverdag, hvor man kan gå ind og nyde en af de mange bøger fra reolen og drikke en økologisk kaffe/te. Et rum, hvor man kan komme og være med til forskellige litterære og kreative arrangementer: events, digtoplæsninger, oplæg, talks og holde til med sin egen lille læseklub. En slags litteratursalon og et lille litterært åndehul." (My translation from Danish to English).

where the preconditions for connectivity, community building and confirmation are part of the logic of media, as defined by van Dijck and Poell (see Chapter 5).

During the Corona pandemic, Det lilla rum was like many cafés and cultural institutions forced to close temporarily. In this context, they established alternative digital arenas for literature and poetry. Det lilla rum created the Instagram service and hashtag #digtfix, where they published readings of poetry. The poetry readings are tagged with the poet's name, the title of the poem read and the topic of the poems, and they range from more topical and time-limited hashtags such as #coronalockdown and #stayhome to haghtags containing more general or political keywords such as #literature, #støtforfatteren (#supportauthors), #støtmikroforlagene (#supportmicropublishers) and, of course, their own hashtag #digtfix. The first poetry reading was published on 1 April 2020, featuring the Danish poet Tina Paludan who reads "Hvidvin" ("White Wine") from her collection of poetry *Skyskraber* (2018; *Skyscraper*).

Det lilla rum's #digtfix serves as a good example of the diversity of recorded poetry readings on Instagram. Their poetry readings are aesthetically and stylistically heterogeneous. There is no music accompanying the readings, but a dark monotonous sound is added to the readings and is played in the background, as a leitmotif, a coherence marker that is similar for all the readings, regardless of the poem that is read and the mood that the reading otherwise creates. The poetry readings are short, compared to the readings on Podpoesi and to what is usually the length of a poetry reading. On Podpoesi the length of reading runs between 5 to 10 minutes, whereas at a festival a poet's reading would as mentioned typically last between approximately 8 and 20 minutes. Most of the poetry readings on Det lilla rum are less than one minute, implying that the length of the reading is also adapted to the platform.

Reading Instagram readings

Many of the poetry readings on Det lilla rum's Instagram profile appear to be instantaneous. The technical standard is not high, many readings appear "amateurish", and the videos are obviously comprised of raw footage. One example of this type of reading is by Mette Moestrup, which is also distributed on YouTube and on Det lilla rum's Facebook page (see Fig. 13). For more than two decades, Moestrup has been one of the most important poets in Scandinavia. She has a strong voice and an intense and engaging presence, both in print and in her performances. She made her debut with *Tatoveringer* (*Tattoos*) in 1998, followed by *Golden Delicious* (2002), *Kingsize* (2006), the novel-collage *Demolished* (2009), *Dø, løgn, dø* (2012; *Die, Lie, Die*) and *Til den smukkeste* (2019, *To the Most Beautiful*). Her poems are at once immediately accessible and challenging. They are also performative, a dimension that is strengthened in the poem by how Moestrup uses her voice and body in her performance-centered reading.

In the video on Det lilla rum, Moestrup reads Eileen Myles' poem "Peanut Butter" from the collection *Not Me* (1991), which was translated into Danish in 2017 by Moestrup herself and which in Danish is titled *Ikke mig*. There is no prologue. Neither is there any introduction to the collection of poems that Moestrup reads from. The information that is given in the comment field below the video includes a short presentation of Moestrup that is mixed with information about different activities on Det lilla rum.

Moestrup's reading begins immediately. She reads the title of the poem, "Peanut Butter" and then continues to read the poem in Danish. The camera angle is fixed during the reading. The upper part of the book is shown in the lower left corner of the video, while the video image is otherwise close to Moestrup's face, which is filmed halfway from below. She is standing somewhat restless, and her gaze changes between focusing on the book and the camera.

Fig. 13: The Danish poet Mette Moestrup reads at Det lilla rum's #digtfix.

Myles' poem is fairly long. It contains short lines, each one comprised of two to five words. In total, it consists of 139 lines. In the video, though, Moestrup only reads 49 of them. The video ends abruptly with the lines: "Tilfældigvis læste jeg alle Prousts værker. | Det var sommer. | Jeg var der, | det var han også" ("Accidentally I read all the works of Proust |It was summer | I was there | so was he"). The reading takes less than one minute. From a poetic perspective, there is no particular reason why the video stops where it does. In this sense, it seems accidental, leaving one with the feeling that the poetry reading is unfinished. Nevertheless, it is more likely that the length of the reading is determined by technological affordances and established conventions on Instagram. A video of nearly one minute is considered to be a long video on Instagram, but as a poetry reading one minute is not particularly long. Therefore, based on the lack of convergence in conventions between Instagram videos and poetry readings, it seems fair to claim that Instagram's media constraints are given priority over the poem and the art form poetry reading.

Moestrup reads the poem by following her own breath, and she pays no attention to the many enjambments in the poem. For instance, she reads "Jeg er altid sulten, og har altid lyst til sex. | Sådan er det bare" ("I am always hungry and wanting to have sex. | This is a fact"). In the original, there are line breaks after "sulten", "sex" and "bare". Rather than marking the line breaks with a short pause at the end of the line, she pauses after "sex" and before "Sådan." Most of the time, her reading follows the punctuation. In a few places she hesitates or repeats a word, but this does not affect her reading, nor does she interrupt the recording in order to start over.

The reading is professional, but the video recording seems unprofessional. It gives the impression of being immediate, recorded in one take and without either a professional director or an editing process. Indeed, not even the reading appears to be well prepared but is rather instant. Still, with a few exceptions, because Moestrup is a well-trained reader and performer, the reading flows. It does not seem to matter that, in some places, she hesitates or unintentionally stops reading for a brief moment. The poetry reading has a rawness and immediacy to it. It is an event, and it becomes what it becomes in that situation, there and then, in that take.

A similar aesthetic for poetry readings on social media is partly visible in another reading on Det lilla rum. Nanna Storr, a young Danish poet who has thus far published three collections of poems, reads from her book *Spektakel* (2017; *Spectacle*).[8] The reading takes 46 seconds. Storr faces the camera; there is a background that seems to have been chosen randomly, giving the impression that she is reading from a private place – perhaps her apartment, perhaps her office. A cupboard and a door with a shelf with books on it are included in the camera frame. She reads the poem with variations in tone and with a rhythmic variation that also settles in her body.

Unlike the reading by Moestrup, which was recorded in one take, Storr's reading contains three takes that are stitched together in a way that does not hide the sutures. The first cut appears after 19 seconds. Something falls from a table in front of Storr, interrupting the reading. A new cut then appears after another two seconds. Moestrup's seemingly unedited reading and Storr's slightly edited reading both represent an aesthetic for social media in which the videos appear to be as sincere as possible, emphasizing the presence of media and the situation of the

---

8 *Spektakel* is Storr's debut. She later published three more books of poems: *Mimosa* in 2018, *Lyngtarm (Ling gut)* in 2019 and *Bøgetid (Subatlantic)* in 2022.

poets as they read. Both recorded readings represent a kind of unfinished aesthetic (see Chapter 6) and the reading as a performance, giving the impression of a certain nowness. Moestrup's reading is unfinished in the sense that the video includes only one third of the poem before it is suddenly interrupted. Both Moestrup and Storr's reading reveal, in a sense, how they could have been different and how they likely will be different in another take. Further, these readings resonate with David Foster Wallace's trust in the return of sincerity in contemporary society, reflecting a more general tendency in the aesthetic of contemporary culture in which authenticity and sincerity are emphasized as cultural dominants (Kirby 2009; Bourriaud 2015). In Alan Kirby's concept of digimodernism, haphazardness and evanescence are two defining features (Kirby 2009, 155; see also Chapter 2). These recorded poetry readings both include unexpected events and appear to be made for the moment, the occasion and the media platform rather than being produced so as to be archived for eternity.

In contrast to these poetry readings that appear as if they were instant recordings, are those poets on Instagram who perform a formal and stylistic way of reading. These recordings tend to be of higher technical standards in terms of video image quality, camera framing, sound, light and cut. Maja Lee Langvad's reading on Det lilla rum's #digtfix is one of the readings that appears more planned, complete and finished. Langvad is another significant Danish poet, who since her debut in 2006 with *Find Holger Danske* (*Find Ogier the Dane*), has questioned identity, nationality and issues of language and translation. In 2019, Langvad published her most recent book, *Madalfabet* (*Food alphabet*) together with Kristina Nye Glaffey.

Langvad reads from the manuscript of the poetry book, *Tolk* (*Interpreter*), which at the time of the performance (28 April 2020) was still in the publication process. Langvad sits behind a desk. There is a bookshelf in the background. Her face is turned towards the camera. As with Moestrup and Storr, Langvad's gaze alternates between looking down at the manuscript that she holds in her hand and staring into the camera. The reading is structured according to the poem's logic. The poem alters between two subject positions, the "I" of the poem and a translator. While Langvad lends her voice to the "I," whereas there is silence when the translator speaks. "Jeg sier: Opp gjennom min oppvekst har jeg lært at amerikanerne var de gode og kommunisterne de onde (. . .)" ("I say: Throughout my childhood I have learned that the Americans were the good ones and the Communists the bad ones (. . .)." Then Langvad reads "min tolk sier" ("my translator says"). The sentence is followed by a silence of about 12 seconds. Langvad's gaze is also turned towards the manuscript in these parts of the reading, a gesture that denotes that she is reading the blank spaces on the paper. The phonetics correspond with the semantics. The absence of Langvad's voice represents the absence of words in this part of the poem. Both the absence of sound in the reading and the absence of words in the printed poem coincide with the speaker's lack of understanding of what the translator says, as he translates from a language that she does not know. Langvad's reading of the lack of words is also a reading. It is not a pause or a break but an indexical sign, a trace of the absence of meaning for the speaker. Langvad uses her gaze performatively, as she looks down even when there are no words to read. In this respect, Langvad utilizes a dimension of the visual part of the reading. Obviously, this would not have been possible in a podcast or in other audiotexts.

The examples I have drawn from above demonstrate how Instagram, like other social media platforms, constitutes a culture of poetry readings that are heterogeneous and where media at least partly have an impact on the art form. At the same time, the videos of poetry readings show how these constitute an alternative to other digital poetry in terms of user participation and interactivity. The platform with the videos of the poetry readings does not give the listener an opportunity to pause or rewind. One can either watch and listen to the poetry reading as it is being played or stop the reading and start it all over again. On the one hand, this can be interpreted as a paradox in the computational network environment where digital media often offer a high degree of interactivity. Actually, many have discussed interactivity as one of the main defining features of digital media and its literature (Aarseth 1997; Manovich 2001; Rettberg 2019). Further on, according to Henry Jenkins among others, digital culture is a participatory culture in which one feels that one participates in what takes place on the screen (Jenkins 2019, 13–20). On the other hand, poetry reading is most often not an art form that invites participation from listeners. This will of course vary. For slam poetry, for instance, the participatory culture is a crucial part of the genre where the readings are fueled by the feedback loop from the audience (Mønster, Rustad and Schmidt 2022, 176–184). Still, for the type of digital poetry readings that I have looked at in this chapter, there is little, if any, interaction between the poet and the listener. Thus, Instagram seems to be a media platform that is well adapted to the traditional poetry reading, text-centered or performance-centered, the purpose of which is to conjure a contemplative state in the audience. This, together with the way the readings are presented and organized, can be said to be part of Instagram's media-specificity.

Nonetheless, other media-specific elements, such as likes, comments, regramming, archiving and hashtags, do invite some interactivity. Let us not forget, this interactivity might well establish or support an imagined community. On Det lilla rum's #digtfix, the number of likes varies between the poetry readings from about 30 to about 200 likes, though there are rarely any comments. "Likes" are traces left by other listeners and can thus create a sense of community. Likewise, regramming establishes a form of participatory culture in which listeners feel that they contribute by sharing readings with others. In so doing, they feel that they are engaging in something that matters, an engagement that is included in Jenkins' participatory culture (Jenkins 2019). Still, it is interesting to observe the absence of comments, which might indicate that this kind of poetry reading barely constitutes communities.[9] Rather, the comment field is mainly used by the owners of the Instagram account to provide information about the poets in question. Additionally, the comment field includes information about other activities provided by Det lilla rum, such as the reopening of the café and cultural events that will take place off- and online after the prolonged closure following the outbreak of the COVID-19 pandemic. Admittedly, the responses from viewers seem to concern Det lilla rum's initiative #digtfix in general, more than specific readings. The number of likes varies; still, there seem to be more likes for the first poetry readings that were posted, while recent ones seem to have fewer likes. I am confident that this reduction in the number of likes has little to do with the poetry readings in question. It is more likely that the higher number of likes in the beginning of the project expresses support for and appreciation of these kind of events in the digital media environment when societies were closed down.

Poetry reading on demand and archived

We are (most likely) still in the beginning of the digital area. Nonetheless, we can already recognize significant transformations in the concept and practices of archiving (see e.g. Røsaak 2010). Wolfgang Ernst identifies a shift in the function of archiving from traditional storage media to networked media. He writes that the twenty-first century

> will increasingly be an epoch that exceeds the archive. With data-streaming and network-based communication, the perspective shifts: the privileged status accorded in Western civilization to 'permanent' cultural values and tradition [. . .] is increasingly giving way to a dynamic exchange, a permanent transfer in the most literal sense. (Ernst 2010, 58; see also Hansen 2015, 41)

Ernst argues that with the intensification of networked media, we will experience a change in the practice of archives, from what he calls archives to anarchives.

---

9 In the study *Digtoplæsning. Former og fællesskab* (2022; *Poetry Reading: Forms and Communities*), Louise Mønster, Michael Schmith and I provide a similar argument and show that this is different for poetry readings at physical bookshop cafés and slam poetry, where the communities have a strong presence (see Mønster, Rustad and Schmith 2022).

This shift can already be observed in poetry in the computational network environment and is exemplified by digital poetry reading. Rather than archives of poetry readings that support long-term storage, social media reflect contemporary dynamic processes where cultural expressions including digital poetry readings are distributed for short-term purposes. They are to be experienced in the here and now.

It seems obvious by now that Podpoesi follows strategies for performance and archiving that fit with a more traditional way of thinking about archives. Actually, Podpoesi appears, in every meaning of the word, as a digital archive for poetry reading. The poets represented are – or are about to be – canonized. Those poets who are not, are organized under the heading "debutanter" ("newcomers"), but they are still included. Therefore, even in its contemporariness, the archive is oriented towards a past, present and possible future canon. Furthermore, the poet reads in a way that does not challenge the traditional poetry reading. The readings are not tied to a specific time or place. Rather, they are suitable for any occasion beyond the current website for which they were made and are presented on. In addition, the organization of the poetry readings on Podpoesi reflects that the website functions both as site for poetry readings and as an archive. This does not apply to the same extent to social media platforms, where many poetry readings are organized according to popularity or the latest published readings, both of which make the videos appear at the top of the feed as the most "relevant".

The immediacy and short-term temporality of the readings on #digtfix do not only reflect the fact that they were events initiated during the COVID-19 pandemic. In line with Ernst, we might say that poetry reading on social media indicates "a shift of emphasis to real time or immediate storage processing, to fast feedback," which have replaced the traditional archive function (Ernst 2010, 67). Poetry reading appears immediately on the feed of social media platforms, where immediacy does not generate the feeling that the readings are stored somewhere in advance but that they take place more or less at the same time as you see and listen to them. They are part of what Jacob Lund has referred to more generally as a contemporary culture or as an aesthetics of the contemporary, a culture "on demand" (Lund 2016, 110). Poetry readings on social media reflect an "on demand" culture, in which the viewers can experience immediate access to a poetry reading, when they want and where they want. This experience challenges the distinction between the notion of something as archived from the past and the impression of a nowness and immediacy. As I have shown, the poetry readings on social media primarily reflect such immediacy in style. Several of the recordings seem to have been made by the poets themselves, as if they were in a private home with their private camera or mobile phone. In other words, the readings are more time-bound, more colored by the here and now in the time of the performance than the archived recordings on Podpoesi, which serve as a traditional digital archive for poetry readings.

The argument made above does not indicate that social media platforms cannot function as archives. By entering a profile, say for instance Det lilla rum on Instagram, all the readings are of course stored and available. The point is rather that digital media alter our conception and practice of archiving. This alternation does not only concern social media but is also relevant for traditional websites. If, during the summer of 2022, one followed the link www.podpoesi.nu, one would have been met with the message that Podpoesi.nu has been closed down: "The project has been closed down and is no longer available for the public. We offer our gratitude to all the readers and listeners who visited us during these years. / the team behind podpoesi.nu"[10] In fact, this is the situation of much poetry in the computational network environment. Due to institutional structures, made for and adapted to poetry in a different era, poetry – and, in this case, poetry reading – in digital media is an event under constant threat of becoming homeless, of disappearing and of no longer being available for the public. The situation is well known for digital and electronic literature. Here, the number of archives is impressive. In this regard, the ELO collection, volumes 1–3, and ELMCIP are two out of several important places to go to discover old and new work.[11] Likewise, there is the invaluable restoration and reconstruction work done by a team of researchers at Electronic Literature Lab, led by Dene Grigar. They have pursued the aim of preserving and making available digitally born work.[12] Still, we must ask towards what end does one preserve and archive poetry in digital media? Archived in national libraries, one might assume that poetry is archived for as long as there is hardware and software available to run the poems. Alternatively, at a minimum, individual works including poetry readings should be available long enough to make sure that they are properly documented for the future. This is a goal, similar to the aim for the Electronic Literature Lab work. Grigar writes that her group's aim is not to secure individual works for eternity but rather until the works can "be properly documented for posterity." (Grigar 2021, 244) The diversity of poetry readings, as well as critical readings of and the variety of voices in the encounter with digital poetry reading, is threatened by shutdowns of archives. Even though Grigar's pragmatic argument is understandable, the question still remains who should decide when a work no longer should be available or when a work is properly documented for future generations.

---

[10] My translation from Swedish to English: "Projektet har avslutats och är inte längre tillgängligt för allmänheten. Vi tackar er alla som besökt oss under åren. /teamet bakom podpoesi.nu".
[11] https://directory.eliterature.org/; https://elmcip.net/ (13 December 2022).
[12] http://dtc-wsuv.org/wp/ell/author/denegrigar/ (5 December 2022).

Between imitation and intensification

In an early phase of digital media history, digital poetry readings were mainly digitalizations and remediations of poetry reading conducted in an analog media, i.e. digitalization of sound clips stored on a gramophone record or on tape. Today, poetry readings exist in a variety of formats and forms, and they travel across different media platforms.

As this chapter has shown, poetry reading can be regarded as an art form that differs in terms of imitation and intensification. Some digital poetry readings are close to poetry reading practices in analog media. These are poetry readings that only in modest ways utilize the opportunities provided by digital media to create new forms and practices of and contextual frameworks for poetry reading. They imitate more than they intensify and appear as less media-specific. Even in length, some types of poetry readings are closer to non-digital poetry readings, as if they insist on not being touched by the aesthetic and culture of digital media. Other digital poetry readings are adapted to the media technology and culture. This is the case for many poetry readings on Instagram, where the readings are video recordings that appear as if instantly recorded. They contribute to the development of new forms of poetry readings, that is, poetry readings that would not have even taken place if it had not been for social media and its culture. On the one hand, one can argue that the readings performed by Moestrup and Storr are exactly the kind of poetry readings that we would experience in a physical room, at a café or on a stage at a poetry festival. They are situated; the place and the atmosphere that surrounds the poets are included as part of the experience of the readings. Indeed, the place and the atmosphere will most often have an impact on a particular reading. The two readings, Moestrup, who reads with a few minor hesitations and Storr, who is interrupted by a sound in the room, could just as well have been events on a stage with an audience. They are authentic in the situation, there and then. On the other hand, both of the readings also differ from poetry readings in physical places. They are short in length. Moestrup's reading is not complete, or, to be more precise, the reading does not include the whole poem. Storr's video is vaguely edited, as if both the unfinished aesthetic and the sutures, as acts of hypermediacy, are part of the aesthetic of the digital poetry reading in social media.

Digital poetry reading on Instagram is in the process of finding its form, where it both imitates older forms of poetry reading and creates new aesthetic expressions through intensification. Differences in the play between imitation and intensification coincide in the examples that I have given, reflecting fundamental differences in the readings on web-based media platforms, such as Podpoesi, and on social media platforms, such as Det lilla rum's digtfix. In the former, the platform appears as an archive and a place where one can closely and deeply listen to poetry readings. In the latter, one can listen to and see poetry readings on an app, give feedback and feel that one is part of the network and community of the respective project and that one is engaged in a poet's reading as if it takes place in the present. On Instagram, many of the readings reflect an aesthetic that implies that it could always have been different and where the mediation process is highlighted. Actually, the readings by Moestrup and Storr tell us that they are just two of many readings of the same poems, that they are two performances in the poems' ecologies.

Regarding prologues, we have entered a point where most of the material in this chapter coincides. Unlike what we saw with the video of Ashbery at Pioneer Works, neither of the two sites, the recorded readings on Det lilla rum and on Podpoesi, include a verbal prologue, which in most cases would have been part of poetry readings at physical locations. The lack of a prologue might reflect that there is no room or time for this kind of information in either of the two, or it could be that because paratextual information is provided on the websites or in the field for comments on Instagram, it would be redundant to repeat it in the actual performance. Furthermore, the material demonstrates that while YouTube serves mainly as a place for distribution, Instagram is also about connectivity, in addition to popularity and datafication, as claimed by van Dijck and Poell (see Chapter 5).

Moreover, while poetry readings from a stage in a physical room are unique performances, events that happen only once, digital poetry readings can, like other recordings, be archived for the future and thus be viewed and listened to repeatedly. With respect to the question of performance and archiving, there is a striking difference between the kind of reading conducted by Moestrup and Storr and the kind of reading presented on Podpoesi and represented by Langvad on Det lilla rum's Instagram profile. The unfinished and apparently unedited videos by Moestrup and Storr carry traces of their time, place and situation in a different way than Langvad and the readings on Podpoesi. Langvad's reading is similar to Podpoesi in the sense that it reflects a finished aesthetics. The readings on Podpoesi are taken out of time and place, and the situation of the reading is played down as if they are recordings for eternity. They appear more timeless and place-less than Moestrup and Storr's videos, where the place for the recordings and the site for distribution are of significance for the experience of the readings. The place where Langvad situates herself is also significant, but her surroundings are more formal. Therefore, the place along with the finished aesthetics seem to reflect that her reading is recorded for a more stable archive and can be reused in the future in almost any situation.

These differences between unfinished and finished, contextualized and non-contextualized readings, readings that are situated and readings that are abstracted from their original situation and location can be regarded as results of a poetics of poetry reading, as they are choices made by the poets themselves, a curator and/or a director. In addition, these changes reflect the notion of archives in the computational network environment.

Chapter 8
Poetry Film as Political Activism: A Language for the Experience of War and Exile in Ghayath Almadhoun and Marie Silkeberg's *Your Memory Is My Freedom* (2014)

Marie Silkeberg poses for the camera on a black-and-white photograph, leaning nonchalantly against a brick wall with a cigarette in her hand. She is positioned to the left-hand side of the photograph, with her eyes fixed on the camera. In the background is an alley from a city with rubbish bins, fire escape stairs, air conditioning systems and downspouts that run vertically along the sides of buildings. The photograph is aesthetic and serves as a classic staging of the modern artist and writer, as a modern version of Gisèle Freund's portraits of Virginia Woolf, Simone de Beauvoir, Paul Valéry, Walter Benjamin, James Joyce and others who also posed with a cigarette in their hands.[1]

The photograph is the background image on Silkeberg's website. On her website, Silkeberg presents herself, her works and the works of other poets. Here, excerpts from Silkeberg's poetry are made available. The website contains information about Silkeberg's poems, books, translations and essayistic works, as well as photographs, audio files, poetry films, a selection of interviews and conversations in which Silkeberg has participated available for downloading. The phenomenon of an author's website is, of course, not new, although it is probably more common today for authors to present and manage their authorship on Facebook, Twitter or Instagram. Silkeberg also uses social media platforms where some of the information from her website also appears. Additionally, as previous chapters in this book suggest, it has become more or less expected that poets use the potential of digital media to distribute poetry, although there are also those poets who consciously and actively try to keep their paths free of digital media and social media platforms. Silkeberg's website serves several functions. It serves as a contact surface, as a platform among many in the network of digital media and as a digital archive for some of her publications. Furthermore, the website is a platform for distributing various types of texts, representing a way for Silkeberg to stage herself and her writing.

Silkeberg made her debut in 1990 with the collection of poems *Komma och gå* (*To Come and Go*). She has since published nine books of poetry, the last of which, *Revolution House*, was published in 2021. Silkeberg is a professor of creative writing

---

[1] https://www.mariesilkeberg.com/ (15 December 2022).

at the University of Gothenburg. She has published essays, translations of poetry and essays by other poets and has contributed with significant essays on other poets, including the Danish modernist Inger Christensen. In this sense, it is worth mentioning the extensive edited collection *Verden ønsker at se sig selv* (*The World Wants to See Itself*) from 2018, containing Inger Christensen's unpublished and lesser-known poems, manuscripts, prose poems and sketches, collected and published by Silkeberg and Peter Borum. It is a work that confirms Silkeberg's commitment to poetic thinking and the poetic wor(l)d and suggests the possible impact of Christensen's poetry on Silkeberg's own poetic work. Silkeberg is also a filmmaker. In collaboration with the Palestinian-Syrian poet Ghayath Almadhoun – who lives in exile in Sweden – Silkeberg has made a number of poetry films. These poetry films are part of Almadhoun and Silkeberg's project exploring poetic language as politically engaged language. The poetry films can be regarded as both independent from and complementary to other publications by the two poets as individuals and collaborators. These poetry films are sometimes included in Silkeberg's poetry readings. Therefore, just as much as the poetry films can be approached as single, independent works, they are also intermedial works included in an ecology of poetry by Almadhoun and Silkeberg. This ecology is constituted by single poems, poetry readings with and without video materials and poetry films. The poetry films are available on Silkeberg's website, YouTube and Vimeo.

This chapter discusses the poetic art form of poetry film as it is situated in digital culture. Moreover, I show how this art form in the computational network environment seems to have gained new significance. Poetry film is another example of how poets relate to digital media and how digital media impact and alter established poetic art forms and practices. The practice in question is poetic activism. In the computational network environment, poetry film has moved out of museums and festivals for experimental film. It has become part of a digital culture on websites and social media platforms. Poetry film travels across analog and digital platforms. Thus, poetry film's social impact has the potential of increasing further due to the distribution networks of digital media. Sarah Tremett makes the same point in her significant and voluminous study of poetry film and its sub-genres, *The Poetics of Poetry Film* (2021), highlighting the potential of poetry film on social media to share subjectivity and political positions widely and to perform activist poetry (Tremlett 2021, xxiv). As in many of the previous chapters of this book, I will discuss poetry film by focusing on one work. Here, a media-sensitive close reading constitutes the preferred method of approach. In the approach to digital poetry film, one can discuss the extent to which remediation entails an intensification or an imitation (see Chapter 7) and to what extent digitalization of poetry film contributes to changing the art form. In addition to examining poetry film in digital culture, I will argue for how poetry film is a form of political activism, exemplified here by Almadhoun and Silkeberg's poetry films and, in particular, the poetry film *Your Memory Is My Freedom* (2012). *Your Memory Is My Freedom* is, as I will show, a media-specific way of representing war and oppression, of exploring a poetic language of exile and of providing a form of poetry of witness through the use of language, sound and video. This poetry film is one out of several collaborative projects between Almadhoun and Silkeberg. Still, because this poetry film was based on a poem written by Silkeberg, and because the poetry film reflects a poetics that is recognizable in much of Silkeberg's work, the presentation and analysis in this chapter will focus more on Silkeberg than Almadhoun.

Poetry film

Poetry film is a verbal-visual art form in which the different media involved engage in a mutually dependent intermedial interaction centered on poetry in film. Similiarly, Tremlett defines poetry film as

> a genre of short film, usually combining the three main elements of the poem as: verbal message – voice-over or on-screen narration – or subtitles (repeating or replacing voice), and as visual text-on-screen; the moving film image (and diegetic sounds); and additional nondiegetic sounds/music to create soundscape. The often complex interweaving of the elements could be said to give poetry films their uniquely associative character. (Tremlett 2021, xxi)

Poetry film includes a poem that is performed and made visual or audible for an audience. This makes poetry film different from the film poem, which does not contain verbal language (see Ieropoulos 2019, n.p.). Poetry film is comprised by an encounter between a poem, a video performance and, most often, sound. The goal, one might say, is to create a synthesis between the media or modes involved so that sensations and experiences, imagination and connotation, cannot be traced back to the verbal, visual or sonic but is the result of a unique interplay.

Poetry film developed from experimentation with film in the early twentieth century, particularly the French film impressionism of Germaine Dulac and Louis Delluc and later by such visual artists as Man Ray (Emmanuel Radnitzky) and Hans Richter. Man Ray set an early example with the experimental combination of film and poetry. The 1928 film *L'Étoile de mer* contains poems by Robert Desnos appearing in combination with visual images by Man Ray. The film is an attempt to translate Desnos' poems into a visual language.[2] Another, somewhat more recent example, is

---

[2] Another term for this kind of experimentation is "cinepoem" (see Wall-Romana 2012), a French term for cinepoetry, where one explores the different relationship between poetry and film.

Ian Hugo's film *Bells of Atlantis* from 1952. This pioneering film is an adaptation of Anaïs Nin's fictional surrealist work *House of Incest* from 1936. The film includes written text and has a narrator who reads parts of Nin's 72-page book. *Bells of Atlantis* is an abstract poetry film that, because of its artistic experimentation, can be associated with the avant-garde.

As an art form, poetry film became more present in the 1960s and 1970s, especially in the US with Beat poets like Herman Berlandt, Lawrence Ferlingetti and Allan Ginsberg and such festivals as the Poetry-Film Festival in Bolinas, California, held for the first time in 1975 (see Tremlett 2021, 8). According to Fil Ieropoulos, the increase of poetry festivals in the 1990s had a significant impact on the distribution of poetry films. Ieropoulos writes that "[i]n the UK, poetry films became an almost popular genre (for art film standards) [. . .]. Literary poetry societies soon got interested and the 1990s saw the publication of *Film Poem. Poem Film*, a periodical brochure of the South London Poem Film Society." (Ieropoulos 2019, n.p.) A similar development also has taken place in Scandinavia. In Norway, Sweden and Denmark, festivals devoted to literature in general and to poetry in particular have increased extensively in number over the last three decades. Poetry films are included in events as part of significant festivals like Oslo Poetry Film Festival, Nordic Poetry Festival | The Rolf Jacobsen Days, Sommertid – Copenhagen International Poetry Festival and Textival in Gothenburg.

The purpose of the experimental movement was to develop a poetic film language, where the films transformed a poetic verbal language into a visual language. In other words, this movement created an art form – the film poem – that was "pure" and which developed its own language. As Ieropoulos points out, "it struggles to work within the specifics of its own language." (Ieropoulos 2019, n.p.) According to Ieropoulos, the development of film poems meant that "poetics should be incorporated into the very visual nature of the film. [. . .] [T]hey believed that verbal languages should be redundant in modern film." (Ieropoulos 2019, n.p.) In this respect, the film poem can be read within the same high modernist thinking as Paul Valéry's conception of realistic literature. With the invention and development of photography, Valéry argued that literature, and especially the novel, would be better prepared to meet the "new" medium if it intensified the peculiarities of literary language rather than try to compete with photography in the presentation of reality (Valéry 1980, 193).

As this short presentation shows, poetry film is historically situated in and has developed from poetic and artistic movements whose similarities in the use of media are striking. For this reason, with his *Videopoetry: A Manifesto* (2011), Tom Konyves aims to distinguish "videopoetry from poetry films, film poetry, poemvideos, poetry videos, cyber-poetry, cine-poetry, kinetic poetry, digital poetry, poetronica, filming of poetry and other unwieldy neologism." (Konyves 2011, n.p.)

In opposition to film poems, Ieropoulos points out, that the different media involved in poetry film are explicitly present. Therefore, while a film poem is a pure visual expression, the verbal-poetic language is explicitly expressed in poetry film, where it is combined with visuals and sounds. Furthermore, while the definition of the film poem is clear, Konyves argues for videopoetry as the end of an evolution of a long period of experimentation with poetry and video: "from poetry film to film poems to poetry videos to *videopoetry*." (Konyves 2011, n.p.) Poetry film is an art form whose borders to related art forms or, for that matter, media art or digital poetry are not transparent. The distinction between poetry film and similar art forms are porous and will not, in this chapter, be made to sharp.

William Wees, one of the pioneers in the exploration of poetry film, explains precisely that the hybridity of poetry film challenges attempts to link it to a specific institutional and academic field of research. Therefore, Wees points out that the field of literary studies has long shown little interest in poetry film. He writes that in contrast to the genre of film poems, which has been recognized as important in the avant-garde film movement, "poetry-films have received little special attention [. . .] because poetry-films are a kind of hybrid art form and, therefore, seem less 'pure', less essentially cinematic, in the high modernist sense." (Wees 2005, n.p.) In this regard, Tremett's recent study, *The Poetics of Poetry*, is a significant exception. Poetry film is partly a verbal expression and should, for this reason, be treated as literature and more precisely as poetry, as I do in this chapter. Still, because of the visual dimension of poetry film, it should also be an object of study for visual studies, film studies and media studies. Moreover, it is often approached as visual art, although it also often contains sound. In this sense, it is also fair to explore poetry film in the context of the broader history and development of media art.

Poetry film as digital poetry

Research on media art typically emphasizes media aspects and the temporal and spatial organization of this art form. For example, Julia Noordegraaf defines media art as "[t] ime-based artworks that rely on media technologies for their creation and exhibition such as slide-based installations, film, video, and computer-based artworks, and net art." (Noordegraaf 2013, 11; here from Benthien 2019, 11) Noordegraaf's definition emphasizes the presence of media in media art. However, her definition does not count for the various functions that media might have, nor how they affect the understanding of media art as art. She therefore runs the risk of regarding media technology as a tool rather than as a creative agent in the making of art. Claudia Benthien, Jordis Lau and Maraike M. Marxsen give a broader and more applicable definition. The authors write that they "use 'media art' as an umbrella term for audiovisual time-based artworks that rely on analog and digital media technologies for their creation and exhibition, and that make palpable the cultural practices surrounding and the communicative contexts enabled by these technologies." (Benthien, Lau and Marxsen 2018, 12) This broad definition denotes that they include experimental film, video art, video performance, video installation, multimedia installations and poetry films. Still, even an inclusive definition where "media art" functions as an umbrella term for art forms that are similar in form, necessitates attention to the specific art form in question. The term "poetry film," in contrast to "media art," represents an emphasis on the significance of poetry, that is, the significant role that verbal language, written or oral, plays in the tradition of poetry film.

Poetry film can be regarded as a kind of digital poetry. More specifically, it can be integrated in the generation of multimedia digital poetry. Moreover, the art form as such is considered by many to be an important precursor to the development of screen-based digital poetry (Funkhouser 2007, 164; Bootz 2012). Philip Bootz describes the French scene for experimental literature and highlights how phonetic and visual poetry on the screen, such as poetry films, more or less naturally slipped into arenas of digital poetry in France (Bootz 2012, n.p.). Today, all film can of course be considered digital. As Manovich describes, film has developed from being an analog medium where data is organized in a continuum, in a continuous process, to being one in which information is represented as numeric codes (Manovich 2001, 28). Needless to say, digital media technology dominates the production, distribution and presentation of films, including poetry films. This development of poetry films blurs the distinction between poetry in digital media that contains moving images and poetry films that contain written poems. When I, nevertheless, maintain a distinction between poetry film and other poetry in digital media, it is because poetry films are structured in terms of film as a medium and because poetry films emphasize and relay on moving images to a greater extent than poetry in digital media, such as the poetry I have otherwise dealt with in this book. We might even say that while verbal language is the primary medium for the progression, or lack of progression, in digital poetry, in poetry film, moving images, words and sound collaborate as primary vehicles for the poetic expression.

I mentioned earlier that poetry film belongs to the multimedia generation of digital poetry. Given that many poetry films are distributed though social media networks and are presented on social media platforms, one could argue that poetry films can be regarded as both multimodal poetry and as social media poetry. Digital platforms like Vimeo and social media platforms like YouTube have become a place where poetry films are exhibited and distributed. Even though poetry film in digital media is not necessarily interactive or distinctive from non-digital poetry in other ways, digital media technology has put its mark on the art form and poetic practice. It has both made it easier to create poetry film and made poetry film more accessible due to the distribution possibilities of networked media. Further, and more important for the computational network environment perspective, poetry films are often included in the media ecological environment where they interact with print poetry, poetry readings and other medializations of poetry. Therefore, it has become more visible and accessible, and it can be more easily included in activist poetry. Just think of the Media City Film Festival, first held in 1994, where exhibitions have been prolonged as digital exhibitions. Likewise, Radical Acts of Care, curated by Greg de Cuir Jr., includes digital exhibitions of poetry films that explore vulnerability, illness and care in society. Among the material in Radical Acts of Care is the Iranian poet Forugh Farrokhzad's 1962 poetry film *The House Is Black*, which portrays people who suffer from various physical illnesses. This and other classic and contemporary poetry films are made available for a wide audience. Therefore, the computational network environment has also strengthened the potential political effect of poetry films. This is also the case for the poetry films by Almadhoun and Silkeberg, which I will focus on later in this chapter.

In this chapter, I demonstrate an open approach to poetry film. This openness reflects an interest in the function of poetry film in digital media and in Almadhoun and Silkeberg's poetry film in particular. With respect to contemporary digital works, moreover, we could classify them as media art or as digital poetry, since they appear as cross-over works. This is due as much to the nature of the works as to the nature of the computational network environment. Here, poetry films change in function and also in form, depending on the media in which the works are distributed and displayed. In this environment, these works travel across institutional borders and contexts. The same poetry film can be displayed at a museum, at an art or poetry festival or on a digital platform, be it a digital exhibition place or on a social media platform.

Three examples of Scandinavian poetry film as digital poetry

In *Crystal World* (2006), inspired by the novel of the same name by J.G. Ballard, the Norwegian-Danish artist Ann Lislegaard explores a future apocalyptic world using text, animation, photography, video, sound and digital technology. Similar to the world in Johannes Heldén's *Astroecology* (see Chapter 4), the explorative point of view in Lislegaard's work is a laboratory abandoned by humans. The work consists of two large screens, one with animation and one with text. The work also includes sound. On one of the screens, a destabilized and slowly changing world is depicted as white crystals develop and create new patterns. On the other screen, the text, which is descriptive, narrative and poetic, heightens moments of metamorphosis in the world depicted on the first screen. It reads: "everywhere the process of crystallization is advancing", "trees are covered in white frost" and "the empty buildings from a labyrinth of crystal caves / as if the exterior world is losing its existence." *Crystal World* has been performed at the twenty-seventh Bienal de São Paulo in 2006, the National Gallery in Copenhagen in 2007, MOCAD – Museum of Contemporary Art in Detroit in 2009, Kyoto Art Center in 2015 and Aaros in Aarhus in 2022. In addition to the media art installation, it was also published as a print version in 2022. *Crystal World* is an installation and work of media art. Moreover, with respect to the verbal language, one can also approach it as poetry and poetry film in the digital age. It is one example of how poetry film, or media art, works in the computational network environment, in which media, art forms and modalities complement each other in an ecology of intermediations.

While Lislegaard is well known for her visual art, another example from the Scandinavian scene of contemporary experimental poetry film is Ottar Ormstad, usually known for his conceptual poetry. Ormstad's poetry film "Når" ("When") from 2009 combines video and music with conceptual poems, utilizing the dual aspect of letters as both visual and verbal, to explore the possible ways conceptual poetry can interact with other media expressions. Here, the question of which expression is the primary one, or the most important, is subject to the effect and potential of meaning-making that lies in the encounter between video, music and language. "Når" is a collaborative project between Ormstad, the German documentary filmmaker Ina Pillat and the musicians and music producers Hallvard W. Hagen and Jens P. Nilsen. The poetry film explores the organic entwining of nature and culture. It depicts misplaced old rusty car wrecks that are left in nature, which already has begun to transform the car wrecks into objects that are neither culture nor nature but something in between. The images are disturbing and warn us about an environmental disaster that has already taken place. Along with dramatic and gloomy music, they create a dystopian atmosphere. In contrast, the verbal text constitutes a web of phrases that appear playfully on the screen in yellow, a color that is characteristic for Ormstad's work and performances.

The poetry film thematizes nature in the age of Anthropocene and highlights different conceptions of time. Everlasting nature is juxtaposed with impermanent, human-made objects that represent the industrial revolution, modernism and, possibly, civilization. Moreover, within the nature-culture motif layers of medializations are engaged to explore and to add conceptions of time. The video is made of photographs, on which the camera with its focal point pans vertically and horizontally. Little by little, each photograph is exposed, as if the panning imitates an investigating gaze of a viewer. The movements supply the photographs with a temporality that they otherwise would not have. As such, the poetry film highlights photography as both a punctual medium and a medium with temporal aspects in the event of perception. Likewise, the conceptual poems on the screen are spatial and temporal as words and letters become events due to Ormstad's animations.

The importance of the materiality of language is embraced more explicitly in Cia Rinne's poetry films. Rinne had her poetic breakthrough with *Zaroum* in 2001, a multilingual poetry book that combines visual poetry, sound poetry and sound symbolism. In 2008, *Zaroum* was made into an online work, *Archives Zaroum* with animations and interactive elements.[3] The term "zaroum" refers to the artificial language zaum, developed by the Russian futurists. In these and later works by Rinne, the combination, mix and materiality of languages, often referred to as translingualism, constitute the core of exploration. Through continuous displacements of words, sounds and typography, new meanings appear. As with several of the poets I have mentioned in this book, Rinne also makes use of different media and materialities for her poetry. For instance, *Zaroum* is a print book; *Archives Zaroum* is digital poetry and media art; *Indices*, first shown in 2003, is an installation; *The Roma Journeys* (2007) is a documentary photobook in collaboration with Joakim Eskildsen; *Sounds of Soloists* (2013) is an exhibition with sound, text and visual material; and *L'usage du mot* (2020) and *Sorry Future* (2021) are poetry films.

L'usage du mot is a nearly eight-minute-long poetry film, depicting the artist as she performs in a white neutral exhibition room. The installation *A Slightly Curving Place* at Haus der Kulturen Welt in Berlin serves as a creative and performative space. The poetry film is a visual performance that includes dance. Language is represented in Rinne's reading of one of her poems in a voice over, in letters written on papers in one of the filmic sequences and in translations into dance. The poetry film begins by simulating the situation of writing. A woman sits behind a desk with a pencil in her hand and white piece of paper in front of her. Rather than writing, she seems to be drawing to the voice of Rinne reading a poem. Then the sequence changes to Rinne performing a modern dance. The dance illustrates how the performing body translates the poem that is being read and hence both transforms and expands the poetic language. Language is made present in its absence or as intermedial translations into dance. In print, the poems, 16 in total, are organized with titles. In the poetry film, the poems become one continuous event as they are read. Here, titles that appear in the print book, such as "sent a letter" or "bonjour lettriste," do not appear. The final poem, "épilogue" also is not featured in the film. Instead, one might argue that the poetry film includes an epilogue of its own.

---

3 See http://www.afsnitp.dk/galleri/archiveszaroum/ (5 December 2022).

Admittedly, Ormstad's film reflects an aesthetic we might associate with late modernism. Still, poetry films can no longer be regarded as (neo) avant-garde. Rather, as both Lislegaard's and Rinne's works demonstrate, poetry film has developed into a widespread aesthetic practice among poets and artists in and outside of Scandinavia. Furthermore, poetry film is an art form that destabilizes the borders between visual art, media art and poetry: it has become more and more common to include poetry film both at poetry and film festivals, as well as on social media and poets' websites.

Poetry films as political activism

In the poetry films by Almadhoun and Silkeberg, poetry is a form of poetic and political activism. The two poets have collaborated on several poetry films, of which six are presented on Silkeberg's website: *Destruction III* (2008), *Ödeläggelse* (*Destruction*, 2009), *Your Memory Is My Freedom* (2012), *The City* (2012), *The Celebration* (2014) and *Snow* (2015). Several of these are available on YouTube and Vimeo. They are intermedial parts developed from or in interaction with print poems collected in the collaborative poetry book *Till Damaskus* (*To Damascus*) (Almadhoun and Silkeberg 2014).[4] This is a collection of poems about the experience of war, oppression and exile, with the war in Syria as a recurring point of reference. The book is in itself an intermedial work with color and black and white photographs of the city of Damascus and with poems that have wandered across media. They have been staged as a radio piece for Swedish radio, some poems have been included in multimedia readings by Silkeberg and some have made it into the digital environment as poetry films.

The poetry films are political: they thematize war, oppression and destruction through image, sound and language. For instance, the film *Snow* juxtaposes moving images of people in need with artistic images of trees and a sky filled with falling snowflakes, while a female voice reads a poem in Swedish and a male poet reads in Arabic.[5] In addition, the poem appears in both English and Arabic on the screen. The moving images that are juxtaposed turn the film into a collage of realistic and contemplative expressions that give way to (self-)reflection. In this respect, the moving images function both as anchor and relay for the poem. They direct our attention towards specific contexts for the poem, and they

---

4 The title refers to *The New Testament* story about the conversion of Paul, which took place on the road to Damascus and is also a reference to August Strindberg's play of the same name.
5 https://www.youtube.com/watch?v=vnfPLnExwBw (13 December 2022).

supply the poem with new meaning as the two collaborate in presenting sensations and experiences of war and suffering. Lines like "the hand movements / as he described / how they filled a truck full of rockets / that failed to explode on impact" are accompanied by moving images of snowflakes falling in the dark.[6] "Images of snow" is read in Swedish and Arabic while the film shows a little girl in the snow in what most likely is a refugee camp. The lines "a collection of snow figures to mourn the dead / the dead in the snow" is followed by images of an installation with snow figures representing a funeral.

The poem, the moving images, the combination of images and words, the rhythm that is made out of the alternation of images and multilingual expressions create a performance and an experience that are specific for poetry film as an art form, demonstrating the poetic-political potential of poetry film.[7] Likewise, the poetry film *The Celebration* shows pictures of cities that have been bombed during a war, while a voice reads in Arabic with English subtitles: "I was exploring the difference between revolution and war | when a bullet passed through my body".[8] Almadhoun and Silkeberg collaborated in directing the poetry film. The poem, however, is by Almadhoun and is titled "The Details." Almadhoun also reads the poem. The last line in the quote from the poem could refer to a real, individual experience or an imagined experience. It could also be read as a metaphor: experiences from the war zones create a particularly bodily experience that is conveyed in the semantics, syntax and phonetics of language. The former interpretation renders the poet a victim, a witness and a survivor, while the latter indicates that the body in question is not only the speaker's but also a collective body, since the speaker expresses a feeling on behalf of the many victims of war and persecution. It is worth observing the title of the poetry film: an obvious response would be that there is nothing about war that is worth celebrating. Likewise, the music from Chopin's *Nocturne*, opus no. 9 that is played throughout most of the film, immediately seems as a bizarre aestheticization of war or misplaced as it contrasts the images of bombed cities.

The poem and the poetry film thematize war and destruction and include a metapoetic dimension. The speaker is an Arabic poet who discovers the beauty of war: "It was the most beautiful war | I've been in in my life | full of metaphors and poetic images." The poem is an epideictic speech where the speaker encourages listeners to leave everything they know to take part in the war:

---

[6] Each clause appears one by one on the screen, creating a sense of line breaks. These deviate from the line breaks in the print poem.
[7] Tremlett elaborates on the function of rhythm in poetry film (see Tremlett 2021, in particular Part One).
[8] https://www.youtube.com/watch?v=QLm_MyOSj1A (15 December 2022).

come let's give up poetry | [. . .] | leave behind | Rumi | Averroes | Hegel | and bring along | Machiavelli | and Huntington | and Fukuyama | for we need them now | leave behind your laughter | your blue shirt | and warm bed | and bring your teeth, and nails | and hunting knife || and come

The poem could be either an ironic gesture or a short manifesto for a revolution. More than this, though, the poem and poetry film are structured around opposing expressions, images and concepts in order to highlight the destruction and non-rationality of war and to show that rather than poetic and artistic representations of war – perhaps because representing war is impossible – war and the experience of it must represent themselves. As we hear in the poem: "bring on the real Guernica | with its smell of fresh blood". These real things, the sensations and materializations of war, are necessary to turn the world, readers and viewers as well as poets' attention to war and the deep historical interconnection between humans across cultures.

Almadhoun and Silkeberg's poetry films exsist and perform in the computational network environment that strengthens their potential to reach a wide audience and to be included in different situations it can be used. According to Evelina Stenbeck, political and activist poetry demonstrates the "power of literature." (Stenbeck 2017, 13)[9] The term "power" captures the effect that literature might have outside of the literary text and its medium. It makes us imagine and experience what literature can do when it is used. According to Stenbeck, the power of literature contains "both the political forces of society and the ability that poetry has to create new spaces, actions and paths of thought." (Stenbeck 2017, 13)[10] As political poetry films in the computational network environment, the films by Almadhoun and Silkeberg give new legitimacy to arguments about the political potential of culture. Poetry film can create opportunities to say or make visible something that has not previously been possible to say: it can function as part of the starting point for new opportunities. We might even argue, with careful reference to Hannah Arendt, that poetry film is an important supporter of political activism. Arendt points out that political action and activism require places where they can appear, where revolution can take place (Arendt 1963). Such places include streets, squares and music venues; they could also include books, the benefits of which lie in the combination of distribution, mobility and archiving; they could also be digital platforms for the creation, distribution, exhibition and discussion of political poetry films.

---

9 My translation. In Swedish the quote reads: "litteraturens verkanskraft."
10 My translation. In Swedish the quote reads: "både samhällets politiska krafter och poesins förmåga att skapa nya rum, handlingar och tankebanor."

In the argument above, Arendt is not a randomly chosen philosopher. In the poetry book *Till Damaskus*, the opening epigraph includes two quotations from Arendt's *On Revolution* (1963). One of the two cites Plato: "For the beginning, because it contains its own principle, is also a god who, as long as he dwells among men, as long as he inspires their deeds, saves everything." The second epigraph is a quote from the Greek historian Polybios: "The beginning is not merely half of the whole but reaches out towards the end." (Almadhoun and Silkeberg 2014, 8) Both quotations draw attention to the concept of beginning and are both politically contextualized. According to Arendt, a beginning contains both opportunities and challenges (Arendt 1990, 20). In Arendt's philosophy, the idea of beginnings contains humanity's ability to create changes or to give way for something new to take place. At the same time, there will always be a possibility that beginnings limit the possibility of creating change and revolution in the future. The complexity of a revolution philosophically consists in, among other things, giving it integrity so that the beginning does not bring about an outcome that is only for the good of some or that holds back future revolutions. In other words, the beginning of a revolution can lead to democracy, justice and a society where everyone has the opportunity to participate. The question or challenge is how this can be done. The epigraphs in *Till Damaskus* from Arendt function as statements about poetry and poetic language and suggest that poetry can offer or be part of a beginning.

Stenbeck claims that the poetics of activism implies transgression on several levels. One form of transgression that is particularly relevant for this chapter, is poetry's transgression of media and institutions. Stenbeck writes that "[p]oems call for activism by seeking ways out of the pages of the books and the literary public in a narrow sense." (2017, 11)[11] In this sense, books are perceived as a medium included in literary institutions that potentially might restrain the effect of political poetry. Therefore, in order to make poetry matter in specific situations, the poet can create poetry that is not only adaptable for print but also available in another media in ways we have seen in previous chapters in this book. This is also a way to make poetry accessible in different public situations in which poems can reach out to people and be used.

The resolution of national and geographical borders in the network of programmable media gives new opportunities for contemporary poetry like poetry films to reach a broad audience, to be used as activist poetry and to demonstrate the political power of poetry. Still, as claimed by Alexander Halavais (2000), even though social media can be seen as international media, one might argue for the

---

[11] My translation. In Swedish, the quote reads: "[d]ikten manar till aktivism genom att söka vägar ut från boksidan och den i strikt mening litterära offentligheten."

existence of social structures and practices on websites that underline traditional national borders. In addition, some countries do practice censorship of social media platforms and social media content. Still, most poetry films distributed online are, due to networked media and media ecological structures, available for anyone with online connection and knowledge about the languages in question.

Almadhoun and Silkeberg's poetry films reflect a strong political commitment, which in their performativity is directed outwards and which both demands and creates a space of appearance. In this way, political poetry films generally demonstrate how contemporary poetry in the computational network environment can serve as activism even when, or perhaps because, it is entwined in symbiotic relationships with digital technology. Their poetry films reflect an international engagement that also involves a deep interconnection between humans on the planet, regardless of religious, cultural and national differences. All except one of the titles of their poetry films are in English. Furthermore, the poems that are included in the poetry films are multilingual: there are poems in Swedish, English and Arabic. What is more, the poetry films are distributed, seen and potentially discussed on social media platforms, giving weight to the political and activist potential of the art form. Anita Harris, for instance, writes that the movement for young and marginalized women was among the early political groups that established themselves as an activist "online culture" and that utilized the potential of digital technologies for political performances (Harris 2012, 214–216). Likewise, as I describe in Chapter 5 and 6, poetry on Instagram and Facebook is a more recent example of how poets use social media in poetic activism. Through connectivity, users' networks and algorithms, social media platforms such as Instagram, YouTube and TikTok ensure the rapid distribution of poetry films to many, connect many to many and, in so doing, contribute to the awareness of crisis in the world, hence maintaining, mobilizing and establishing activist network communities.

Montages and the experience of war

One significant technique used by Almadhoun and Silkeberg is montage. Collected images, music and voices are combined to present a dense image of war, intensifying the experience of war. The moving images in many of Almadhoun and Silkeberg's poetry films are selected and organized in a poetic system. They do not follow a pre-conceived chronology or narrative structure. Rather, the classic structure of selection and combination, outlined by Roman Jakobson as a "projection of the principle of equivalence from the axis of selection on to the axis of combination" (Jakobson 2014, 240) is applied to the poetry films. The images are composed of material from different sources, as segments taken out of narrative and documentary contexts and combined on the syntagmatic level of the film. They may include images from a specific war, in a specific time and place, combined using the principle of resemblance and difference. In some poetry films, the material used is from one war-torn city, such as in *The Celebration* where film clips from Berlin on 2 July 1945 are combined with music from Chopin's *Nocturne*. In *The City*, the principle of combination is resemblance. This poetry film is a montage of images, poems, music fragments and voices. Silkeberg's poem "What Gas", read by male voices, is combined with Almadhoun's poem "The City", read by female voices. Randomly chosen people from the street of Stockholm read both of the poems. Furthermore, the poetry film depicts buildings that collapse, accompanied by music, poetry reading and the visualization of the poem in English on the screen. In these and other poetry films, the montage has several possible functions. One is that the repetition of shocking images reinforces the representation of war at the same time as it draws attention to poetry film as an art form and media for the representation of war. Rather than a chronological representation of war, war and destruction are represented through a global imagination that emerges because of the montages and the applied principle of equality that is projected onto the principle of proximity, combinations that are engaged on the syntagmatic level of the poetry films.

As I pointed out with regard to *Celebration*, the poetry film problematizes poetry's (and literature's) representation of war. Presenting war, distress and the pain of the other are always challenging, as Susan Sontag famously reminds us (Sontag 2003). Fredric Jameson goes further, arguing that a holistic narrative representation of war is impossible. According to Jameson, any literary attempt to present or thematize war ends with "various forms of the impossible attempt to represent it [war] may have taken." (Jameson 2009, 1533) He suggests that literature that depicts war must be read as a laboratory for exploring other aspects of the human being and the world, such as anxiety, class struggle, solidarity, politics, etc. His main target is literature that has the ambition of representing war entirely. Therefore, Jameson writes: "It is not to be imagined, however, that we can return to some earlier state of wholeness, in which, as in Homer, individual hand-to-hand combat would at one and the same time somehow epitomize the totality." (Jameson 2009, 1536) Jameson concludes: "War is one among such collective realities, which exceed representation fully." (Jameson 2009, 1547) The complexity of war and, we might add, of poetry make Jameson emphasize collage, fragmentation and decentralized perspective as more adequate for representing war than narrative and holistic attempts.

In the poetry film *Your Memory Is My Freedom*, Almadhoun and Silkeberg utilize the technique of montage and cross-cutting in order to avoid the problem of representation outlined by Jameson. Moreover, they seek to create a poetry film that presents the experience of war and exile. In the poetry film, images are dramatic and somewhat aggressive or provocative, and they are combined in a confrontational style, probably to create an effect of shock. The poem that is materialized in written and oral form is without emotional engagement, as if it represents the poets' restrained mode. This implies that the poetry film is neither propagandistic, nor resigned. Rather than compelling viewers to go out into the streets to protest, the film informs, shocks, problematizes and alienates. Through a particularly poetic and cinematic language, it seeks an adequate way of portraying others' pain as well as the experience of war and exile.

Your Memory Is My Freedom

The poetry film *Your Memory Is My Freedom* includes video clips from Stockholm and Damascus. Its duration is 5 minutes and 40 seconds and begins with a prologue of 55 seconds in which Silkeberg reads from one of her print poems in *Till Damaskus* (2014). During the prologue, the screen is black and the sound of a heavy and somewhat mechanical breath accompanies Silkeberg's reading. The prologue is followed by the main part of the film, which is introduced with the title "Your Memory Is My Freedom" that appears on the screen to Arabic music. The main part of the poetry film shows videos of the streets of Stockholm from a first-person viewer perspective. These images are juxtaposed with others from the streets of Damascus. The film presents an unpleasant encounter between the peaceful everyday life of Stockholm and war zone that is Damascus. Silkeberg lends her voice to the poem, though the sound of heavy breathing continues. These sounds are then combined with someone's footsteps, as if he or she is running or walking fast. The sound of the breathing and the footsteps reflect a bodily presence of a subject. Because of the filming, the heavy breathing and the fast footsteps, this subject seems misplaced and defamiliarized in the surroundings of harmonious and safe Stockholm. At the same time, the breathing, the footsteps and Silkeberg's voice, which carries the poem across the shifting images of the two cities and situations, join to create a sense of continuity. The striking contrast between the images and the two situations in question is tuned down and the individual subject's embodied experiences are foregrounded.

The cross-cutting of images positions the two places and situations in dialogue with one another, creating a condensation of time and space. The form of the poetry film correlates with the poem that Silkeberg reads, which is also dialectic and temporally and spatially dense (see Fig. 14). It presents the voice of a speaker who appears as privileged and safe despite the war and a "he", whose voice represents the oppressed and persecuted. The poem corresponds with one of the longer print poems in the book *Till Damaskus*. This print poem is untitled and appears in a section called "Your memory Is My Freedom." The section contains a number of poems: some are single-lined poems, while others are longer poems. They deal with war, mostly in Damascus, with the oppression and persecution of certain ethnic groups in Palestine and Syria and with the experience of exile.

> now the killing will start, he says. when i ask him about the veto. about what will happen now. looks at the clock. only five. he shows me his passport. they see it here, he says, and points at nationality stateless. i look at his palestinian passport, a photo of him as much younger. can hardly recognize him. so long ago i say, is it a long ago. see that it's almost six. we must go i say. will you accompany me to the bus. no. he replies. will you help me with the suitcase. no he replies. takes it from me. moves towards the bus. an experience of violence. an insight into it. to bear the memory of it. nakba sadness. he says they call it. that the men died from it. that nobody could explain why. no sickness in the body. like the africans, the native americans. the people in australia. i read in lindqvists book. but not the parallel. the similarity. they floated. were floating. in the library. the leaves that swirled. their presence. light. reflection. clear lucid colors. running water. long before the frozen. to reflect oneself in the foreign. find one's picture. some picture. skin. to take the world in through. opening the eyes. turning the head. the signal. the siren. an emergency. a need. what would the next step be. some words out of the night. or giving the word to the night. or taking it. risking the word. i saw my hand when I tried to imagine my face in the mirror. the devastation. to be broken down. into parts. to let the parts speak. or. or. I couldn't pronounce his name. without feeling it was an abyss I moved over. when the languages fell silent. the foreign ones. the shared. a reaching out. in so many directions. if the massacre in hama 1982. if the world had condemned in time. not kept silent. it wouldn't be repeated now. maybe. if the west was the eastern state dissident's hope. what then was the hope in Syria? did one hope anything? where did the impulse come from? the demand for justice, freedom? one generation to forget. the killing. the outrageous. grief. loss. silencing. the disappeared in prisons. the hope that they were still alive. would come back. they who managed to leave the country. how long the pressure remains. the fear. we weren't allowed to say that the bread was bad, nothing. each morning we were forced to rattle off a homage to the president. the truth a function of the power. of the economy. I thought about the whisper in the child's ear. when it is born. to have the dream still. make reality of it when possible. if it becomes possible. live for it. to whisper in the child's ear. that god is great, greater. to be put in touch with the relatives. the generations. the father's names in a long row, far back in history. to be in revolt against the world. is that a universal truth, that revolt. a deeply human movement. deep inside. dark wedding. homelessness. don't laugh he said. I'm not laughing. the language of exile. of poetry. maybe. to accept. bare it. know. to see. to have seen. that skin. the hand mark against the inner wall

Marie Silkeberg. From *Till Damaskus* 2014

Translation: Agneta Falk-Hirschmann

Fig. 14: The poem in question, published on Marie Silkeberg's website in an English translation.[12]

In the print poem in question, both the left and the right margin are straight, providing the poem with the shape of a black square, as if it is a poem's visual-verbal reply to Kazimir Malevich's *Black Square* (1950) or to the photographs of the city

---

[12] https://www.mariesilkeberg.com/_files/ugd/eb057a_5692ee6169b848a993a1e750300464c2.pdf (7 December 2022).

of Damascus in the book. The photographs show Damascus from a distance. The houses are positioned close to each other, similar to the poem that is without blank spaces. The poem is written without capital letters and the use of punctuation, other than full stops. The words in the poem are placed close together, making the poem appear visually dense. The visual and syntactic density of the poem reflects the poem's theme. There are no visual pauses, as if the poet does not want to give readers a break from the words that tell about war, continuous oppression and other dramatic events. The poem is intense and reflects visually and semantically entwined sensations and memories belonging to subjects who have been there.

Still, the material in the poetry film and in the book differs. There is no prologue in the print poem. There is no indication of a change or turn, a line break or an enjambment between "går mot bussen" ("walk towards the bus"), which is the last line of the prologue in the poetry film and "en erfarenhet av våld" ("an experience of violence"), which is the first line in the main part of the film. Furthermore, most of the visual material is different, even though it also contains photographs of Damascus that is similar to the photographs in the book. What is more, the poem is performed in Silkeberg's voice as it simultaneously appears visually in the form of single lines on the screen, not in the form of a square as in the print version. Here, the interplay is between words and images and between Silkeberg's voice and the video images in first-person viewer perspective. Indeed, the poetry film contains layers of voices, events and experiences that are presented in the print poem, but the poetry film is in itself a process of layering that heightens the opacity of the work.

Both the print poem and the poetry film can be regarded as independent works, even though the print poem appears in the poetry film, both in oral (read by Silkeberg) and visual form. Still, they are part of an intermedial and media ecological environment, connected through layers of media, motif, theme and poetic language that transcend differences in media and art forms. As I outline in the following, both are attempts to develop a language for the experience of war in exile.

Layers of media and memory

In *Your Memory Is My Freedom*, the images from Damascus represent memories from war and persecution. Likewise, the heavy breathing, most likely from a male subject, represents a bodily response to the memories that reappear. These affective responses imply that the experiences of war and persecution are present as flashbacks and body memories. They are, as the poem says, "en erfarenhet av våld. en insikt i det. att bära minnet av det" ("an experience of violence. an insight into it. to bear the memory of it"). Likewise, the film alternates between presenting what the haunted subject sees and hears, as he runs or walks quickly through the streets of Stockholm, and showing short glimpses of what haunts him in his memory. It is a palimpsestic layering of past and present – an analogy that potentially shows how traumatic memories work. Traumatic memory is, according to Jonathan Shay, "not narrative. Rather, it is experiences that reoccur, either as full sensory replay of traumatic events in dreams or flashbacks, with all things seen, heard, smelled, and felt intact, or as disconnected fragments." (Shay 1994, 172; see Brison 1999, 42–43) In the poetry film, the experiences of war are presented in a layered montage of images. Actually, the layering technique in the poetry film is informed by the traumatic memories and past experiences that become part of the subject's present.

The process of layering is a much-used technique in media art and poetry film. Tremlett points at how the use of laying techniques in poetry film foreground a mnemonic space, thereby showing how the past haunts the present (Tremlett 2021, 95, 135). In media art, Benthien, Lau and Marxsen write, layering techniques provide works with "a form of semantic as well as aesthetic layering, resulting in a heightening degree of opacity." (Benthien, Lau and Marxsen 2018, 218) Integrated in the process of layering is the intermedial layering of video, the written poem and the oral performance of the poem. In this respect, the act of reading and the visualization of the poem on the screen are of sensational and semantic significance, not least because the film foregrounds embodied experiences, languages and the poem in question. In so doing, the poetry film reflects upon itself as a literary work.

The technique of layering is an intermedial phenomenon that takes place on different levels in the poetry film. In this way, layering strengthens the thematization of traumatic memories of war. One level of layering is the engagement with different media aesthetics, which takes the form of intermedial references. Irina O. Rajewsky writes that intermedial references are used "to refer to a specific medial subsystem (such as a certain film genre) or to another medium qua system (Systemreferenz, "system reference")." (Rajewsky 2005, 53) In the poetry film, the first-person viewer perspective is both a way of exploring trauma, a point supported by the claim made by Susan Brison, and an intermedial reference. In order to explore an individual's trauma and the presence of past experiences of war in exile, the film reproduces the perspective from the genre of first person documentary film. Nevertheless, this intermedial reference is not a linear one-way reference since the chosen perspective is a well-developed aesthetic from computer games. However, this first-person viewer perspective imitates the situation where one engages in the dramatic world, even though the viewer is not able to move about on his or her own in the mediated environment. The poetry film positions a subject in the two situations and provides a perspective that presents the world as if it is perceived directly through the eyes and breathe of this subject. The moving gaze, breath and footsteps all reflect bodily presence and embodied experiences of war and exile. In this regard, the first-person viewer perspective is an attempt to position the reader-viewer as an observer, as one who sees what the subject sees and remembers and one who hears the subject's embodied responses to a situation in which the past is part of the present, where memories of war are present in exile.

The cross-cutting, layering and fragmentation absorb and reinforce Silkeberg's fragmented poetic language. This is a language for the literary (re)presentation of war and trauma. Therefore, the poetry film, including Silkeberg's poem, can be read as an implicit response to Jameson's claim regarding the impossibility of representing war. The individual parts are allowed to speak; in the words of one of the poems in *Till Damaskus*: "att vara nedbruten. i delar. att låta delarna tala. eller. eller." ("to be broken down. in parts. to let the parts speak. or. or.") (Almadhoun and Silkeberg 2014, 16).[13] Neither the poetry film nor the poetry book *Till Damaskus* are attempts to create a holistic narrative presentation or to develop a coherent language for the experience of war. Rather, the poetry film contains layers and fragments from different places and of different voices, underlining that the poetry film is itself a rupture. In this respect, it is a rupture that corresponds with ruptures created by the experience of war and exile.

"exilens språk" ("the language of exile")

To thematize the experience of war and exile, the poetry film reflects a search for a poetic-cinematic language that is adequate to these experiences. *Your Memory Is My Freedom* is structured in terms of a "now." This now is made dense: it is filled with traumatic memories of war and persecution. The combination of these two aspects – i.e. the present, represented by the poem and the poetry film as an event, and the past, represented by memories – join to make the poetry film a powerful poetic statement and event.

The opening line of the poem establishes a dramatic situation: "Now the killing will start". This statement corresponds with images from Damascus that depict corpses among other things. In addition to referring to something that has happened and that the video shows, it provides the poem and the poetry film with a nowness. It gives the impression that the killing is happening now. Moreover, because of the present tense, the poem is an account of what happens repeatedly, as unfinished events. This aspect, one could argue, is what makes the poetry film so

---

[13] Here, the poem in Swedish is quoted from the print poem in the book *Till Damaskus*. The English version is how the poem appears in the poetry film.

powerful. Here, event and enunciation coincide. This "now" makes the poetry film an event in the present, rather than a representation of past events.

The opaque "now" replaces a chronological presentation of events, constituting a temporal space, a container that comprises "en erfarenhet av våld" ("an experience of violence"). This experience, in turn, is represented through memories that are both individual and collective: "att bära minnet av det" ("to bear the memory of it"). In this sense, the black background of the poetry film's prologue is a visualization of such a space, the black screen as a visualization of repressed memories. This background seems to demonstrate Jameson's point that there are no ways to represent war in a holistic way. As an alternative, the poetry film follows poetic principles that we can identify in what Silkeberg herself calls "the language of exile."

The poetry film is composed in the language of exile. This is a language of embodied experiences of a world torn asunder. For the traumatized subject in exile, this world appears as non-coherent. As argued in my analysis so far, this language of exile is a non-narrative, verbal-poetic language. Furthermore, it is a language of activism that posits an alternative to the prosaic language of everyday life. The poem and the poetry film are in search of a non-quotidian language. This is no peacetime language but one adequate to rupture. It is as if the poem and film say: it is a paradox that the same language used for everyday situations should be used for experiences that are anything but ordinary. In other words, the poem and poetry film are in search of a poetic-cinematic language that could more fully serve a referential function for the exceptional, for the experience of war and exile.

Lines like "exilens språk. diktens. kanske. att acceptera. stå ut. veta. att se. att ha sett. den huden. handavtrycket mot den inre muren" ("the language of exile. the poem's. maybe. to accept. stand out. know. to see. to have seen. the skin. the handprint against the inner wall") reflect possible connections between poetic language and a language for certain experiences. Simultaneously, the poetry film is an attempt to develop a poetic language that expresses the vulnerability of both the privileged and exposed subject, how the privileged subject is affected by what she has seen, from the inside. It is an attempt to touch and engage the audience though words, sentences, images and sounds that represent memories and experiences of violence.

To explore a language for the exiled is about more than trying to bridge the distance between language, what one sees and has experienced and the other's memories and experience. Here, we can recall Sontag's words in *Regarding the Pain of Others*: "(T)here are many uses of the innumerable opportunities a modern life supplies for regarding – at a distance, through the medium of photography – other people's pain." (Sontag, 2003 11) Sontag is concerned with how representations of war and the other's pain in photography and film turn humans into objects. Among others, she refers to Simone Weil who in her essay "The Iliad, or The Poem of Force" writes that "violence turns anybody subjected to it into things." (Weil 1965, 6)

Later in her book, Sontag returns to this issue: "(T)he scale of war's murderousness destroys what identifies people as individuals, even as human beings. This, of course, is how war looks when it is seen from afar, as an image." (Sontag 2003, 49) The distance in space, the imagination and the medializations, whether in words, photographs or videos, turns subjects into dead objects or things.

In Almadhoun and Silkeberg's poetry film, language as both sign and action has been supplied with a verbal-cinematic language that is specific to certain experiences. It might be that Almadhoun and Silkeberg, through a poetic verbal-cinematic language, are trying to create a connection between worlds and experiences with the aim of connecting with "the other" and the unknown. However, the challenge is not only a representational one. It is also a poetic one, related to the poetic language and to Silkeberg's other concerns. In an essay on Inger Christensen, Silkeberg writes that poetic language expresses a sense of belonging and that language is grounded in the world (Silkeberg 2005, 11). Likewise, the poetry film is an attempt to develop a language that is connected to the world and poetic language as an extension of the world and other. Words like "belonging," "connection" and "extension" serve as bridges. What is more, they also work to measure the distance between language and the world, the speaker and the addressee, the "I" and "the other." Silkeberg explains elsewhere that poetic language measures the distance to the other, the unknown, simultaneously as it stretches out towards the world "as a sensitive instrument of approaching." (Silkeberg 2005, 248) In this respect, the poetic language serves a double function. The reflection is at once poetic and ethical. In this case, we find an ethic not disconnected from poetic language but which is part of a poetic language that makes visible a divergent world with, as Silkeberg writes, "differences, conflicts, displaced languages, interest, unwritten history." (Silkeberg 2005, 12)

The poetry film both develops and demonstrates a language of exile, "exilens språk," which becomes a language of exception that disperses a given order and that brings forward a new beginning. War, oppression and vulnerability are presented in a fragmentary visual and verbal language in which the grammar of verbal language and the linear temporality of the film are broken. The spatial and temporal continuity is exceeded in favor of fragments, repetitions, displacements and the environmental combination of images from two cities, Stockholm and Damascus, one as the representation of a privileged place, the other depicting a war zone. Likewise, the poem is remnants of dysfunctional dialogues, sometimes in an introverted style and often paradoxical. Early in the poetry film, for example, it says: "följer du mig till bussen. no svarar han. hjälper du mig med väskan. no svarar han. tar den från mig. går mot bussen." ("do you follow me to the bus. no he answers. will you help me with the bag. no he answers. take it from me. goes towards the bus"). This is how the poetry film shows the language of exile as a beautiful but broken and paradoxical language. It is a language affected by the logic of war; "now the killing will start", it says in the beginning of the poem. Further, it is a language that is exposed to violence, appropriate to the experiences of violence that the poetry film conveys. In this way, the poetry film reflects the state of exception that is the governing logic of war and destruction.

Furthermore, the language of exile is the language of the misplaced subject. This traumatized subject in exile may be situated in a time and place distant from war and oppression, but the experience of war and oppression are continually present through memories and flashbacks. With the language of the poem and the poetry film, the gap between language and these experiences is not bridged but measured: it is the only way, according to the poem and the poetry film, that one can be engaged with the other's experience. Both the poem and the poetry film allow us to be in an opaque moment, a spatial and temporal now with sensations, experiences, memories, repetitions and shifts. Therefore, rather than the chronology of a narrative, the poetry film provides an opportunity to be in a mood and in a dwelling over time, as a standstill, without turning the poetic language into a narrative language where the events are organized in a linear and causal order that involves a development and a change. In the poetry film, there is no change, no future or horizon, as it often is in linearly structured narratives.

Voice, body, witness

Your Memory Is My Freedom is an event made out of a poetic-cinematic language of exile, a language that in the film is presented by different subjects. The poem and the first-person viewer perspective in the poetry film represent two different perspectives and functions. The speaker in the poem is privileged, one who is not persecuted, in opposition to the "he", who is the persecuted. In the poetry film, the perspective that is represented in images is from the traumatized other and, as mentioned, probably one who is in exile in Stockholm. The first-person viewer perspective, the breathing and the footsteps all create continuity in the crosscutting of images from Damascus into the sequences of images from the streets of Stockholm. In Stockholm, he is haunted by his memories of war and persecution in Damascus. Here, the images from Damascus represent memories and documentation of war and the pain of the other.

The two perspectives, the perspective of the speaker in the poem and the perspective of the subject in the poetry film, contrast and complement each other. These again are juxtaposed with the presence of Silkeberg who lends her voice to the poem. A significant contrast occurs between the thematization, carried forward by the dramatic images and sounds, and Silkeberg's voice, who reads the poem in a way that is controlled and unaffected by what takes place on the screen and what the poem is about. Silkeberg reads the poem with a restrained and almost mechanical voice that appears as distant from and unaffected by the situation, the images, the sounds and the appearance of embodied experiences. Silkeberg's voice and way of reading offer a different form of empathy and immersion than the video images and the sounds. With regard to the way Silkeberg reads, we can say more generally that it invites an aesthetic contemplation that is often associated with her poetry readings (see Mønster, Rustad and Schmith 2022, 54). This is a poetry reading that puts its attention on an in-depth immersion into the voice's material qualities and the poem's phonetic and semantic dimensions. While the poetry film with its many layers might call for hyper attention, the poetry readings, isolated, invite contemplative deep attention.

Poetry, including poetry films, can, as a form of activism, uncover memories, experiences and voices that are not otherwise seen and heard. These genres offer forms other than conventional or narrative representations in order to explore the topics of war, oppression and exile. Here, the poem and poetry film position the subjects in two different roles as witnesses. One is an individual and direct witness of war and suffering, which in the poetry film is represented though memories and embodied experiences from "the other," the "he" in exile. The other position is the one taken by the poets who, whether as direct eyewitness or not, can make the poem and the poetry film become a witness. These two functions, which are not necessarily mutually exclusive, are reflected in the title of the poetry film. The one's memory becomes the other's freedom to create. Carolyn Forché argues for a similar expansion of the understanding of the function of witness. In *Poetry of Witness: The Tradition in English 1500–2001* (2014) she writes that "[i]n the poetry of witness, the poem makes present to us the experience of the other, the poem is the experience, rather than the symbolic representation." (Forché 2014, 26) It is worth noting that Forché writes "experience". In this way, she emphasizes a contextual discourse and avoids confusing witnessing with valuations of whether something said is true or false.

It is precisely this type of understanding of the function of witness and activism that *Your Memory Is My Freedom* performs. It provides other ways and a different language to convey experiences and memories of war, oppression and exile. Almadhoun and Silkeberg show video clips from Stockholm and Damascus, clips that emphasize the subject who is running or walking fast through the cities with the camera. This implies that the subject with necessity must have been there and that the video images convey how it was at the exact time when this person ran through the streets. The testimony of the poetry film is precisely the combination of images, sounds and poetic texts that make up the world of the poetry film and that are put together without ignoring the differences. Nevertheless, because the poetry film is not a narrative, a retelling of an event but a poetic performance, these images and sensations are turned into events which create the sense of concurrency, that they take place simultaneously as the poetry film is shown on the screen. More than a witnessing of events that has taken place, the poetry film, as poetry, is a witness and a presentation of something as if it is happening in the present. The poetry film is structured in accordance with a now, giving us the impression that this takes place in the present and that these events continue to take place.

The poetry film demonstrates that the experience of violence and the language of exile and witness testimony are not only reflected in verbal language. They are also acts of materialized voices and bodies. This is a specification of Stenbeck's argument that activist poetry is performative and bodily. Moreover, these embodied experiences are one side of a double logic of the poetry film as a witness. Whether as a witness or as a victim, it is impossible not to be affected by acts of war. Still, as a witness and victim it is necessary to establish a distance from what one sees and hears, perhaps as a survival strategy, to bear what one has seen and experienced and to bring these forward. In this sense, the untouched and mechanical voice of Silkeberg as she reads, reflects a necessary position for the speaking subject to take. It is a way of surviving, of being able to be a witness and of being able to talk about what one sees or imagines through the other's memory. Likewise, the sound of breathing is a vehicle of continuity in the film, as it appears almost throughout the whole film. It is stable and controlled and indicates that it comes from a body that is in control, despite what he sees and remembers. The breathing is detached both from the action of running and the content of the poem. As with Silkeberg's reading, the breathing does not change in character throughout the film. Rather, it can be perceived as a mechanically and physically-emotionally disconnected event. The running or the fast walking in the touristic area of Stockholm or among dead bodies in Damascus or lines like "Now the killing will start" do not affect the body that breathes or the body that reads.

"[A]n experience of violence. An insight into it. To bear the memory of it," it says in Silkeberg's poem. This insight requires the other's survival and experience. Likewise, in order to present this experience and insight as not one's own but as belonging to the other, she needs to maintain a distant voice and to lend her voice to these experiences and insights without engaging herself emotionally. In this way, she avoids turning the poem and the poetry reading in the film into her own experience of and insight into the other's experience and insight.

Poetry film in the computational network environment

Your Memory Is My Freedom is a digital poetry film, distributed on YouTube, among other channels. The social media platform functions primarily as a distribution channel. The viewers' opportunities to comment on and discuss the film have been turned off and the number of likes, dislikes and sharing are not available. The available paratextual information tells us that the video was uploaded on 1 September 2015, that is, approximately three years after it was produced, and that it had 265 views before the registration for number of views was turned off or stopped working. This implies that the poets and the poetry film make little use of the opportunities that the platform provides for interaction and sharing. Some of the media technological features for social media, among others defined by José van Dijck and Thomas Poell (2013), are nevertheless operational (see Chapter 5). The algorithms and network organization can still affect the distribution of the poetry film. It is still possible for viewers to like, possibly dislike, as well as to share the poetry film via other platforms. This means that the number of viewers who have made use of one or more of these features is available to programmers and algorithms and that popularity can be measured, even if this information is not available to the average viewer.

The fact that some of YouTube's default settings have been turned off, may in itself be a display of activism. If these are choices made by Almadhoun and Silkeberg, it implies that the two poets do not want the poetry film to be part of a like economy controlled by social media. It suggests that they want the poetry film to be distributed, seen and discussed on the premises of poetry and poetry film. It may also be that the field for commenting is made unavailable due to unwanted comments. A consequence of this is, for whatever reason, that the opportunity for discussions on the theme of the poetry film and the opportunity to continue a conversation about war, oppression and exile on the platform have not been realized.

In addition to the platform with its facilities, network organization and algorithms provide some opportunities for political and activist poetry films like *Your Memory Is My Freedom*. These features remind us that a literary text rarely makes political changes by itself. Rather, it gains its power and effectiveness in a media ecology with other texts, other bodies and other media. Poetic-political activism is thus a collaboration between (re)medializations and (re)materializations. This necessity of collaborations to gain a political effect can for some works become even clearer in the digital culture. Poetry film is multimedia, intermedial social media poetry, and in the digital environment in which it and other digital poetry films are inserted, their power to make changes is also determined by the media's network organization and distribution capabilities.

Poetry film and its aesthetic practice in the computational network environment emphasize that there is no competition between the various medializations and materializations, in this case the poetry film produced in 2012 and the poem published in 2014. Rather, they are part of and exploit some of the opportunities that lie in digital culture. They do so in order to reach out in a poetic language that explores the experience of war and exile. Here we find an attempt to touch readers and viewers on a social media platform. The poetry film thus demonstrates Bolter and Grusin's claim that rather than competition, remediations help to make a medium, a genre, a theme and a poetic language accessible to more and more senses (Bolter and Grusin 1999, 68). *Your Memory Is My Freedom* it not a total work of art but rather a poetry film that exists simultaneously with, sometimes independent of and other times in collaboration with, the print poems in *Till Damaskus* and poetry readings from the section "Your Memory Is My Freedom."

Chapter 9
Between Idea and Media: A Note on Some Preconditions for the Making of Poetry in the Computational Network Environment

There are numerous suggestions for how to grasp the contemporary situation of poetry (and literature and the arts). These attempts to conceptualize the present time not only emphasize the intervention of digital media in most parts of our everyday life, they also highlight some aspects of the cultural and aesthetic epoch sometimes referred to as post-postmodernism. More than two decades ago, Linda Hutcheon claimed that the postmodern era had passed. She encouraged, perhaps as an ironic gesture, researchers to come up with alternatives to what the post-postmodern era should be termed and described as: "Post-postmodernism needs a new label of its own, and I conclude, therefore, with this challenge to readers to find it – and name it for the twenty-first century." (Hutcheon 2002, 181) The proposals are by now many. Some draw attention to aesthetic-cultural peculiarities such as hypermodernism (Lipovetsky 2005), automodernism (Samuels 2008), altermodernism (Bourriaud 2009) and metamodernism (Vermeulen and van den Akker 2010). Others have more specifically linked the period to the dominant role digital media play in how we write, read, think and behave. These include Hayles' "computational regime" (Hayles 2006), Allan Kirby's "digimodernism" and Hansen's "computational networks" (Hansen 2015). My contribution to this list is "computational network environment."

In this book, I have presented, analyzed and discussed a selection of contemporary Scandinavian poetry in the computational network environment. I have done so in order to reflect upon some of the medial premises for contemporary poetry in digital media. More broadly, I have also been interested in questions regarding reading, writing and thinking in the age of the digital. Implicit in my explorative method is an interest in both the preconditions for poetry in an environment dominated by programmable and network media and the possibilities and limitations of this environment. Although there are several outcomes of this study, such as the analysis of the works I have discussed, I will use this concluding chapter to highlight two important findings in particular. Firstly, I have argued in favor of the importance of perceiving the situation of contemporary poetry as one in which poetry is embedded in a media environment. Moreover, I have suggested that this environment is a computational network environment. Secondly, I have argued for the necessity of closely reading poetry in programmable and network media, demonstrating its benefits, and, based on this, suggested contributions made by the poets and poems in question. With regard to the question of method, I have followed in the path of such scholars as Roberto Simanowski in *Digital Art and Meaning* (2011) and N. Katherine Hayles and Jessica Pressman in *Comparative Textual Media* (2013), in addition to the work conducted in *Analyzing Digital Fiction* (2014). One significant difference vis-à-vis these earlier studies is that I direct my attention solely to poetry. By focusing on poetry, the method of close reading appears specific to the art form and the respective media under consideration. This method proves to be well suited to the computational network environment, helping us to grasp the medial situation of poetry without losing sight of the poems in question and these poems as poetry.

Medialized future, present and past

The material of contemporary Scandinavian poetry that I have analyzed is diverse. It contains both digitally born and digitalized poetry that is part of a media ecology in the computational and network environment. This environment makes the distinction between digital and digitalized less relevant, if relevant at all, and represents medializations that engage the respective works in conversation with some of the tendencies in contemporary theories of arts and media.

In Chapters 3 and 4, I explored two works, one by Johannes Heldén and Håkan Jonson and one by Heldén, in which digital parts are intimately linked in their formation to their respective platforms. These platforms' structure and interface are unique to the works. This is interesting for at least two reasons. First, we can assume that the platforms are part of the poet's or poets' aesthetic practice in creating poetry. The platforms are, so to speak, internalized in the works themselves and are part of the poetics of the works. Obviously, poetry in digital media needs a platform to be materialized and to be experienced by readers, but in *Evolution* and *Astroecology*, these two works are part of an intimate collaboration between poets, the materiality of language and media and digital technology. This collaboration takes place between human and non-human subjects and continues through the entire aesthetic process that precedes and follows other parts of the ecological work. In this ecology, it is a potentially never ending or unfinished process. Secondly, by studying the platform and programming language of the two works, one can identify aesthetic and communicative characteristics that can be linked more specifically to the poets' style, their way of writing, drawing, composing, taking photographs, designing, programming, creating intentions and moods and engaging readers. For the kind of poetry that *Evolution* and *Astroecology* represent, the platform, its design and interface can establish connections to other individual texts by Heldén and Jonson.

Another common feature of these two chapters is that they both explore one or more possible and probable "near" future(s). In this sense, the chapters not only draw attention to representations of possible futures but more specifically to the significance of media and the processes of medialization that are at stake in the performances. "Mediated futures" is a term that is also relevant for other works referred to in this book. Possible mediated futures are, for instance, staged in Ann Lislegaard's *Crystal World* (2006), a work that, at least in terms of this concept, shares certain similarities with Heldén's *Astroecology* (2016). Moreover, "mediated futures" is a trend that is not unique to poetry in digital media but which can also be found in contemporary art, literature and film. Jussi Parikka engages in the question of possible future(s) in the article "Planetary Goodbyes: Post-History and Future Memories of an Ecological Past" (2015) and asks what kind of future and memories contemporary art is able to produce (Parikka 2015, 130). There may be several reasons why such an aesthetic has appeared in contemporary literature and art, including as reflections on the end of history (Fukuyama 1989/1992), utopian pragmatism (Ingels 2013), our time as a planetary time (Moraru and Elias 2015), interrupted future prospects (Stiegler 2020) or our awareness of the Anthropocene. This last point implies that human interventions on Earth are irrefutable, that actions performed by humankind have made the Earth and, hence humans, vulnerable and that the present time bears traces of a future without humans, as is suggested by Roy Scranton in *Learning to Die in the Anthropocene* (2015). Additionally, I would point out that the media situation for contemporary poetry, the computational network environment with collaborations between human and non-human subjects, or our awareness of these collaborations all open up new ways of reflecting not only upon our past and present but also upon our (lost or found) possible futures.

Both Heldén and Jonson's *Evolution* (Chapter 3) and Heldén's *Astroecology* (Chapter 4) thematize artificial intelligence. In so doing, they show how computers might create poetry and hence replace the poet (in this case Heldén), fieldwork and observations otherwise made by humans. Obviously, this media situation that they refer to, is contemporary, but because the development does not stop here, there is also a possibility, either utopian or dystopian, that is recognized on the horizon. Heldén's *Astroecology* is a work that can be read as a response to or as a continuation of work by Scranton and others. Here, Heldén uses poetry as a way of thinking and imagining our present time and our future in an environment that is driven by evolutionary forces, wherein past, present and future are interconnected. *Astroecology* demonstrates a particular ecological mode of thinking and imagination and medializes a future in the Anthropocene. Moreover, it shows what kind of future and what memories of a past and future poetry can create.

In Chapters 5 and 6, I turned my attention to poetry in social media. Again, the poems that are discussed vary in form and expression, and they represent different genres and practices in social media. Chapter 5 focuses on Instagram poetry. Here, the analyses and discussions show how poets to a great extent, intentionally or not, accept the preconditions given by the logic of social media. Therefore, my analyses offer new insights and enhance new dimensions of the relationship between poetry and social media platforms. In this way, the chapter argues that platforms dictate or encourage certain types of poems, poetic styles and ways of writing. Instagram poetry is platform poetry, one wherein the platform is fixed, serving as a vehicle for the distribution of poetry, connecting people to people and people to algorithms. The platform and the given technical medium, most often a smart phone or tablet, set the conditions for responses to the poems, for how poets write and for when they publish their poems. As I have argued, Instagram poetry is typically occasional poetry and is often oriented towards a present now.

Rather than creating a sensory environment for the experience of a future, as is the case with *Evolution* and *Astroecology*, Instagram poetry, with its orientation towards a now, medializes the experience of a present. The poems contribute to a sense of a now in which presence is intensified. This presence is made possible by the platform technology and its culture and has come to replace a physical absence. This aspect is not only specific to Instagram. As Jérôme Bourdon (2019) claims, it is often the case for social media in general. This now is experienced and shared by many, because of network media, leading Jacob Lund to describe this experience as one of simultaneity (Lund 2016, 110; see also Chapter 7). For this reason, it is fair to say that Instagram poetry is made for the moment, not for the future. Generally, it is difficult to imagine how Instagram poetry could be canonized, unless the poems – as many of them indeed do – travel from digital to print, from Instagram to books.

Likewise, the poems that I analyze in Chapter 6 are medializations of a contemporary, subjective and collective experience expressed through a poetic language. Still, poetry on Facebook, which is the material analyzed in this chapter, is not a genre. The platform seems to be more of a tool for distributing poetry and a medium for testing unfinished poems. Where social media logics like programmability, connectivity, popularity and datafication comprise a framework for Instagram poetry, these social media logics seem less significant for the understanding of poetry on Facebook, the goal of which seems to be to preprint-publish poetry, at least for the material I have analyzed. Of course, if a poem does not receive many likes, it might be that the poet chooses not to publish it in print. Nevertheless, the value of responses from readers (expressed in likes, comments and sharing) – at least in the case of Nils-Øivind Haagensen's practice – are not part of a financial economy but are concerned with the function and quality of the poems as print poems. These poems, in contrast to Instagram poetry, are not in any particular way media- or platform-specific. Overall, it is not obvious to what extent the logic of Facebook affects the conditions and rules of social interaction. It is also not clear that this logic informs the way the poet writes, except insofar as the poems that are published on Facebook are typically revised to a greater or lesser degree before being printed in a collection of poetry.

The perspective taken in this chapter denotes a counter-chronology from medialized futures to medialized presents, potentially suggesting a time reversibility that ends in a medialized past. Chapters 7 and 8 do not deal with the past in this sense but engage in two poetic practices that represent remediations in the network environment: digital poetry reading and digital poetry film. Remediation is to be understood here neither as an inverted process, nor as a concept that underlines a linear change of poetry. Rather, it is applied as a perspective that allows us to explore how two poetic practices and genres, developed in other media and for other situations, appear in digital media. It is a dynamic interaction of imitation and intensification in which digital poetry reading and digital poetry film are informed both by old and new practices and genres. The analyses in chapters 7 and 8 show how digital poetry reading and digital poetry film can be approached in terms of a continuum between a "traditional" approach based on imitation and one that is "innovative" or "adaptable" and, therefore, emphasizing intensification.

Some poetry readings are easily adapted to their new media situation, while others have evolved and changed the media, genres and practices from which they have unfolded. Some are distributed on already-existing platforms, while others are elaborated in accordance with the production of a specific platform. Some are distributed for the present moment, while others are archived for the future. One might argue that the play between imitation and intensification is easier to identify in digital poetry reading than in digital poetry film. By and large, digital poetry film tends to utilize the affordances of digital technology to develop the art form less than digital poetry reading. For instance, poetry films on YouTube might be intermediations of certain poems and of a poetry film in analog media, but the computational and network environment in which the films are produced, distributed and viewed, does not, in any significant way, interfere with the development of the art form in a strict sense.[1] Still, it is important to notice that digital media have indeed left their marks on poetry film. Techniques like layering are easier to implement with digital technology. Further, digital

---

[1] Here it is important to recall my discussion about poetry film from Chapter 8 and the discussion of similarities and differences between media art and poetry in digital media in Chapter 1.

poetry film is based on codes and, for this reason, can easily travel between media platforms. The history of poetry film implies that the art form has always developed by exploiting media affordances and combining them with features of poetry like voicing, rhythm, syntactic sequence, movements through time, rhyme, meter and enjambment.

The variety of poetry readings in digital media implies that poetry readings more than ever are available for a vast number of listeners. These readings are available (in the so called Western world) in almost any situation that a listener might be in. This simple observation underlines claims that poetry is more often heard than seen nowadays (Middleton 2005, 7; Mønster, Rustad and Schmidt 2022, 9). Similarly, the contemporary media situation has provided digital poetry film with new possibilities, because it is more available than ever before and can be watched on demand. Still, even though the distribution situation in the contemporary network environment provides new possibilities for both poetry reading and poetry film as well as their political potential, the situation also highlights how vulnerable the accessibility of poetry in digital media might be. This does not only relate to the two practices and genres in question but for poetry in digital media more generally. Distribution and availability of poetry depend on the existence of platforms, on private, public and semi-public archives and on initiatives taken with the purpose to restore and preserve poetry in formats that rest on a certain hardware and software. The situation of poetry in digital media is also one in which, if deprived of adequate platforms, archives and initiatives for restoring and preserving poetry, this poetry will no longer be available, seen or heard (see Chapter 7).

Digital media as inspiration

The questions I posed at the beginning of Chapter 1 concerned the situation of poetry in the digital age. Over the course of this book, these questions have been narrowed down to a consideration of the impact of the computational network environment on poetry. This involves, for instance, how poetry is an event, how poetry can be regarded as unfinished, how poetry relates to preconditions identified in and made by media and how poetry is part of an environment that often involves collaborations between poets, programmers and computers. Some of these aspects are new or different with digital media. Many of these aspects, though, are not new or different but are rather intensified by the computational network environment. In short, this shows that digital media inspire and are co-creators of poetry. As discussed in Chapter 2, this claim is consistent with the theoretical position of this book and with arguments put forward by such scholars as

N. Katherine Hayles and Bernard Stiegler. The challenge for poetry research, as I see it, is how this interaction between human and non-human can be inscribed in the understanding of poetry and the making of poetry in order to recognize mutuality, reciprocity and the cessation of binaries like subject-object, dominator-dominanted.

Research into literature in digital media often presents media technologies as important sources of inspiration and motivation for the development of literary texts. Scott Rettberg, among others, claims that digital media, more than merely being a tool for production and distribution, also inspires the authors. In his book *Electronic Literature* (2019), Rettberg writes that authors are "energized by the potentialities of the networked computer as a medium." (Rettberg 2019) Similarly, Bronwen Thomas in *Literature and Social Media* (2020) rejects any assumptions that there should be a contradiction between social media and literature and claims that encounters between the two can be fruitful and lead to innovative literary works. Both Rettberg and Thomas argue that digital media technology can be a driving force for the development of new forms of literature. Embedded in such a notion is the idea that authors explore new technologies to discover the opportunities that these technologies offer literature. Hence, both Rettberg and Thomas emphasize the importance of programmable and network media for the creative process. While it is difficult to disagree with this view, it is not obvious what it implies that media can inspire the creation of literary and poetic texts, during which stage in the process this inspiration occurs or how we can understand the relationship between a poetic idea and media technology.

In the contemporary network environment, the making of poetry has to be considered in relation to the role of the media as both environment and situation. This position implies that the artistic idea and the creative process are always intertwined with other materialized ideas and media. Here, the freedom to create is not considered from the outside, as an a priori quality, but rather freedom and creativity are always situated and negotiated. This is a freedom, we might say, that is an emancipation from media regarded as tools or as deterministic, as being solely objects or subjects for each other, and toward media as part of the creative subjectivity at work.

In *The Poet's Freedom: A Notebook on Making* (2011), Susan Stewart distinguishes between negative and positive freedom. Negative freedom refers to a freedom where the artist tries to move away from boundaries, limitations and other structures that control the creative process and the making of art. Such limitations can be art and genre conventions, or they can involve material and medial affordances, even though Stewart herself does not engage the question of media. In opposition to this, Stewart defines a positive freedom in which the artist approaches restrictions, not only in order to embrace them but, most importantly, to avoid being defined by these restrictions, in terms of the artist's creative process and work. Stewart writes that positive freedom involves an act of affirmation (Stewart 2011, 6). Following Kant's notion of freedom as the only fact that bridges posteriori and a priori knowledge, that is, the knowledge we gain of the world through experience and knowledge made by reason – knowledge acquired regardless of our experience – Stewart elaborates on positive freedom as performed, constituted in the poet's action in and towards the world: "[F]reedom is exercised or played upon the world rather than wrested from it." (Stewart 2011, 6) Rather than to read this statement as a claim that one is free or independent of space, time and causality, it implies that positive freedom is freedom performed through these "limitations." This is, as Dan Ringgaard (2020b) writes, a way of thinking of creativity where the poet seems to be in control and have agency in the process of creation.

To Stewart's elaboration of the poet's freedom to make, one should also add the dimension of media as an active subject in the creative process. From this perspective, negative freedom would imply the poet's attempt to break free from the determining processes of media, that is, to overcome restrictions defined by media. Following Stewart's reflections, these attempts would only end in a situation in which media defines poetry and thus the poet's freedom. In the computational network environment, we might imagine that the poet will not let herself be restricted, because her writing, reading and thinking are also always writing, reading and thinking in media environments. She always already performs her freedom of making in this environment. To some extent, the conception of positive freedom applies well to this environment. Still, Stewart's reflections on the artistic freedom to create takes on a humanistic perspective, one in which the artist, through the idea of positive freedom, is placed at the center of the creative event. As should be clear by now, with regard to the computational network environment, poets think and work with and through programmable and network media. Hence, a positive freedom in this sense is a freedom not from thinking about media restrictions but a freedom located in the environments constituted by the poet and computational machines, poetry and media.

With regard to the making of poetry in the computational network environment, the idea of media as an environment implies that a binary thinking of negative and positive is dissolved. The romantic notion of a non-material poetic idea is replaced by the notion that information, ideas, experiences, sensations, subjectivity, etc., are always embodied and medialized. This implies that in the (liberal) humanities, one would assume that a poet possesses certain qualities; the poet is an autonomous individual who is essentially the proprietor of her own capacity to create (see e.g. Hayles 1999b). This too is a freedom to create because one is in possession of certain qualities or talents. This is a talent for poetry, for exploring and discovering the materiality of language, for making images and music, but it is also a talent for programmable and network media and an ability to see the potential for poetry in the encounter between computers and words, images and music. In the computational network environment, and in posthuman thinking more generally, poetic and aesthetic properties are not regarded exclusively as the poet's. Rather, they derive from a network of actors directly and indirectly, explicitly and implicitly involved in the creative process. Similarly, the freedom of making is a freedom that springs from this network as a consequence both of the poet's talent and the qualities of the network, which are both constituted by and constitute the poet and the poetry.

The computational network environment is both a human and non-human environment in which the role of digital media for poetry varies. Poetry and digital technology can collaborate to create an environment in which the creative process that presents poetry on the screen is partly run by algorithms and where the poet appears (partly) as a technological subject (see Chapters 3 and 4). Further, social media as environment gives way to the testing and distribution of poetic texts at the same time as social media appears as a new sensory and social world for poetry (see Chapters 5, 6 and 8). Similarly, digital remediations and intermediations of forms of poetry demonstrate how particular artistic arrangements are inscribed in the computational network environment. While imitating some features of poetic forms and genres, developed in non-digital media, a practice of imitation that is crucial for recognizing the remediated forms as remediations, the new environment provides these remediated forms with new functions, intensifying them as digital artistic arrangements in the computational network environment (see Chapters 7 and 8).

In short, in this environment, creativity in writing, reading and thinking are both human and non-human activities. Therefore, digital media technology must be regarded as a creative agent in collaboration with a poet or poets. In this respect, Stiegler's notion of a co-evolution of the human and technology and Hayles' concept of contemporary technogenesis and the posthuman comprise a philosophical rationale for the understanding of contemporary poetry and its media situation. Here, creativity is performed and experienced as a collaboration of human and non-human agents, underlining how, in the media environment, the freedom of poets' is not a freedom from medial constraints or a freedom to overcome restrictions made by media but a freedom that is always situated in a contemporary media environment. For this reason, the freedom of making is not a concept that can be measured against negativity and positivity, an attempt to escape or embrace media affordances, because creativity and the freedom to make poetry are always already embedded in the media environment. To the extent that we can consider such a concept as freedom, it is a freedom conditioned by an environment that is more than human. It is an environment of posthuman and technological subjectivity – a subjectivity, moreover, located in deep rationality with computational and networked media. Consciously or subconsciously, such media are the poet's fellow non-human agents.

Work Cited

Aarseth, Espen. *Cybertext. Perspective on Ergodic Literature*. Baltimore: Johns Hopkins University Press, 1997.
Agamben, Giorgio. *The End of the Poem*. Stanford: Stanford University Press, 1999.
Agamben, Giorgio. *The Open: Man and Animal*. Stanford: Stanford University Press, 2002.
Almadhoun, Ghayath and Marie Silkeberg. *Destruction III. Warzshava Osviecim*. https://www.youtube.com/watch?v=KXIMmBT_8Y0, 2008 (13 January 2017).
Almadhoun, Ghayath and Marie Silkeberg. *Ödelägelse IV Stockholm | Gaza*. https://www.youtube.com/watch?v=L11ubnRGOPw, 2009 (23 September 2022).
Almadhoun, Ghayath and Marie Silkeberg. *The City*. https://www.youtube.com/watch?v=w8ZoxPv2W3I, 2012 (23 September 2022).
Almadhoun, Ghayath and Marie Silkeberg. *Your Memory is My Freedom*. https://www.youtube.com/watch?v=d6RKa4JcxYI, 2012 (23 September 2022).
Almadhoun, Ghayath and Marie Silkeberg. *The Celebration*. https://www.youtube.com/watch?v=QLm_MyOSj1A, 2014 (23 September 2022).
Almadhoun, Ghayath and Marie Silkeberg. *Till Damaskus*. Stockholm: Albert Bonniers Förlag, 2014.
Almadhoun, Ghayath and Marie Silkeberg. *Snow*. https://www.youtube.com/watch?v=vnfPLnExwBw, 2015 (23 September 2022).
Anker, Elizabeth S. and Rita Felski. *Critique and Postcritique*. Durham: Duke University Press, 2017.
Arendt, Hannah. *On Revolution*. London: Penguin Books, 1990.
Aristotle. *Aristotle's Politics*. Book 1, section 4. Grinnell: Peripatetic Press, 1986.
Attridge, Derek. *The Experience of Poetry. From Homer's Listener to Shakespeare's Readers*. Oxford: Oxford University Press, 2019.
Azzam, Fuad. "The Poetics of Facebook Poem." http://www.psp-ltd.com/JIEB_72_7_2019.pdf. *Journal of International Education in Business* 7 (2019).
Backman, Frida. "Kris, Kritik, Teori. Postkritik och den nya offentligheten." *Norsk litteraturvitenskapelig tidsskrift* 2 (2020): 87–99.
Bajohr, Hannes (ed.). *Code und Konzept. Literatur und das Digitale*. Berlin: Frohmann, 2015.
Balpe, Jean-Pierre. "Principles and Processes of Generative Literature. Questions of Literature." http://www.dichtung-digital.de/2005/1/Balpe/. *Dichtung Digital* 1 (2005).
Barthes, Roland. *S/Z. An Essay*. London: Farrar, Straus and Giroux, 1974.
Beck, Ulrich. *Risk Society. Towards a New Modernity*. London: Sage, 1992.
Bell, Alice, Astrid Ensslin and Hans Kristian S. Rustad. *Analyzing Digital Fiction*. New York: Routledge, 2014.
Benthien, Claudia, Jordis Lau and Maraike M. Marxsen. *The Literariness of Media Art*. New York: Routledge, 2018.
Benthien, Claudia. "Poetry in the Digital Age." https://lyricology.org/poetry-in-the-digital-age/. *Lyricology. A Reader* 1.1 (2019).
Benthien, Claudia and Norbert Gestring. *Public Poetry. Lyrik im urbanen Raum*. Berlin: De Gruyter, 2023.
Berens, Kathi Inman. "E-Lit's #1 Hit: Is Instagram Poetry E-literature?" https://electronicbookreview.com/essay/e-lits-1-hit-is-instagram-poetry-e-literature/. *Electronic Book Review* (2019).
Bernstein, Charles. *Close Listening. Poetry and the Performed Word*. Oxford: Oxford University Press, 1998.

Bishop, Claire. "The Digital Divide: Contemporary Art and New Media." https://www.artforum.com/print/201207/digital-divide-contemporary-art-and-new-media-31944. *Art Forum* September (2012).

Björk. *Björk*. New York: MoMa, 2015.

Bolter, Jay D. *Writing Space: The Computer, Hypertext, and the History of Writing*. Hillsdale: Lawrence Erlbaum, 1991.

Bolter, Jay D. and Richard Grusin. *Remediation. Understanding New Media*. Cambridge: MIT Press, 1999.

Bootz, Philip. "From OULIPO to Transitorie Observable. The Evolution of French Digital poetry." https://mediarep.org/bitstream/handle/doc/18713/Dichtung-Digital_41_1-12_Bootz_OULIPO_Transitoire_Observable.pdf?sequence=1. *Dichtung Digital* 41 (2012).

Bourdon, Jérôme. "From Correspondence to Computers. A Theory of Mediated Presence in History." *Communication Theory* 30.1 (2019): 64–83.

Bourriaud, Nicolas. *Altermodern. Tate Triennal 2009*. London: Tate Publishing, 2009.

Bourriaud, Nicolas. *The Radicant*. Cambridge: MIT Press, 2009.

Bourriaud, Nicolas. *The Exform*. London: Verso, 2015.

Braidotti, Rosi. *The Posthuman*. Cambridge: Polity Press, 2013.

Breeze, Mez. *Attn. Solitude*. Victoria: Cordite Publishing, 2017.

Brison, Susan. "Trauma Narrative and the Remaking of the Self." *Acts of Memory. Cultural Recall in the Present*. Ed. Mieke Bal, Jonathan Crew, and Leo Spitzer. London: University Press of New England, 1999. 39–55.

Burdorf, Dieter. "The I and the Others. Articulations of Personality and Communication Structures in the Lyric." *Journal of Literary Theory* 11.1 (2017): 22–31.

Burges, Jean, Alice Marwick and Thomas Poell. "Editors' Introduction." *The SAGE Handbook of Social Media*. New York: Sage Publishing, 2018. 1–10.

Bush, Vannevar. "As We May Think." https://www.theatlantic.com/magazine/archive/1945/07/as-we-may-think/303881/. *The Atlantic* July (1945).

Carpenter, J.R. *The Gathering Cloud*. Axminster, Devon: Uniformbooks, 2017a.

Carpenter, J.R. *The Gathering Cloud*. http://luckysoap.com/thegatheringcloud/. 2017b (23 September 2022).

Carpenter, J.R. *This is a Picture of Wind*. https://luckysoap.com/apictureofwind/. 2017c (23 September 2022).

Carpenter, J.R. *This is a Picture of Wind*. https://longbarrowpress.com/films/this-is-a-picture-of-wind-short-films/, 2017d (23 September 2022).

Carpenter, J.R. *This is a Picture of Wind*. Sheffield: Longbarrow Press, 2020.

Clüver, Claus. "Ekphrasis Reconsidered. On Verbal Representation of Non-Verbal Texts." *Interart Poetics. Essays on the Interrelations of the Art and Media*. Ed. Ulla Britta Lagerroth, Hans Lund and Erik Hedling. Amsterdam: Rodopi, 1997.

Coover, Roderick and Scott Rettberg. *Toxi City: A Climate Change Narrative*, http://www.crchange.net/toxicity/. CRChange Production, 2017.

Cramer, Florian. "Digital Code and Literary Text." https://www.netzliteratur.net/cramer/digital_code_and_literary_text.html. *Dichtung Digital. Journal für Kunset und Kultur digitaler Medien* 20.3 (2001).

Cramer Florian. "What Is 'Post-digital'?" *Postdigital Aesthetics*. Ed. David M Berry and Michael Dieter. London: Palgrave Macmillan, 2015, 12–26.

Crepax, Rosa. "The Aestheticisation of Feminism: A Case Study of Feminist Instagram Aesthetics." *ZoneModa Journal* 10.1 (2020): 71–81.

Culler, Jonathan. *Theory of the Lyric*. New York: Cornell University Press, 2015.

Culler, Jonathan. *"Theory of the Lyric." Nordisk poesi. Tidsskrift for lyrikkforskning* 2.2 (2017): 119–133.
Daugaard, Solveig. *Collaborating with Gertrude Stein. Media Ecologies, Reception, Poetics*. Unpublished doctoral dissertation, Linköpings universitet, 2018.
Deleuze, Gilles and Felix Guattari. *A Thousand Plateaus. Capitalism and Schizophrenia*. Minneapolis: University of Minnesota Press, 1987.
Derrida, Jacques. *Specters of Marx. The State of the Debt, the Work of Mourning and the New International*. New York: Routledge, 2006.
Dijck, José van and Thomas Poell. "Understanding Social Media Logic." https://www.cogitatiopress.com/mediaandcommunication/article/view/70. *Media and Communication* 1.1 (2013).
Donnachie, Karen Ann and Andy Simionato. *The Library of Nonhuman Books*. Computer Art, 2019.
Douglas, Jane Y., "'How Do I Stop This Thing': Closure and Indeterminancy in Interactive Narratives". *Hyper/Text/Theory. Reading Hypertext*. Ed. George Landow. Baltimore: Johns Hopkins University Press, 1994. 150–188.
Douglas, Jane Y. *The End of Books – or Books Without End?* Michigan: University of Michigan Press, 2001.
Drucker, Johanna. "Sight." *Further Reading*. Ed. Matthew Rubery and Leah Price. Oxford: Oxford University Press, 2020. 167–178.
Eagleton, Terry. *How to Read a Poem*. Oxford: Blackwell Publishing, 2006.
Elias, Amy J. and Christian Morau. *The Planetary Turn. Relationality and Geoaesthetics in the Twenty-First Century*. Evanston: Northwestern University Press, 2015.
Ellefsen, Bernhard. "Ikke mobb kameraten min." https://www.morgenbladet.no/boker/2020/02/28/ikke-mobb-kameraten-min/. *Morgenbladet* (28 February 2020).
Elleström, Lars. "The Modalities of Media. A Model for Understanding Intermedial Relations." *Media Borders, Multimodality and Intermediality*. New York: Palgrave Macmillian, 2010. 11–48.
Eliot, T.S. *Ash Wednesday*. London: Faber and Faber, 1930.
Engberg, Marie. *Born Digital. Writing Poetry in the Age of New Media*. Unpublished doctoral dissertation, Uppsala universitet, 2007.
Engberg, Marie. "Chance Operations." *Evolution*. Johannes Heldén and Håkan Jonson. Stockholm: OEI, 2014.
Ensslin, Astrid. *Canonizing Hypertext*. London: Bloomsbury Publishing, 2006.
Ensslin, Astrid. *Literary Gaming*. Cambridge: MIT Press, 2014.
Ernst, Wolfgang. "Cultural Archive versus Technomathematical Storage." *The Archive in Motion. New Conceptions of the Archive in Contemporary Thought and New Media Practices*. Ed. Eivind Røssaak. Oslo: Novus Forlag, 2010. 53–76.
Fallo, Alexander. @alexanderfallo. *Instagram*, (26 September 2022).
Fallo, Alexander. *du fucker med hjertet mitt nå*. Oslo: Cappelen Damm, 2020.
Felski, Rita. "Introduction." *New Literary History* 45.2 (2014): v–xi.
Ferlinghetti, Lawrence. *San Francisco Poems*. San Francisco: City Lights Books, 2001.
Fischer-Lichte, Erika. *Ästhetik des Performativen*. Berlin: Suhrkamp, 2004.
Foer, Jonathan Safran. *Tree of Codes*. London: Visual Editions, 2010.
Forsché, Carolyn and Duncan Wu. *Poetry of Witness: The Tradition in English 1500–2001*. New York: W.W. Norton and Company, 2014.
Foucault, Michel. *The Order of Things. An Archeology of the Human Sciences*. New York: Routledge, 1970.
Foucault, Michel. *The Birth of Biopolitics*. New York: Palgrave Macmillan, 2010.
Fukuyama, Francis. "The End of History." *The National Interest* 16 (1989): 3–18.

Fuller, Matthew. *Media Ecologies. Materialist Energies in Art and Technoculture*. Cambridge: MIT Press, 2005.
Funkhouser, Chris. *Prehistoric Digital Poetry*. Tuscaloosa: The University of Alabama Press, 2007.
Funkhouser, Chris. *New Directions in Digital Poetry*. New York: Continuum, 2012.
Gerlitz, Carolin and Anne Helmond. "The Like Economy: Social Buttons and the Data-Intensive Web." *New Media and Society* 15.8 (2013): 1348–1365.
Glazier, Loss Pequeño. *Digital Poetics. The Making of E-Poetries*. Tuscaloosa: The University of Alabama Press, 2002.
Goody, Alex. *Technology, Literature, and Culture*. Cambridge: Polity, 2011.
Gramsci, Antonio. *Utvalgte tekster 1916–1926*. Oslo: Cappelen Damm Akademiske, 2019.
Grigar, Dene. "Challenges to Archiving and Documenting Born-Digital Literature. What Scholars, Archivists, and Librarians Need to Know." *Electronic Literature as Digital Humanities. Contexts, Forms, and Practices*. Ed. James O'Sullivan. New York: Bloomsbury Academics, 2021. 1–5.
Haagensen, Nils-Øivind. *God morgen og god natt*. Oslo: Cappelen, 2012.
Haagensen, Nils-Øivind. *Det uregjerlige*. Oslo: Cappelen, 2020.
Haagensen, Nils-Øivind. "Detnorskearbeiderpartidiktet." https://www.facebook.com/people/Nils-%C3%98ivind-Haagensen/624120737/. *Facebook*, 2019 (26 September 2022).
Halavais, Alexander. "National Boarders on the World Wide Web." *New Media & Society* 2.1 (2000): 7–28.
Hansen, Mark B. "New Media." *Critical Terms for Media Studies*. Ed. W.J.T. Mitchell and Mark. B. Hansen. Chicago: University of Chicago Press, 2010. 172–186.
Hansen, Mark B. "The Operational Present of Sensibility." *The Nordic Journal of Aesthetics* 47 (2015): 38–53.
Haraway, Donna. *Staying with the Trouble. Making Kin in the Chthulucene*. Durham: Duke University Press, 2016.
Harris, Anita. "Online Cultures and Future Girl Citizens." *Feminist Media: Participatory Spaces, Networks and Cultural Citizenship*. Ed. Elke Zobl and Ricarda Drüeke. Bielefeld: Transcript, 2012. 213–225.
Hassan, Yahya. *Yahya Hassan*. Copenhagen: Gyldendal, 2013.
Hayles, N. Katherine. *How We Became Posthuman*. Chicago: University of Chicago Press, 1999a.
Hayles, N. Katherine. "The Illusion of Autonomy and the Fact of Recursivity. Virtual Ecologies, Entertainment, and 'Infinite Jest.'" *New Literary History* 30.3 (1999b): 675–697.
Hayles, N. Katherine. *Writing Machine*. Cambridge: MIT Press, 2002.
Hayles, N. Katherine. "Print Is Flat, Code Is Deep: The Importance of Media-Specific Analysis." *Poetics Today* 25.1 (2004): 67–90.
Hayles, N. Katherine. *My Mother Was a Computer*. Chicago: The University of Chicago Press, 2005.
Hayles, N. Katherine. "The Time of *Digital Poetry*: From Object to Event." New Media Poetics: Contexts, Technotexts, and Theories. Ed. Adalaide Morris and Thomas Swiss. Cambridge: MIT Press, 2006. 181–206.
Hayles, N. Katherine. *"Electronic Literature: What is it?"* https://eliterature.org/pad/elp.html. The Electronic Literature Organization January 2, 2007 (31 March 2023).
Hayles, N. Katherine. *Electronic Literature. New Horizons for the Literary*. Notre Dame: University of Notre Dame Press, 2008.
Hayles, N. Katherine. "How We Read. Close, Hyper, Machine." *ADE Bulletin* 150 (2010): 62–79.
Hayles, N. Katherine. *How We Think. Digital Media and Contemporary Technogenesis*. Chicago: University of Chicago Press, 2012.
Hayles. N. Katherine. *Unthought. The Power of the Cognitive Unconscious*. Chicago: Chicago University Press, 2017.

Hayles. N. Katherine. "Literary Texts as Cognitive Assemblages: The Case of Electronic Literature." https://doi.org/10.7273/8p9a-7854. *Electronic Book Review* (2018).
Heffernan, James. *Museum of Words. The Poetics of Ekphrasis from Homer to Ashbery*. Chicago: Chicago University Press, 1993.
Hegel, G. W. F. *Aesthetics*, vol. 2. Oxford: Oxford University Press, 1975.
Heldén, Johannes. *Elect*. https://anthology.elmcip.net/works/valjarna.html. 2008 (17 May 2019).
Heldén, Johannes. *The Prime Directive*. http://www.afsnitp.dk/galleri/primardirektivet/. 2006 (26 September 2022).
Heldén, Johannes. *Entropy*. https://www.johanneshelden.com/, 2010 (9 April 2019).
Heldén, Johannes *The Fabric*.https://www.johanneshelden.com/, 2013 (9 April 2019).
Heldén, Johannes and Håkan Jonson. *Evolution*. http://www.textevolution.net/. 2014a (26 September 2022).
Heldén, Johannes and Håkan Jonson. *Evolution*. Stockholm: Albert Bonniers förlag, 2014b.
Heldén, Johannes. *Astroekologi*. https://www.astroecology.se/en.html. 2016a (26 September 2022).
Heldén, Johannes. *Astroekologi*. Stockholm: Albert Bonniers förlag, 2016b.
Heldén, Johannes. *New New Hampshire & Clouds*. Moss: H // O // F, 2017.
Hermansson, Gunilla and Jens Lohfert Jørgensen. *Exploring Nordic Cool in Literary History*. Baltimore: Johns Benjamins Publishing Company, 2020.
Heyward, Megan. *Of Day, Of Night*. Sydney: Eastgate Systems, 2002.
Hillis Miller, Joseph. *On Literature*. New York: Routledge, 2002.
Horace. *Ars Poetica / The Art of Poetry. An Epistle to the Pisos*. https://gutenberg.ord/ebooks9175. Project Gutenberg, 2005.
Hutcheon, Linda. *The Politics of Postmodernism*. London: Routledge, 2002.
Ieropoulos, Fil. "Poetry-Film & The Film Poem. Some Clarifications." https://5metrosdepoemas.com/index.php/poesia-y-cine/56-el-cine-en-las-artes/611-poetry-film-the-film-poem-some-clarifications. *British Artists' Film & Video Study Collection Archive*, 2019.
Ingels, Bjarke. *Yes is More. An Archicomic on Architectural Evolution*. Cologne: Taschen, 2013.
Ingvarsson, Jonas. *Towards a Digital Epistemology*. New York: Springer, 2021.
Jackson, Virginia. *Dickinson's Misery. A Theory of Lyric Reading*. New York: Princeton University Press, 2005.
Jackson, Virginia. "Who Reads Poetry?" *PMLA* 123.1 (2008): 181–187.
Jakobson, Roman. "Closing Statement: Linguistics and Poetics." *The Lyric Theory Reader: A Critical Anthology*. Ed. Virginia Jackson and Yopie Prins. Baltimore: Johns Hopkins University Press, 2014. 234–248.
Jameson, Fredric. *Postmodernism, or, the Cultural Logic of Late Capitalism*. Durham: Duke University Press, 1991.
Jameson, Fredric. "War and Representation." *PMLA* 124.5 (2009): 1532–1547.
Jenkins, Henry, Sam Ford and Joshua Green. *Spreadable Media. Creating Value and Meaning in a Networked Culture*. New York: New York University Press, 2013.
Jenkins, Henry. *Participatory Culture. Interviews*. Cambridge: Polity Press, 2019.
Jonson, Ben. *The Cambridge Edition of the Work of Ben Jonson*. Vol. 5. Cambridge: Cambridge University Press, 2012.
Joyce, Michael. *afternoon, a story*. Watertown: Eastgate systems, 1989.
Kaur, Rupi. *Milk and Honey*. Kansas City: Andrews McMeel Publishing, 2015.
Kennedy, David. *The Ekphrastic Encounter in Contemporary British Poetry*. London: Routledge, 2012.
Kirby, Alan. *Digimodernism. How New Technologies Dismantle the Postmodern and Reconfigure Our Culture*. New York: Continuum, 2009.

Kirby, Alan. "The Possibility of Cyber-Placelessness." *The Planetary Turn. Relationality and Geoaesthetics in the Twenty-First Century*. Ed. Amy J. Elias and Christian Moraru. Evanston: Northwestern University Press, 2015. 71–88.

Kirschenbaum, Matthew. "ELO and the Electric Light Orchestra: Lessons for Electronic Literature from Prog Rock." *MATLIT: Materialities in Literature* 6.2 (2018): 27–36.

Kittang, Atle and Asbjørn Aarseth. *Lyriske strukturer*. Oslo: Universitetsforlaget, 1968.

Kittler, Friedrich. *Grammophon, Film, Typewriter*. Berlin: Brinkmann & Bose, 1986.

Kittler, Friedrich. *Gramophone, Film, Typewriter*. Cambridge: Routledge, 1999.

Kjerkegaard, Stefan, and Dan Ringgaard. *Dialogues on Poetry. Mediatization and New Sensibilities*. Aalborg: Aalborg University Press, 2017.

Kjerkegaard, Stefan. *Den menneskelige plet. Medialiseringen af litteratursystemet*. Aarhus: Dansklærerforeningens forlag, 2017.

Konyves, Tom. *Videopoetry. A Manifesto*. https://issuu.com/tomkonyves/docs/manifesto_pdf, 2011.

Kovalik, Kate and Jen Scott Curwood. "#poetryisnotdead: Understanding Instagram Poetry within a Transliteracies Framework." *Literacy* 53.4 (2019): 185–195.

Khilnani, Shweta. "Moving Poetry. Affect and Aesthetic in Instapoetry." *Inhabiting Cyberspace in India*. Ed. Simi Malhotra, Kanika Sharma, and Sakshi Dogra. New York: Springer. 135–142.

Kolberg, Elizabeth. *The Sixth Extinction: An Unnatural History*. New York: Henry Holt Books, 2014.

Korecka, Magdalena. *Instagram Poetry as a Site of Empowerment: Advocating Equality, Anti-Racism, and Mental Health Awareness*. Unpublished master's thesis, Schwerpunkt Kultur- und Medienwissenschaft, Universität Wien, 2021.

Korecka, Magdalena. "Political Visibilities and Intentional Aesthetics in Social Media Poetry." *Lyrik und zeitgenössische Visuelle Kultur / Poetry and Contemporary Visual Culture*. Ed. Magdalena Korecka and Wiebke Vorrath. Berlin: De Gruyter, forthcoming.

Kvinnsland, Ranveig 2021. *'har du hört vad som har hänt i syrien?'. Om traumer, tilskuere og den andres smerte i Ghayath Almadhoun og Marie Silkebergs* Till Damaskus *(2014)*. Unpublished master's thesis, Scandinavian literature, Universitetet i Oslo, 2021.

Landow, George. *Hypertext: The Convergence of Contemporary Literary Theory and Technology*. Baltimore: Johns Hopkins University Press, 1992.

Landow, George P. *Hyper/text/theory*. Baltimore: Johns Hopkins University Press, 1994.

Larsen, Deena. *Marble Springs*. Watertown: Eastgate Systems, 1993.

Larsen, Peter Stein. *Poesiens ekspansioner. Om nordisk samtidsdiktning*. Copenhagen: Spring, 2016.

Larsen, Peter Stein. *Lyriske linjer. Fem tendenser i nyere litteratur*. Hellerup: Forlaget Spring, 2018.

Latour, Bruno. *Reassembling the Social. An Introduction to Actor-Network-Theory*. Oxford: Oxford University Press, 2007.

Latour, Bruno. *Down to Earth. Politics in the New Climatic Regime*. Cambridge: Policy Press, 2018.

Leaver, Tama, Tim Highfield, and Crystal Abidin. *Instagram. Visual Social Media Culture*. New Jersey: Wiley, 2020.

Lessing, Gotthold Ephraim. "Fra Laokoon, oder über die Grenzen der Malerei und Poesie." *Estetisk teori. En antologi*. Ed. Kjersti Bale and Arnfinn Bø-Rygg. Oslo: Universitetsforlaget, 2008.

Lewis, Jason Edward. *P.o.E.M.M.* https://www.poemm.net/. 2007–2013 (26 September 2022).

Liestøl Gunnar. "Wittgenstein, Genette, and the Reader's Narrative in Hypertext." *Hyper/text/theory*. Ed. George Landow. Baltimore: Johns Hopkins University Press, 1994. 87–120.

Lipovetsky, Gilles. *Hypermodern Times*. Cambridge: Polity Press, 2005.

Lislegaard, Ann. *Crystal World*. Copenhagen: SMK Forlag, 2006.

Longenbach, James. *The Art of the Poetic Line*. Saint Paul: Graywolf Press, 2007.

Lund, Jacob. "Samtidighedens æstetik. Teknik, tid og politik." *Agora* 33.1 (2016): 101–117.

Lunenfeld, Peter. "Unfinished Business." *The Digital Dialectic. New Essays on New Media*. Ed. Peter Lunenfeld. Cambridge: MIT Press, 1999. 6–23.
Mangen, Anne. *New Narrative Pleasures? A Cognitive-phenomenological Study of the Experience of Reading Digital Narrative Fictions*. Unpublished doctoral dissertation, NTNU, Trondheim, 2006.
Mangen, Anne, Bente Rigmor Walgermo and Kolbjørn Kallesten Brønnick. "Reading Linear Text on Paper versus Computer Screen. Effects of Reading Comprehension." *International Journal of Educational Research* 58 (2013): 61–68.
Manovich, Lev. *The Language of New Media*, Cambridge: MIT Press, 2001.
Marino, Marc. *Critical Code Studies*. Cambridge: MIT Press, 2020.
Sans soleil. Chris Marker. Narr. Florence Delay. Argos Films, 1983.
Matthews, Kristin L. "'Woke' and Reading: Social media, Reception, and Contemporary Black Feminism." *Journal of Audience and Reception Studies* 16.1 (2019): 390–411.
Matter, Marc. "The Experimental Media Alchemy of E.E. Vonna-Michell and Balsam Flex." https://janmot.com/files/janmot-130.pdf. *Newspaper Jan Mot* 26.130 (2022).
McLuhan, Marshall. *The Gutenberg Galaxy. The Making of Typografic Man*. Toronto: University of Toronto Press, 1962.
McLuhan, Marshal. *Understanding Media. The Extensions of Man*. Toronto: McGraw-Hill, 1964.
Mitchell, W.J.T. *The Pictorial Turn*. New York: Routledge, 1992.
Mitchell, W.J.T. and Mark B. Hansen. *Critical Terms for Media Studies*. Chicago: University of Chicago Press, 2010.
Middleton, Peter. *Distant Reading: Performance, Readership, and Consumption in Contemporary Poetry*. Tuscaloosa: University of Alabama Press, 2005.
Moi, Torill. *Revolution of the Ordinary. Literary Studies After Wittgenstein, Austin, and Cavell*. Chicago: University of Chicago Press, 2017.
Montero, David. "Film also Ages. Time and Images in Chris Marker's *Sans soleil*." *Studies in French Cinema* 6.2 (2006): 107–115.
Montfort, Nick and Ian Bogost. *Racing the Beam. The Atari Video Computer System*. Cambridge: MIT Press, 2020.
Montfort, Nick. "A Web Reply to the Post-Web Generation." https://nickm.com/post/2018/08/a-web-reply-to-the-post-web-generation/. *Post Position* (2018).
Moravic, Hans. *Mind Children. The Future of Robot and Human Intelligence*. Harvard: Harvard University Press, 1990.
Morton, Timothy. *The Ecological Thought*. Cambridge: Harvard University Press, 2010.
Mose, Gitte. Johannes Heldéns *Astroekologi*. Et mesh af konstellationer og mellemrum." *Tidsskrift för litteraturvetenskap* 50.1 (2020): 51–59.
Mossner, Alexa Weik von. *Affective Ecologies: Empathy, Emotion, and Environmental Narrative*. Columbus: Ohio State University Press, 2017.
Moulthrop, Stuart. *Victory Garden*. Watertown: Eastgate Systems, 1995.
Müller, Ralph and Henrieke Stahl. "Contemporary Lyric Poetry in Transitions between Genres and Media." *Internationale Zeitschrift für Kulturkomparastik* 2 (2021): 5–24.
Mønster, Louise. *Ny nordisk*. Aalborg: Aalborg universitetsforlag, 2016.
Mønster, Louise. "Det politiskes genkomst i dansk samtidslyrik." *Edda. Nordisk tidsskrift for litteraturforskning* 106.2 (2019): 142–157.
Mønster, Louise, Hans Kristian S. Rustad and Michael Kallesøe Schmidt. *Digtoplæsning. Former og Fællesskaber*. Bergen: Fagbokforlaget, 2022.
Nachtergael, Magali. *Poet against the Machine: Une Histoire Technopolitique de la Littérature*. Marseille: Mot et le reste, 2020.

Naji, Janeen. *Digital poetry*. Chem: Palgrave Macmillian, 2021.
Nelson, Jason. "Poetic Playlands. Poetry, Interface, and Video Game Engines." *Electronic Literature as Digital Humanities: Contexts, Forms, and Practices*. Ed. James O'Sullivan. New York: Bloomsbury Academic, 2021. 335–350.
Nelson, Theodor Holm. "Complex Information Processing: A File Structure for the Complex, the Changing, and the Indeterminate." *Proceedings from ACM National Conference*. Cleveland: Association for Computing Machinery, 1965, 84–100.
Noordegraaf, Julia. "Introduction." *Preserving and Exhibiting Media Art. Challenges and Perspectives*. Ed. Julia Noordegraad et al. Amsterdam: Amsterdam University Press, 2013. 11–20.
Novak, Julia. *Live Poetry. An Integrated Approach to Poetry in Performance*. Vienna: Brill, 2011.
Nykvist, Karin. "Creative Destruction in Multilingual Sound Poetry. The Case of Eiríkur Örn Norðdahl." *Canadian Review of Comparative Literature* 47 (2020): 514–532.
Orphal, Stefanie. *Poesiefilm. Lyrik im audiovisuellen Medium*. Berlin: De Gruyter, 2014.
Otto, Fabian. *Erich Kästners Konzept von Gebrauchslyrik*. Magisterarbeit. Universität Koblenz-Landau, 2003.
Pâquet, Lili. "Selfie-Help: The Multimodal Appeal of Instagram Poetry." *Journal of Popular Culture* 52.2 (2019): 296–314.
Parikka, Jussi. "Planetary Goodbyes: Post-History and Future Memories of an Ecological Past." *Memory in Motion. Archives, Techology and the Social*. Ed. Ina Blom, Trond Lundemo and Eivind Røssaak. Amsterdam: Amsterdam University Press, 2016. 129–152.
Pedersen, Frode H. "Kvinne, redd meg." *Morgenbladet* (31 Januar 2020a).
Pedersen, Frode H. "Instapoesi er ikke uten videre poesi". *Bokvennen litterære avis* 24 Februar 2020b.
Penke, Niels. "#instapoetry. Populäre Lyrik auf Instagram und ihre Affordanzen." *Zeitschrift für Literaturwissenschaft und Linguistik* 49.3 (2019): 451–475.
Pressman, Jessica and N. Katherine Hayles. *Comparative Textual Media. Transforming the Humanities in the Post Era*. Minneapolis: University of Minnesota Press, 2013.
Pressman, Jessica. *Digital Modernism. Making It New in New Media*. Oxford: Oxford University Press, 2014.
Proust, Marcel. *À la recherché du temps perdu*. https://openlibrary.org/books/OL33198615M/A_la_re cherche_du_temps_perdu. Paris: University of Toronto Libraries, 1919.
Prytz, Øyvind. *Litteratur i digitale omgivelser*. Bergen: Fagbokforlaget, 2015.
Queneau, Raymond. *Cent mille milliards de poèmes*. Paris: Gallimard, 1961.
Rajewsky, Irina O. "Intermediality, Intertextuality, and Remediation. A Literary Perspective on Intermediality." *Intermédialités: histoire et théorie des arts, des lettres et des techniques / Intermediality: History and Theory of the Arts, Literature and Technologies* 6 (2005): 43–64.
Rancière, Jacques. "What Medium Can Mean." *Parrhesia* 11 (2011): 35–43.
Rettberg, Scott. "Communitizing Electronic Literature." http://www.digitalhumanities.org/dhq/vol/3/2/000046/000046.html. *Digital Humanities Quarterly* 3.2 (2009).
Rettberg, Scott. *Electronic Literature*. Cambridge: Polity Press, 2019.
Ringgaard, Dan. *Årsværk. En kritikers dagbog*. Aarhus: Aarhus Universitetsforlag, 2017.
Ringgaard, Dan. "Stemninger i Regnet i Buenos Aires." *Nordisk samtidspoesi. Særlig Hanne Bramness' forfatterskap*. Ed. Ole Karlsen and Hans Kristian S. Rustad. Oslo: Novus forlag, 2020a. 89–108.
Ringgaard, Dan. *Chaplins pind. Et essay om litteratur og kreativitet*. Aarhus: Aarhus Universitetsforlag, 2020b.
Roberg, Sofia. "'The Overwhelming Indifference of Ingen'. On the Dark Ecopoetics of Aase Berg and Johannes Heldén". *Perspectives on Ecocriticism. Local Beginnings, Global Echoes*. Ed. Ingemar Haag,

Karin Molander Danielsson, Marie Öhman, and Thorsten Päplow. Newcastle upon Tyne: Cambridge Scholars Publishing, 2019. 113–132.

Rosenthal, M.L. and Sally M. Gall. *The Modern Poetic Sequence: The Genius of Modern Poetry*. Oxford: Oxford University Press, 1983.

Ross, Christina. *The Past is the Present; It's the Future too. The Temporal Turn in Contemporary Art*. London: Continuum, 2012.

Rustad, Hans Kristian Strandstuen. *Digital litteratur. En innføring*. Oslo: Cappelen Damm, 2012.

Rustad, Hans Kristian Strandstuen. "Digital litteratur." *Litteratur mellem medier*. Ed. Tore Rye Andersen et al. Aarhus: Aarhus universitetsforlag, 2017. 177–198.

Rustad, Hans Kristian Strandstuen. "Comme en pregnant des photographies. La poésie contemporaine au-delà de l'ekphrasis moderne, https://lyricology.org/comme-en-prenant-des-photographies/?lang=fr. *Lyricology. A Reader* 1.1. (2020).

Ryan, Marie-Laure. *Narrative as Virtual Reality: Immersion and Interactivity in Literature and Electronic Media*. Baltimore: Johns Hopkins University Press, 2001.

Samuels, Roberg. "Auto-Modernity after Postmodernism. Autonomy and Automation in Culture, Technology, and Education." *Digital Youth, Innovation, and the Unexpected*. Ed. Tara Mcpherson. Cambridge: MIT Press, 2008. 221–240.

Sandahl, Ann-Louise. *Temporalitet i visuell kultur. Om samtidens heterokrona estetik*. Unpublished doctoral dissertation, Guthenburg Studies in Art and Architecture, Göteborg universitet, 2016.

Schmidt, Lisa. *Radera. Tippex, tusch, tråd och andra poetiska tekniker*. Göteborg: Glänta production, 2018.

Schmidt, Michael Kallesøe. "(U)muligheder. Multilingvistiske strategier hos Cia Rinne og Christina Hagen." *Edda. Journal for the Study of Scandinavian Literature* 106.1 (2019): 24–38.

Scranton, Roy. *Learning to Die in the Anthropocene. Reflections on the End of a Civilization*. San Francisco: City Lights Books, 2015.

Serup, Martin Glaz. "Digtoplæsning." *Litteratur mellem medier*. Ed. Tore Rye Andersen et al. Aarhus: Aarhus Universitetsforlag, 2017. 137–158.

Shakespeare, William. *The Complete Works of Shakespeare*. London: Spring, 1979.

Shanahan, Murray. *The Technological Singularity*. Cambridge: MIT Press, 2015.

Sharon, Tamar. *Human Nature in the Age of Biotechnology. The Case of Mediated Posthumanism*. New York: Springer, 2013.

Shay, Jonathan. *Achilles in Vietnam. Combat Trauma and the Undoing of Character*. New York: Scribner, 1994.

Silkeberg, Marie. *Avståndsmätning*. Göteborg: Autor, 2005.

Simanowski, Roberto. "Understanding New Media Art Through Close Reading. Four Remarks on Digital Hermeneutics." *Dichtung Digital* 40 (2010): 1–10.

Simanowski, Roberto. *Digital Art and Meaning. Reading Kinetic Poetry, Text Machines, Mapping Art, Interactive Installations*. Minneapolis: University of Minnesota Press, 2011.

Skaug, Trygve. @trygveskaug. *Instagram*. (26 September 2022)

Soelseth, Camilla Holm. "When is a Poet a Instapoet?" *Baltic Screen Media Review* 10 (2022): 96–120.

Soffer, Oren. "The Oral Paradigm and Snapchat." *Social Media + Society* July–September (2016): 1–4.

Sontag, Susan. *Regarding the Pain of the Other*. New York: Farrar, Straus and Giroux, 2003.

Stenbeck, Evelina. *Poesi som politik. Aktivistisk poetik hos Johannes Anyuru och Athena Farrokhzad*. Eureka: Ellerströms akademiska, 2017.

Stern, Frederick C. "The Formal Poetry Reading." *The Drama Review* 35.3 (1991): 67–84.

Stewart, Susan. *The Poet's Freedom. A Notebook on Making*. Chicago: University of Chicago Press, 2011.

Stiegler, Bernard. *Technics and Time*. Stanford: Stanford University Press, 2008.

Stiegler, Bernard. *Philosophising by Accident. Interviews with Elie During*. Berlin: De Gruyter, 2017.
Stiegler, Bernard. *The Age of Disruption. Technology and Madness in Computational Capitalism*. Cambridge: Polity Press, 2020.
Store-Ashkari, Sabina. @ingentingusagt. *Instagram*. (26 September 2022).
Strickland, Stephanie. *To Be Here as Stone is*. https://www.stephaniestrickland.com/stone, 1999 (16 February 2023).
Strickland, Stephanie. "Born Digital. A poet in the forefront of the field explores what is–and is not–electronic literature." https://www.poetryfoundation.org/articles/69224/born-digital. *Poetry Foundation* (2009).
Strotsev, Dmitij. *Беларусь опрокинута* (trans. *Belarus på hodet*). Moss: H/O/F, 2021.
Tallmo, Karl Erik. *Iakttagarens förmåga att ingripa*. Self-published, 1992.
Thomas, Bronwen. *Analyzing Digital Fiction*. Ed. Alice Bell, Astrid Ensslin and Hans Kristian S. Rustad. New York: Routledge, 2014. 94–108.
Thomas, Bronwen. *Literature and Social Media*. London: Routledge, 2020.
Trahndorff, Carl Friedrich Eusebius. *Ästhetik oder Lehre von der Weltanschauung und Kunst*. Berlin: Maurer, 1827.
Tremlett, Sarah. *The Poetics of Poetry Film. Film Poetry, Video Poetry, Lyric Voice, Reflection*. Bristol: intellect, 2021.
Tygstrup, Fredrik. "Affekt og rum." *Kultur & klasse* 116 (2013): 17–32.
Tygstrup, Frederik. "Kultur, kvalitet og menneskelig tid." *Kvalitetsforståelser. Kvalitetsbegrepet i samtidens kunst og kultur*. Ed. Knut Ove Elisassen and Øyvind Prytz. Bergen: Fagbokforlaget, 2016. 23–35.
Uricchio, William. "Reassessing the Situation of the Text in the Algorithmic Age". *Situated in Translation. Cultural Communities and Media Practices*. Ed. Michaela Ott and Thomas Weber. Bielefeld: Transcript, 2019.
Utterback, Camille and Romy Achituv. *Text Rain*. http://camilleutterback.com/projects/text-rain/, 1999 (26 September 2022).
Valéry, Paul. "Centenary of Photography." *Classic Essays on Photography*. Ed. Alan Trachtenberg. New Haven: Leete's Island Books, 1980. 191–198.
Wall-Romana, Christophe. *Cinepoetry: Imaginary Cinemas in French Poetry*. New York: Fordham University Press, 2012.
Wallace-Wells, David. *The Uninhabitable Earth. Life After Warming*. New York: Tim Duggan Books, 2019.
Watts, Rebecca. *"The Cult of the Noble Amateur."* PN Review 239 44/3 (2018). https://www.pnreview.co.uk/cgi-bin/scribe?item_id=10090 (31. March 2023).
Wees, Williams. "Poetry-Films and Film Poems." *The Lux*. http://www.lux.org.uk, 2005 (8 April 2010).
Zuboff, Shoshana. *The Age of Surveillance Capitalism: The Fight for a Human Future at the New Frontier of Power*. New York: Public Affairs, 2019.

Index of Names

Almadhoun, Ghayath 22, 31, 174–176, 180, 183–188, 193, 195, 197, 199
Arendt, Hannah 185–186
Attridge, Derek 42, 44, 46

Barthes, Roland 124–125, 140
Bell, Alice 25
Benthien, Claudia 8, 10, 17, 21–22, 44–46, 178, 192
Berens, Kathi Inman 102, 108, 116, 125
Bernstein, Charles 152, 156–157
Bolter, Jay 41, 93, 151, 154, 200
Bootz, Philip 179
Bourdon, Jérôme 204
Bourriaud, Nicolas 128, 166, 201
Braidotti, Rosi 11
Brison, Susan 192

Carpenter, J.R. 79
Crepax, Rosa 102–103
Culler, Jonathan 33, 42, 44, 46, 137–138

Derrida, Jacques 94
Drucker, Johanna 101, 114

Eagleton, Terry 7
Elleström, Lars 6, 45
Engberg, Marie 8–9, 27, 57, 69
Ensslin, Astrid 9, 25–26
Ernst, Wolfgang 168–169

Fallo, Alexander 1, 99–101, 103, 111–113, 118
Felski, Rita 16–19, 72
Fischer-Lichte, Erika 56–57
Foucault, Michel 38–39
Fuller, Matthew 31, 42
Funkhouser, Chris 8–9, 10, 11, 24, 43, 179

Gestring, Norbert 8, 21
Grigar, Dene 170
Grusin, Richard 93, 151, 154, 200

Haagensen 135, 146–147
Haagensen, Nils-Øivind 2, 21, 126–128, 130–131, 135–136, 139–144, 147–148, 204

Hansen, Mark B. 2, 5–6, 31, 37, 40, 105, 155, 168, 201
Haraway, Donna 14
Hayles, N. Katherine 5–6, 9, 11, 14–15, 17–18, 20, 24–25, 27, 29–30, 33, 35–39, 43–48, 51–53, 56–57, 61–65, 69, 71, 101, 129, 154, 156, 201–202, 207–209
Hegel, Georg Wilhelm Friedrich 33, 185
Heldén, Johannes 1–2, 13, 20–21, 31–32, 50–52, 57–58, 61–75, 78–81, 84, 86–87, 93–94, 97, 110, 112, 129, 180, 202–203

Ieropoulos, Fil 176–178
Ingvarsson, Jonas 39, 57, 89

Jackson, Virginia 7–8, 33
Jakobson, Roman 60, 105, 187
Jameson 194
Jameson, Fredric 188, 193
Jameson, Fredrich 79
Jenkins, Henry 105, 167–168
Jonson, Ben 139
Jonson, Håkan 1, 20, 50–52, 57–58, 61–64, 66, 68–72, 74, 94, 110, 129, 202–203

Kaur, Rupi 1, 99, 102–103
Kirby, Alan 20, 40–41, 166, 201
Kirschenbaum, Matthew 113, 116
Kittler, Friedrich 5–6
Korecka, Magdalena 29, 100–104, 113

Lajta-Novak, Julia 9, 150
Landow, George 41
Larsen, Deena 25–26
Larsen, Peter Stein 5, 9, 79
Lau, Jordis 17, 22, 45–46, 178, 192
Lislegaard, Ann 180–181, 183, 203
Lund, Jacob 169, 204
Lunenfeld, Peter 23, 128–129, 148

Manovich, Lev 43, 60, 167, 179
Marino, Marc 58, 110
McLuhan, Marshall 5–6, 30, 37, 89
Mitchell, W.J.T. 5–6, 23

Moestrup, Mette 2, 163–166, 171–172
Mønster 168
Mønster, Louise 5, 150–152, 167, 197, 206
Morris, Adalaide 8–9, 25, 155
Morton, Timothy 80–81, 92

Nelson, Jason 7, 45–47, 112
Nelson, Ted 31

Ormstad, Ottar 2, 13, 112, 181–183

Parikka, Jussi 203
Poell, Thomas 21, 99, 104–108, 115–117, 122–123, 125, 130, 148, 154, 161, 163, 172, 199
Pressman, Jessica 9, 14–15, 202

Rajewsky, Irina 43, 45, 47, 192
Rancière, Jacques 32–34
Rettberg, Scott 8, 10–11, 18, 31, 46, 59, 79, 167, 207
Rinne, Cia 2, 13, 31, 182–183
Rustad 168
Rustad, Hans Kristian Strandstuen 25, 44, 150–152, 167, 197, 206

Schmidt, Lisa 13, 67
Silkeberg, Marie 2, 13, 22, 31, 174–176, 180, 183–191, 193–199
Simanowski, Roberto 13–14, 17, 46, 69, 202
Skaug 99, 124, 147
Skaug, Trygve 1, 98–100, 103, 109, 118–122, 125, 147
Sontag, Susan 188, 194–195
Stahl, Henrieke 2–4, 8–9
Stenbeck, Evelina 185–186, 198
Stiegler, Bernard 37, 52, 203, 207, 209
Store-Ashkari 98–99
Store-Ashkari, Sabina 1, 98, 112–113, 118
Strickland, Stephanie 25, 27–28
Swiss, Thomas 8–9, 25

Thomas 130
Thomas, Bronwen 9, 34, 101–103, 116, 125, 207
Tremlett, Sarah 175–177, 184, 192

van Dijck, José 21, 99–100, 104–108, 115–117, 122–123, 125, 130, 148, 154, 161, 163, 172, 199
Vorrath, Wiebke 28, 43, 58, 110

www.ingramcontent.com/pod-product-compliance
Lightning Source LLC
Chambersburg PA
CBHW020229170426
43201CB00007B/372